# The Failure of Poetry,
# The Promise of Language

## POETS ON POETRY

**David Lehman, General Editor**
**Donald Hall, Founding Editor**

*New titles*

John Ashbery, *Selected Prose*
Annie Finch, *The Body of Poetry*
Laura (Riding) Jackson, *The Failure of Poetry, The Promise of Language*
Alice Notley, *Coming After*
Charles Simic, *Memory Piano*
John Yau, *The Passionate Spectator*

*Recently published*

Dana Gioia, *Barrier of a Common Language*
Paul Hoover, *Fables of Representation*
Philip Larkin, *Further Requirements*
William Stafford, *The Answers Are Inside the Mountains*
Richard Tillinghast, *Poetry and What Is Real*

*Also available are collections by*

A. R. Ammons, Robert Bly, Philip Booth, Marianne Boruch,
Hayden Carruth, Amy Clampitt, Douglas Crase, Robert Creeley,
Donald Davie, Thomas M. Disch, Tess Gallagher, Linda Gregerson,
Allen Grossman, Thom Gunn, Rachel Hadas, John Haines,
Donald Hall, Joy Harjo, Robert Hayden, Edward Hirsch,
Daniel Hoffman, Jonathan Holden, John Hollander, Andrew Hudgins,
Josephine Jacobsen, Mark Jarman, Galway Kinnell, Kenneth Koch,
John Koethe, Yusef Komunyakaa, Maxine Kumin,
Martin Lammon (editor), Philip Larkin, David Lehman, Philip Levine,
Larry Levis, John Logan, William Logan, William Matthews,
William Meredith, Jane Miller, David Mura, Carol Muske,
Geoffrey O'Brien, Gregory Orr, Alicia Suskin Ostriker, Ron Padgett,
Marge Piercy, Anne Sexton, Karl Shapiro, Charles Simic,
William Stafford, Anne Stevenson, May Swenson, James Tate,
Richard Tillinghast, C. K. Williams, Alan Williamson, Charles Wright,
James Wright, and Stephen Yenser

*Laura (Riding) Jackson*

# The Failure of
# Poetry, The Promise
# of Language

Edited by John Nolan

THE UNIVERSITY OF MICHIGAN PRESS
*Ann Arbor*

Copyright © 2007 by the Laura (Riding) Jackson
Board of Literary Management
All rights reserved
Published in the United States of America by
The University of Michigan Press
Manufactured in the United States of America
∞ Printed on acid-free paper

2010   2009   2008   2007      4   3   2   1

*A CIP catalog record for this book is available from the British Library.*

Library of Congress Cataloging-in-Publication Data

Jackson, Laura (Riding), 1901–1991.
    The failure of poetry, the promise of language / Laura (Riding)
Jackson ; edited by John Nolan.
        p.   cm. — (Poets on poetry)
    Includes bibliographical references and index.
    ISBN-13: 978-0-472-09957-3 (cloth : acid-free paper)
    ISBN-10: 0-472-09957-4 (cloth : acid-free paper)
    ISBN-13: 978-0-472-06957-6 (pbk. : acid-free paper)
    ISBN-10: 0-472-06957-8 (pbk. : acid-free paper)
    1. Jackson, Laura (Riding), 1901–1991—Authorship.   2. Poetry—
Authorship.   I. Nolan, John, 1950–   II. Title.

PS3519.A363Z46   2007
811'.52—dc22                                    2006029797

[T]here must be a reorganizing of the faith put in the promise of poetry into a faith in the promise of language itself.

—*Rational Meaning* 447

# Acknowledgments

This book is published with the permission of, and on behalf of, the Laura (Riding) Jackson Board of Literary Management. I am deeply grateful to Alan J. Clark and Elizabeth Friedmann, who have been as coeditors with me. I am grateful to my other colleagues on the Laura (Riding) Jackson Board of Literary Management: Professor William Harmon, Dr. Mark Jacobs, Robert Nye, Dr. James Tyler, and Joan Wilentz. I would also like to thank René VanDeVoorde, Professor David Lehman, and LeAnn Fields and Rebecca Mostov.

Grateful acknowledgment is made to the following journals and publishers for permission to reprint previously published material.

*Chelsea* (New York) for "Introduction for a Broadcast; Continued for *Chelsea*," published in *Chelsea* 12 (September 1962); "Poetry Log: Random Choices," and "Story, and Story-Style," published in *Chelsea* 35 (1976); and "As To A Certain Poem & Poetry," published in *Chelsea* 47 (1988).

*P. N. Review* (www.pnreview.co.uk) for the extracts from "Some Notes on Poetry and Poets in This Century, and My Influence," published in issue 9, 1979; and from "Twentieth-Century Change in the Idea of Poetry, And of the Poet, And of the Human Being," published in issue 57, 1987.

The *London Review of Books* for Sections 7–10 of "From a Notebook of Essays-In-Little," and "In Gratuitous Witness," published in issue 17(17), September 1995, under the title "The Promise of Words."

The Gale Group for the 1970 statement in *Contemporary Poets*. Copyright © 1970 St. James Press. Reprinted by permission of the Gale Group.

The H. W. Wilson Company for the entry in *Twentieth Century*

*Authors 1942 (Supplement 1955)*. Copyright © 1955 by the H. W. Wilson Company. Material reproduced with permission of the publisher.

Lord John Press for "A Poem: 'How A Poem Comes To Be,'" published as a broadside in 1980.

I am grateful for the additional permissions of the owners of the manuscripts, as detailed in the "Note on the Text": to Elizabeth Friedmann for twenty-nine items; to Alan Clark for one item; to the Berg Collection of English and American Literature, The New York Public Library, Astor, Lenox, and Tilden Foundations, for thirty items; to the Division of Rare and Manuscript Collections, Cornell University Library, for eleven items including the photograph of Laura (Riding) Jackson.

# Contents

# Chronology of Laura (Riding) Jackson's Life

1901    Laura Reichenthal is born in New York City, the daughter of Nathaniel Reichenthal and Sadie Edersheim Reichenthal. As a child, Laura will move from school to school in Ohio, Indiana and Pennsylvania as a result of her father's employment as a manager of clothing stores.

1914    The Reichenthal family returns to New York and Laura attends Brooklyn Girls' High School, graduating four years later.

1918    Enrolls at Cornell University, where she begins to write poetry.

1920    Marries history instructor Louis Gottschalk.

1921    Leaves Cornell without gaining a degree to accompany her husband to teaching appointments in Illinois and Kentucky. Writes poem *Voltaire*, published in 1927.

1923    Her poems, already accepted by magazines such as Harriet Monroe's *Poetry*, are taken up by the Fugitives, a group of southern poets including John Crowe Ransom, Allen Tate, and Robert Penn Warren, who in 1924 award her the "Nashville Prize" and invite her to become a member. It is in *The Fugitive* that Robert Graves comes across her work in February/March 1924. Publishes as Laura Riding Gottschalk.

1925    Divorces Louis Gottschalk, and moves to New York City, where she becomes friends with the poet Hart Crane and other American writers. Her first critical essay, "A Prophecy or a Plea," is published. In December she accepts Graves's invitation to come to England, entering into a literary partnership that will last until 1939.

1926    Spends six months in Egypt with Graves and his wife
        Nancy Nicholson. First book of poems, *The Close Chap-
        let*, is published in America, and in England by
        Leonard and Virginia Woolf's Hogarth Press.
1927    Changes name, by deed poll, to Laura Riding.
1927–28    Five books are published in seven months: *A Survey
        of Modernist Poetry* and *A Pamphlet Against Anthologies* are
        co-authored with Graves, the former pioneering a
        method of close reading which is the seed for what will
        become the New Criticism. *Contemporaries and Snobs*
        and *Anarchism Is Not Enough* appear in February and
        May respectively. Riding and Graves start their private
        Seizin Press in 1927, the first publication being her
        poems *Love As Love, Death As Death* (1928). Contributes
        to Eugene Jolas's magazine *transition*.
1929    Attempts suicide on April 27th, falling from a high win-
        dow of her house in St. Peter's Square, Hammersmith;
        she sustains serious injuries and spends nearly three
        months in hospital. Gertrude Stein's *An Acquaintance
        With Description* is published by the Seizin Press.
1929    Riding and Graves leave England in October to live in
        Deyá, Majorca, where, until 1936, they are the center
        of a group of English and American friends who come
        to visit or stay, including poets Norman Cameron and
        James Reeves, film-maker Len Lye, painter John
        Aldridge, journalists Honor Wyatt and T. S. Matthews,
        and mathematician and writer Jacob Bronowski.
1930    Publishes two volumes of poetry: *Poems: A Joking Word,*
        and *Twenty Poems Less*; and three other books: *Four Un-
        posted Letters to Catherine, Experts Are Puzzled,* and *Though
        Gently.* Gertrude Stein breaks off correspondence with
        Riding and Graves.
1931    *Laura and Francisca* published by the Seizin Press.
1931–32    Riding and Graves design and build their house,
        Canellun.
1933    *Everybody's Letters* published, and two more books of po-
        etry: *Poet: A Lying Word,* and *The Life of the Dead* (illus-
        trated by Aldridge).
1935    *Progress of Stories* published. Riding is consulted by

Michael Roberts in the formation of the *Faber Book of Modern Verse* (1936). In the autumn the first issue of *Epilogue* appears, edited by Riding with Graves as assistant editor. Two more issues of this "Critical Summary" will be published in 1936 and 1937.

1936   Riding and her friends are forced by the outbreak of the Spanish Civil War to evacuate Majorca, and the following three years are spent mainly in England, with spells in Lugano and Brittany.

1937   *A Trojan Ending* published.

1938   *Collected Poems* published; also *The Covenant of Literal Morality,* and *The World and Ourselves.*

1939   *Lives of Wives* published. She returns to the United States in April, accompanied by Graves and others. She meets Schuyler B. Jackson, poet and critic, with whom she resumes work on a dictionary begun with Bronowski in Majorca. Graves returns to Europe in July.

1940–41   Renounces poetry, and discourages republication of her poems, for reasons that she would not feel able to communicate publicly for another fifteen to twenty years.

1941   Marries Schuyler Jackson.

1943   The Jacksons settle in Wabasso, Florida, where they live quietly and simply, without electricity or telephone. They disengage from the literary world, but participate in the life of the local community. They sustain themselves by running (until 1950) a small business growing and shipping citrus fruit. Their dictionary work draws them into exploring the principles of meaning and definition underlying language; the result will be published posthumously as *Rational Meaning: A New Foundation for the Definition of Words* (1997).

1955   Publishes a short biographical statement in *Twentieth Century Authors* in which she gives "a cautious generalization" concerning her renunciation of poetry.

1962   BBC broadcasts a selection of her poems with an introduction, read by herself, stating her reasons for renouncing poetry; "Introduction for a Broadcast" appears in the New York magazine *Chelsea* in September.

1962–65   Composes "The Telling." Throughout the 1960s she is writing "Open Confidences," published in *Chelsea* 35 (1976).

1963   BBC broadcasts a slightly revised version of *Four Unposted Letters to Catherine* in July with a new postscript by the author.

1964   "Further on Poetry" appears in *Chelsea* 14 under the authorial name Laura (Riding) Jackson. She is planning a book to be titled *The Failure of Poetry.*

1965   "The Sex Factor in Social Progress" appears in *Chelsea* 16; "The Bondage" will appear in issue 30/31 (1972).

1967   The 62 numbered passages of "The Telling" appear in *Chelsea* 20/21; they will be republished in 1972 as the "core-part" of a book of the same title. Composes "What, If Not A Poem, Poems?" (published 1974).

1968   Schuyler Jackson dies on July 4th. "The Sufficient Difference" (published 2000) had been composed for him the previous year. She continues work on *Rational Meaning*, completing it in the mid-1970s.

1970   *Selected Poems: In Five Sets* published, with a preface explaining her new evaluation of poetry. Confirms policy of allowing her poems to be reprinted if accompanied by a statement of her renunciation of poetry.

1971   Receives Mark Rothko Appreciation Award.

1972   *The Telling* published in England, and in 1973 in the United States. In January records a reading of her poetry for Lamont Library, Harvard University.

Early 1970s   Begins work on *Later-Life Commentaries,* her literary memoirs (at this time titled *Praeterita*).

1973   Receives Guggenheim Fellowship in support of her work on *Rational Meaning: A New Foundation for the Definition of Words.*

1973–74   Rediscovered 1920s–30s manuscript material is returned to Riding from Deyá, including her letters from Gertrude Stein. Other components subsequently published in *Description of Life* (1980) and *The Word "Woman and Other Related Writings"* (1993).

1976   *Chelsea* 35 appears; bearing the title *It Has Taken Long,* the entire issue is devoted to L(R)J's writings. Begins assembling some of her essays as a book to be titled *Under The Mind's Watch* (published posthumously in 2004).

1979    Receives National Endowment for the Arts Fellowship to assist with work on her literary memoirs. Manuscripts of more than two hundred early poems (pre-1926) rediscovered by a friend in New York and returned to L(R)J; they will be published in 1992 as *First Awakenings: The Early Poems of Laura Riding* with a preface by the author.

1980    *The Poems of Laura Riding: A New Edition of the 1938 Collection* is published with appendices and a new introduction exploring further her revised evaluation of poetry.

1981    Nominated by Danish poet Poul Borum for the Neustadt Prize.

1982    *Progress of Stories* republished with a new Preface and added material. Chapters from *Later-Life Commentaries* are being published in little magazines, e.g. "Backgrounds" and "Interest." "The Missing Story" also appears.

1983    *Some Communications of Broad Reference* published. Begins work on *Literature As Celebration of the Incomplete: A Century of Loss,* consisting of three long essays.

1984    *A Trojan Ending* republished with a new preface. A Spanish translation is published in Barcelona as *Final Troyano* in 1986.

1988    *Lives of Wives* republished, with a new Afterword.

1991    Laura (Riding) Jackson's ninetieth birthday celebrated in the United States by *Chelsea* and in England by *P.N. Review.* She is awarded the Bollingen Prize for her lifetime service to poetry. Dies of heart failure on September 2nd. Leaves behind extensive work-in-progress, some of it gathered in *The Sufficient Difference: A Centenary Celebration of Laura (Riding) Jackson* (*Chelsea* 69, 2000).

# Editor's Introduction
## Poetry, Language, Truth-Speaking

It was in about 1940–41 that Laura Riding renounced poetry and withdrew from public literary life in order to take stock, though it would be fifteen to twenty years before she would feel able to begin publicly exploring her reasons and communicating her findings. From 1962 onward—early April to be more exact, the occasion of her quietly momentous BBC broadcast—Laura (Riding) Jackson wrote and published prolifically until her death in 1991. In her writings of these decades her thinking came to fruition, especially in *The Telling* (1972)—a book she once described, perhaps with a sisterly smile in Shelley's direction, as "my kind of sword."[1] One of the books she was envisaging throughout this period was to be titled *The Failure of Poetry*. Though she never brought it to completion, nor left a plan for its contents or their arrangement, she continued actively to assign pieces to it. In this reconstruction, her intentions have been carried out (subject to restrictions of space) wherever they could be ascertained; the book has been realized from whatever hints and clues she left.

## The Failure of Poetry

To begin with Laura (Riding) Jackson's renunciation of poetry is to begin the story in the middle. The setting for her renunciation is the view of poetry that she had at the time, arrived at in the course of two decades of intensive practice as a poet. Her early descriptions of poetry as "a sense of life so real that it becomes the sense of something more real than life," and, differently, of a poem as "nothing," a "vacuum," had culminated, in the thirties, in her view of poetry as "truth-telling."[2] With a seriousness fully comparable to Shelley's in his "Defence" or Wordsworth's in his "Preface," she had urged in her 1938 preface to *Collected Poems* that "a poem is an uncovering of truth of so fundamental and general a kind that no other name besides poetry is adequate except truth."[3] Steadfast thereafter in her devotion to the end of truth-telling, or truth-speaking, she nonetheless ceased to regard poetry as the means to that end.

Against this backdrop, her eventual case against poetry could be set out in something like the following steps:

1. The failure of poetry is its failure to be truth-speaking.
2. The failure is inevitable because poetry, by its nature, must use the techniques of art, which are extraneous to, and harmful to, the truth-speaking potential inherent in language itself.
3. Therefore poetry can never be more than an imitation of truth-speaking, relying excessively on exploitation of the physical properties of words.
4. This physical imitation of truth-speaking has served as a substitute for the real thing: in former times an honorable anticipation of a hoped-for eventuality of truth-speaking, poetry has tended in recent times to become accepted as a compensatory substitute for truth-speaking, the real thing being assumed to be not practicable.
5. The reason why truth-speaking is assumed to be not practicable is that human beings have become reluctant to believe literally in their capability of truth-speaking and in the truth-potential of language. (The theme of the failure of poetry opens here into the larger themes of human attitudes to language, truth, and human identity.)

Laura (Riding) Jackson does not herself set out her case in this step-by-step manner. She tends, rather, to identify a number of distinct weaknesses in poetry, focusing sometimes on one, sometimes on another. Each piece on poetry presents her revaluation of it afresh, from a different angle; her thought is always in movement as she explores the implications of her underlying position.

Prominent among her criticisms is that there is a contradictoriness or inconsistency in poetry. In her first full statement (1962) the inconsistency is said to be between art and reality, or more exactly between a sought equivalence between poetry and truth on the one hand, and on the other hand their being, the one, *art* and the other, *the reality*. In "The Failure of Poetry" (1965) the contradiction is said to be between poetry's "creed" of truth of word and its "craft" of producing sensuously pleasing and emotionally compelling imitations of truth with words. In subsequent pieces the terms of the contradiction are said to be, variously, the natural versus the artificial, spiritual liberation versus sensuous compulsion, freedom from ordinary restrictions on word-use versus subjection to special poetic restrictions, spiritual intention versus literariness.[4]

Closely linked to the charge of contradictoriness is the charge of ineffectualness. Poetry changes nothing. Our ordinary speaking life is left in its wretched state of unaspiringness by poetry's ephemeral exaltations; they are not intended to extend beyond the time of the poem. "The implicit objective of poetry, that of forming a perfect way of speaking, becomes its ideal objective in *not* being practically pursued."[5] Poetry is only a token activity, a substitute for truth-speaking itself; truth-speaking is postponed for the sake of creating beautiful anticipations of what it might sound like. Poets prefer arguing the possibility of truth-speaking rather than putting its practicability to the test; a poem, by its very nature, prohibits taking belief "to the live proof."[6] This spiritual ineffectuality of poetry is said to be intimately related to its linguistic ineffectuality: its seeming to imply what is presumed to be otherwise inexpressible, by using techniques appearing to suggest more than is explicitly said.[7]

In other pieces it is the charge of incompleteness that is in the foreground. Poetry's subjection of truth to the discipline of art is said to result in incompleteness of thinking that nonetheless presents itself as complete. Part of the theme of the poem is excluded, only the effect of completeness is aimed at. "Poetry offers linguistically incomplete solutions the incompleteness of which can be concealed in sensory supplements."[8] Poetry arbitrarily postulates an inexpressible, for the sake of creating physical impressions of what is left unexplored. This criticism is demonstrated in one piece by means of an unforgettable reconsideration of her early poem "Lucrece and Nara."

Another cluster of criticisms she makes of poetry concerns its exclusiveness, divisiveness, and power-mongering. There is a gratuitous assumption that truth-speaking is attemptable only by a few insiders, who dispense it to a "silent laity" rendered "slavish attendants" by poetic resort to physically compulsive, spell-like devices to sustain attention.[9] Poetry's truth-telling aspiration is weighed down by its status as a social institution, indeed a profession, and by its having, as such, to maintain its social credentials and authority.[10]

Such are the weaknesses of poetry most frequently identified by her—as if she were the Kurt Gödel of poetry, with inconsistency, incompleteness, and undecidability theorems of her own. Though the weaknesses are not explicitly interrelated by her, they can be inferred to be inevitable effects of poetry's being only a physical imitation of truth-speaking, a compensatory substitute for the real thing.

## The Promise of Language

If truth-speaking is what poetry fails to be, nevertheless truth-speaking is what is promised in language. What brought about her renunciation of poetry, Laura (Riding) Jackson says, "was, rather than an experience of a sudden loss of faith in the truth-potential of poetry, an experience of gradual learning of the full potential of language."[11]

Language is perfect, is her eventual estimate (and her husband Schuyler B. Jackson's too), or more exactly, "every language carries a pattern of perfection in it." Words are "linguistically infallible . . . perfectly dependable":

> In this sense of believing—the putting of perfect trust in something as the guiding principle of one's thought, and so of the entire course of one's being—we believe in language. Believing in language may be impossible without believing

in something else, that causes language to be as trustworthy as it is.[12]

This must seem an unusual view, especially nowadays when language tends to be regarded as a system of arbitrary, differential signs traced across an absence left by "the death of God," flawed and slippery, though not without a reservoir of magic that can be conjured up by poets. If the prevailing view nowadays is that language is inadequate, but rescuable from its inadequacies by poetry, her view is the reverse: it is language that contains within itself the potential for truth-speaking, and the poetic use of language that postpones fulfillment of this potential.

Her view that language is perfect is not to be equated with the search for the perfect language, regarded nowadays as a quixotic quest for an original universal language to be rediscovered, or an artificial one to be invented, marked (in the former case at least) by an affinity between words and objects such that words reflect the true essences of things. As it happens, she did once toy with such an idea, though embedded in a fiction-within-a-fiction-within-a-fiction;[13] and it is indeed part of her notion of truth-speaking that "our speaking speaks the actuality"; it is "ever-present to our *evocation*."[14] But her idea of language's perfection is different. It is most closely exemplified by the "expanded normal" diction of the core-part of *The Telling*—an "illustrious vernacular" if ever there was one (to borrow Dante's description of his idea of the perfect language).[15]

The "promise of language"[16] is probably to be construed not as a promise *made* by language (for it does not seem to be her view that language is such that it could itself be a promise-maker) but as the promise *shown* in language: it is promised in the very existence of language that truth-speaking is practicable. Her idea of there being a truth-potential contained in language needs some explanation. "Especially was I unhappy in the language I heard spoken everywhere—sordidly chaotic to my ears," she recalled in 1955, going on to tell how she was drawn "ever closer to the crux of the human problem: the question of the validity of words."[17] There is comparability in this respect with another poet's yearning—Rilke's: "Oh, how often one longs to speak a few degrees more deeply!" But where Rilke looked to "an innermost language" metaphorically described as "a language of word-kernels, a language that's not gathered, up above, on stalks, but grasped in the speech-seed,"[18] she, less romanticist, spiritually more practical, was led to the making of a dictionary: "the meanings of words, I had come to feel, had to be known with perfect distinctness before they could be used with perfect truthfulness . . . for us [herself and Schuyler B. Jackson], the act of definition must involve a total reconstituting of words' meanings."[19]

Language she regards as, at the very least, a provision of word-meanings each possessed of a distinct identity all its own that can be known in relation to its neighbor-words and to one's language as a whole, so that one should endeavor to mean each word distinctly rather than to imply a number of meanings ambiguously. This is one aspect of language's "rationality" (distinguished by the Jacksons from scientific rationality). Her view goes against the grain of modern poetics, over which there has often presided a cult of poetic unreason.[20] But if metaphor, ambiguity, multiplicity of meaning, and wordplay, are, for her, only incidental to the prime language-values of distinctness and determinateness of meaning, the latter are not at all what is exemplified by the careless everyday use of words, nor by the mortific use of them in the various intellectual discourses of the day. Seriously to address her view of language would require a willingness to rethink gratuitous value-oppositions, including the metaphorical versus the literal, poetry versus prose, creativity versus representation. This much is certain: nothing need be lost—fullness of meaning need not be lost—by adoption of her "one-word, one-meaning" principle, understood as a rule of respect for words.[21]

It may help to think of her emphasis on the definability of meanings not as invidiously prescriptive (as if she were seeking to impose her meanings on us) but as unselfish: "To know words well, one must know them unselfishly, as not one's own, but as the words of all."[22] Indeed, this identifies a quality audible in her writings: where speaking is animated by belief in one another, by sense of the value of human beings to one another as proof of the authenticity of one another, the words travel out beyond private contexts of self-referent meaning into the open of presence to one another. To know words thus is to know them as belonging to what she calls "the natural language of our minds."[23]

## Human Truth-Speaking

If truth-speaking is what is promised in language, in what would successful truth-speaking consist? Part of her idea of it is that it could only ever be one's personal own, free of the constraints imposed by religion, philosophy, even poetry; her concern is with the intimately personal, urgently practical need "to live by truth, inwardly arrived at truth, truth that is the utterance of one's own mind."[24] That all formal categories of truth-aspiration—poetry no less than religion and philosophy, if in a less apparent way—skew one's speaking and thinking out of true is axiomatic for her. The failure of poetry is regarded by her as an instance, albeit a special one, of the failure of all the "truth-telling professions"[25] to be truth-speaking whole-and-nothing-but. Truth-speaking is, for her, to be engaged in by each and all "on the common plane," not in the isolation of those professions by specialist practitioners of them.[26] Neither is truth-speaking seen as an isolated individual achievement but as a speaking to one another, "an express mutuality of human life" in which is realized "a spiritual unity of minds."[27] The "objective" is

> a precisely expressive and self-expressive humanity, governed by knowledge and love of the universally shared possibilities of the benevolent, wise, and beautiful intercourse of which words allow . . . conceivable as the naturally proper normal of human articulateness.[28]

"Truth" she regards as "the word of words," but nonetheless as a word to be defined like any other,[29] and she works patiently to dispel the prevailing obtundity, even embarrassment, concerning it. By the 1960s she had come to distinguish explicitly between two words *truth:* truth the quality and truth the thing—that is, truth as a quality of something said, and truth as something said possessing this quality (as in "a truth," "truths," "the truth").[30] She tends, when making the distinction, to identify her concern as being with the first of these "truth" words rather than the second; for instance, "I did not look in poetry for '*a* truth' . . . I believed that poetry offered possibilities of speaking *with* truth, making utterances that achieved the full quality of truth."[31] Concomitantly, she tends to think of truth as something to be made—spoken—rather than something discovered or uncovered: truth "does not lie abroad unfound but exists only by and in our speaking."[32]

Truth the quality she calls "the essential 'truth.'"[33] The quality includes (to cite the provisional definition given in *Rational Meaning*) "animation of words with purpose of mind to make manifest possessed awareness, productive of complete rightness of expression."[34] Finding, and showing, how to get more of this truth-quality, more of the breath of truth, into our speaking lives is a not unjust description of her whole life-endeavor.

The other word *truth*, truth the thing, she is at pains to distinguish from *fact* and *reality*, words with which *truth* is wrongly synonymized in people's minds, also from *truthfulness* the opposite of lying. Rather, the word as used by her, almost always without definite or indefinite article, seems to pick out a subject matter: our great "Subject" as distinct from particular subjects, as she puts it in *The Telling*, "truth in the large" as distinct from the special truths of religion, philosophy, and science.[35] It is also presented as "the one story." What more than anything gives Laura (Riding) Jackson's work its value is her constantly raising this all-important subject, bringing it to life afresh on every speaking occasion.

Several of the threads in her notion of truth and truth-speaking are woven together in the following passage from the Jacksons' *Rational Meaning*:

> Our notion of the nature of truth, manifestly, goes far beyond the conventional ideal of truth as a factual correspondence of words with the objects of thought. We understand it to be a fulfilment in the letter and the spirit of all the beneficent potentialities of language. And we think it to be, in the ultimate whole of its nature, an essentially personal performance—

and experience: we think that language teaches the possibility of a spiritual unity of minds, and that truth is an express mutuality of human life in which the possibility is practically realized. (69)

She came to see human truth-speaking as speaking the truth of "being" (sometimes with initial capital, "Being"),[36] and as having a crucial part to play—literally a speaking part—in the universal scheme of things:

> The greater sense of being, ever lost in infinite extension, cannot let the rendering of it as the finite truth-sense of the human person, which life implicitly urges into being, fail! . . .
> Poetry has explored an involuntary conviction of the human mind that there is concentratedly secreted in human beings the meaning-will of the comprehensive reality of being—that what it is "like" is individualized into revelatory expression of its identity in them, as if *it* had direct presence in the speaking presence of human beings to one another.[37]

But this high valuation of the human task has for obverse her reproof of human shirking it. Examining a variety of human attitudes to the prospect of truth-speaking—including fear, embarrassment, hesitation, the judging it "folly"—she diagnoses a deep-seated malaise affecting human life. At its heart is the "equivocal attitude" adopted by human beings to the *good* as "a right and necessary yet less than entirely sensible and sane objective."[38] The impasse in which they become immobilized as a consequence is depicted as a "delicate balance maintained between decisiveness and indecisiveness in the milieu for the presumed comfort of everyone concerned,"[39] and she presents her life's work as a variety of attempts to demonstrate that the impasse can be broken:

> With a very sympathetic camera I caught modern humanity in a characteristic posture of willed indifference to its fate, yet a posture so strained that it invited hope of a change, any next moment, in the viewer: were these not beings who knew another kind of bravery, that of defending their best against their worst, instead of choosing to be impartial between them?[40]

The failure of poetry can now be situated in the context of this larger failure of human spiritual life heretofore, a failure described in this book as

> a spiritual reservation pinning humanity down like a ball and chain it attaches to itself for its own supposed good and then forgets about, so that it enjoys both the sense of the possibility of freedom of word and the sense of security from the possibility. A balm, poetry has been, to the embarrassment and pain of human reluctance to face in actuality the full potential of truth implicit in words—and in the human speaking-capability.[41]

(That "reluctance," it might be added, she sometimes links with what she regards as the peculiarly *male* propensity to self-separation, and in several pieces in this book the theme of the failure of poetry opens into another of her recurrent concerns, that of the man- and woman-components of human identity.)[42]

No attempt will be made here to place Laura (Riding) Jackson on maps of literary or intellectual history beyond drawing attention to her describing her poetic work as "intellectually modernist yet spiritually traditional";[43] nor to contrast her evaluation of poetry with that of others beyond referring readers to her contrasting herself with two of the usual suspects, Rimbaud and Plato.[44] What is being offered here is a report, drawing on the full range of her later writings, of her professed reason for renouncing poetry: namely, that truth-speaking is what is promised in language and what poetry fails to be.

Despite appearing in the venerable Poets on Poetry series, this book is best thought of not as poetics,[45] not as secondary critical commentary on something else (on the nature of poetry, for instance), but as primary in its own right, part of the author's attempt at truth-speaking outside the "pleasance" of poetry.[46] The same is true of all her writings of the sixties, seventies, and eighties, not just *The Telling*, but also "Open Confidences," "The Missing Story," "Interest," "The One Language. Self-Revealed," "The Only Possible Ending," "The Risks," "On the Continuing of the Continuing," and many others: it was for the sake of something even better that she renounced poetry, and her later, post-renunciation writings are meant to exemplify this something-even-better, rather than being merely a post-mortem commentary on her earlier work.[47] Hers is not a story of a poetic gift lost or spoiled. In renouncing poetry's partial likenesses of truth, she was not giving up on truth-speaking, but intensifying her devotion to "truth singularly itself, unlike its likenesses."[48] As she wrote to a poet in 1962:

> if there are those who think my statements are essentially ex-cuse-making, covering an actuality of burnt-out-ness, I am not going to worry about that. My concern is not what people think of me as once-poet, but to find energy of spirit for keeping faith with the task of words that I see con-fronting me, and all.[49]

Nor, in renouncing poetry, did she renounce her own poems. Though she came to disapprove of the writing of poems by herself or anyone else thenceforth, she judged her own poems to be "an unrenounceable record of the poetically pos-sible," indispensable by their providing evidence that the possi-bilities of poetic expression had been tested to the limit.[50] Nor was her *re*nouncing a *de*nouncing. "I honor what is virtuous in the poetic legacy," she says:[51] indeed, in criticizing poetry she at the same time honors its inspiring motive of dedication to the lin-guistic best. "Don't go rubbing poetry's nose so much in the dirt," she urged a young student of her work: "*I* never have done that."[52]

"It will not pass without vision of something better," she wrote of poetry in 1964.[53] The nub of her revaluation of poetry is that an even better speaking than poetic speaking is possible: if we believe literally in the practicability of speaking with truth, we will no longer need or want poetry. Poetry will come to be seen as no more than the very best next-best-thing to a best that had been gratuitously assumed to be too good to be attainable:[54]

> The total import of what I have to say is a happy one. It is, that truth—the speech of truth—is a real and immediate possibil-ity. But the poetic shadows that veil it must be torn away be-fore it can be seen to be so.[55]

1. "The Telling is my kind of sword and, yes, it is clean, sharp, but with no blood on it, and not made to kill with—yet not as a mere symbol. It is an actual dealing with the fact of the battle—right there, in the battle's midst." Letter to Sonia Raiziss, May 1, 1967, Division of Rare and Manuscript Collections, Cornell University Library. There may be a glancing reference here to Shelley's "Poetry is a sword of lightning" ("A Defence of Poetry").

2. *Contemporaries and Snobs* (London: Cape, 1928), opening sentence; *Anarchism Is Not Enough* (1928), ed. Lisa Samuels (Berkeley and Los Angeles: University of California Press, 2001), 16–17; "Poetry is . . . the joy of comprehensive truth-telling." "An Enquiry," *New Verse* 11 (October 1934): 4. For details of L(R)J's published works see Alan Clark's revised checklist in *Chelsea* 69 (2000): 147–79.

3. "To the Reader," *The Poems of Laura Riding: A Newly Revised Edition of the 1938/1980 Collection*, centennial preface by Mark Jacobs (New York: Persea Books, 2001) 484; also in *The Poems of Laura Riding: A New Edition of the 1938 Collection* (Manchester; Carcanet; New York: Persea Books, 1980), 407; and in *The Laura (Riding) Jackson Reader*, ed. Elizabeth Friedmann (New York: Persea Books, 2005), 193.

4. Poetry is "too much the child of literature to transcend the limitations of literature" ("Backgrounds," *Glasgow Magazine* 1, Winter 1982/83, 29), and is doomed to "insoluble self-contradictoriness, in its putting of its ideal objective under the protection of the logic of literary objectification" ("Engaging in the Impossible," *Sulfur* 10, 1984, 19–20).

5. "Then, And Now," p. 54 of this book.

6. "What, If Not A Poem, Poems?" *Denver Quarterly* 9(2) Summer 1974, 12, also in *The Laura (Riding) Jackson Reader*, 247.

7. "Poetry and the Good," *P.N. Review* 84, March–April 1992, 21, *Reader*, 211.

8. "Then, And Now," 95.

9. *The Telling*, London: Athlone Press, 1972; New York: Harper & Row, [1973]; Manchester: Carcanet Press, 2005, 65; and "The Failure of Poetry," 34.

10. *The Telling*, 65–67.

11. "Background Statement," 179. Compare: "my view is not antipoetic but pro-linguistic," 235. Also, "My View Is Not Anti-Poetic". . . my attitude to poetry, and my poems, is not anti-poetry fanaticism. It is incidental to views as to language generally, and human self-expression generally." To Sonia Raiziss, November 8, 1961, Berg Collection of En-

glish and American Literature, New York Public Library, Astor, Lenox, and Tilden Foundations; also "The Road To, In, And Away From, Poetry," 159.

12. These last three quotations are from Laura (Riding) Jackson and Schuyler B. Jackson, *Rational Meaning: A New Foundation for the Definition of Words, and Supplementary Essays,* ed. William Harmon (Charlottesville: University Press of Virginia, 1997), 71; compare: "Words are the way in which that purity of being associated with the idea of divine nature is immediately achievable by human beings" (570).

13. "An Anonymous Book," in *Anarchism Is Not Enough,* 171; and in *Progress of Stories,* new ed. (Manchester: Carcanet; New York: Dial Press, 1982), 328. As it happens, one of the projects of the magazine *transition,* to which she had in 1927–28 contributed nine poems and six other pieces, was the attempt to rediscover the primeval, perfect, "Adamic" language; see David Bennett, "Chronicle of Quests for a Universal Language," *Australian Higher Education Supplement,* March 6, 1996, 24.

14. *The Telling,* 160.

15. *The Telling,* 68. See Umberto Eco, *The Search for the Perfect Language* (London: Fontana Press, 1997), 45–46.

16. *Rational Meaning,* 447; see 179, 181, 240–41 of this book.

17. "Entry in *Twentieth Century Authors* (1955)," 161–62; see also *Rational Meaning,* 64.

18. Cited in editors' introduction to *Duino Elegies,* trans. J. B. Leishman and Stephen Spender (London: Hogarth Press, 1968), 20–21.

19. "Entry in *Twentieth Century Authors* (1955)," 162. This "total reconstituting" echoes her 1925 description of the poet's task: "By taking the universe apart he will have reintegrated it with his own vitality." "A Prophecy or a Plea," in *First Awakenings: The Early Poems [of Laura Riding],* ed. Elizabeth Friedmann, Alan J. Clark, and Robert Nye (Manchester: Carcanet Press; New York: Persea Books, 1992), 280.

20. Whistling the unsayable (Frank Ramsey's criticism of Wittgenstein's *Tractatus*) is an apt characterization of this strand of poetics, illustratable by this description by a contemporary poet (Harry Mathews) of his central theme: "Language and what it cannot say, or: how poetic language says that it cannot say what it means and so succeeds in meaning what it doesn't say." Cited by David Lehman in *The Line Forms Here* (Ann Arbor: University of Michigan Press, 1992), 31.

21. *Rational Meaning,* 211, also 178–79.

22. *Rational Meaning,* 128.

23. These last few lines are a paraphrase of part of "The Person I Am: The Subject In Extended Perspective," *Later-Life Commentaries* (forthcoming).

24. "For Later Readers," *The World and Ourselves* [Reissue (photographic reprint) of 1938 edition, with new preface] (Ann Arbor M; High Wycombe: University Microfilms, 1969), xi.

25. *The Telling*, Passage 5, also 63–64.

26. "Entry in *Twentieth Century Authors* (1955)," 161; compare 1980 *Introduction to the Poems of Laura Riding, Reader*, 260.

27. *Rational Meaning*, 69. Compare: "I try to live towards truth the Meeting-Place." To Sonia Raiziss, March 10, 1964, Cornell.

28. "A Reading . . . for . . . the University of Florida," *The Sufficient Difference: A Centenary Celebration of Laura (Riding) Jackson*, ed. Elizabeth Friedmann; *Chelsea* 69, December 2000, New York: Chelsea Associates, 2000 [whole issue], 52.

29. "A Modern Legend," 33, Berg; and *Rational Meaning*, 353–54.

30. *Rational Meaning*, 457–58; also "Prologue: Description of Planned Work," 17 of the present volume.

31. Letter to Walter Arnold, October 20, 1970, Cornell. Compare: "I have tried not to be a speaker of 'truths,' but to find the way that each must take to preserve and develop the human faculty of truth." "For *Who's Who in America*," Berg. "As to my having an 'obsession with truth'—my concern with the matter of truth is not with 'my' telling of 'the' truth, but in the general project implicit in the possession and employment of language to which human beings dedicate themselves in using words." To Michael Braziller, February 26, 1981, Cornell. "I do not in *The Telling* present my sentences as 'truth.' I place the burden, the responsibility, of speaking with truth, speaking words of truth, *in* a natural human potential individually possessed." "To Someone who had both seriously pondered on the content of, and seriously questioned the tenor of, my book *The Telling*," collection of Elizabeth Friedmann. "I am of my human nature a thinker, and conscious of need, responsibility of thinking-speaking *with* truth. I do not go about hunting 'truths.'" To Sonia Raiziss, June 1983, *Chelsea* 52 (1991): 63.

32. "Then, And Now," 98; compare "Truth is not just 'there'; it must be made—that is, it must be spoken." "What, If Not A Poem, Poems?" 5, *Reader*, 242.

33. *Rational Meaning*, 458.

34. *Rational Meaning*, 379.

35. *The Telling*, 59ff. Compare "A Covenant," *Chelsea* 69 (2000): 85.

36. For "human," see *The Telling*, 137–38, also "The Word Human, The Living Of Human Life," in *Under The Mind's Watch* (Oxford: Peter Lang, 2004). For "being," see "The Missing Story," *Grand Street* 1(3), Spring 1982, 81—a passage comparable to Heidegger's *What Is Called Thinking*, Part Two, Lecture X.

37. "Twentieth-Century Change," 84–85 (though she is speaking of poetry here, *criticism* of poetry is the context).

38. "For Later Readers," xii.

39. Letter in *The Review* 24 (1970): 76.

40. "For Later Readers," ii–iii.

41. "Then, And Now," 98. See also "Engaging in the Impossible," 23 and 9.

42. "Reading for the Library of Congress," 140–43 of the present volume; "Then, And Now," 89ff. "Miscellaneous General Reflections," 169 of the present volume.

43. "Prologue: Description of Planned Work," 18.

44. For her view of Rimbaud, see "Then, And Now," 65, also "Kinds of Poetic Excitement, Kinds of Poets," 200ff. of the present volume; for her view of Plato, see "Poetry and the Good." Oppen is sometimes mentioned by commentators in this context, but his reason for desisting from writing poetry had to do with his response to depression-era politics; see Jeremy Harding, "Take Out All the Adjectives," *London Review of Books*, May 6, 2004, 17. Augustine's renunciation of rhetoric is mentioned by her in "A Reading . . . for . . . the University of Florida" (*Chelsea* 69, 2000), 51.

45. " . . . what you call my 'aesthetic.' I do not have one. I do not have views on what is called that, as on what is called 'poetics.'" To Michael Trotman, April 19, 1986, Cornell.

46. "From Letters to Robert Nye, 1962," 220.

47. It is his avowed lack of sympathy with the later writings that detracts from Michael A. Masopust's otherwise careful and well-informed account in "Laura Riding's Quarrel with Poetry," *South Central Review* 2(1) (1985): 42–56. The most reliable and helpful accounts of her renunciation of poetry are Alan Clark's "The One Story: Laura (Riding) Jackson, 'The Telling,' and Before," *Stand* 15(1) (1973): 32–37, and Elizabeth Friedmann's *A Mannered Grace: The Life of Laura (Riding) Jackson* (New York: Persea Books, 2005), chaps. 36–37.

48. "Twentieth-Century Change," 72 (here again, though she is describing poetry, *criticism* of poetry is the context).

49. To Jose Villa, December 27, 1962, Berg.

50. "The Principle of the Thing," *Chelsea* 69 (2000): 100.

51. "Then, And Now," 93; compare "I have never ceased to bless the historic fact of poetry." "Body & Mind and the Linguistic Ultimate," *Reader,* 306.

52. "[From] Comments on a study of my work, [1975]," 228. Compare her appreciation of Roy Fuller's remark in *The Review* 23 (1970): 9, that she did not "rat" on poetry in renouncing it, 1980 introduction

to *The Poems of Laura Riding,* 10; (2001), xli; (1980), 10; *Reader,* 260. See also "Something Rather Short," 3, Berg.

53. "Poetry and the Good," 24, *Reader,* 218.

54. This is an adaptation of her closing remark in *Everybody's Letters* (London: Barker, 1933), 253.

55. "Then, And Now," 54.

LAURA (RIDING) JACKSON

# Prologue
## Description of Planned Work

This book collects many comments and commentaries that have accumulated in my years of reflection on poetry since I was moved, a few years after the publication of my *Collected Poems* in 1938, to forswear the writing of poems. References to this renouncing of poetry and varied statements on it of an explanatory kind appear in the course of the presentation of the book's material. But the material has not been organised according to any programme of "position" stressing, systematic advancing of views, or of elaborating on themes regarded by me as critically crucial. The assortment of pieces of writing joined here into loose connectedness is genuinely miscellaneous. What consistency is found to pervade the whole is internal, and progressive.

The work has relation to my past concern with poetry as an active poet: I believe I have report of experience and thinking and study to make, with regard to poetry, poets, and the question of the poetic and the ordinary use of language, of important literary and general interest.

As a poet I applied modern sensibilities to the appreciation of what was implicit in the traditional conception of poetry. This embodies an ideal of eloquent expression in which language is pressed to fulfil a function generally but vaguely recognized in it, that of serving as the instrumentality of truth. Closely related to the linguistic aspect of the ideal is an objective of achieving a truth-quality in poetic expression that unifies the personal and the common human impulses of articulate sensibility in authentically representative human utterance.

I think I was unique as a "modernist" poet in my adherence

to the traditional principle of poetry, which I later called its "creed." All other poets of intellectually modern orientation broke faith, variously, with the creed of poetry. Variously, also, they broke attachment to the physical tradition, which, later, I distinguished from the spiritual tradition, or creed, as the craft component of the historical actuality "poetry."

In devoting myself to poetry as its traditional self, I practised fidelity to the integrities of language, a literalness of verbal faith corresponding to the spiritual literalness of my devotion. I shall treat somewhat of my poetic work, its character as intellectually modernist yet spiritually traditional, with regard to its effect on other poets. Of those in direct association with me, none were affected in full or permanent moral earnest; those who derived, and derive, what is called "influence" from it I judge to be generally in the category of the narrowly literarily-interested. I shall also treat of my ultimate resolution to renounce poetry. But I shall give some main attention to the dissolution of the traditional conception of poetry in the late modern era, and the confusions and aberrancies, accompanying this, in poets' sense of appropriate poet-objectives.

I shall also give some main attention to the discrepancy, which I came to think unresolvable, between the requirements of *creed* and the exactions of *craft*. I see the discrepancy as of a moral order: the craft-urgencies attune the linguistic course of the truth-commitment to a pattern of sensuous word-appeal designed to supplement the humanly representative meaning of poetic expression with physical symbolizations of humanly representative emotionality—the craft-element is, that is, exterior dramatic artifice.

No other poet of this era has, I think, brought, within the actual range of poems-writing, the spiritual ideal of poetic truthfulness of word to crisis-point juxtaposition with the craft principle of dramatic substitutes of verbal sensuosities for veritable word-expressiveness. The prevailing contemporary preoccupation of poets has been, not with the ultimate question of the nature of poetry, and the test to be made of its nature by modern sensibilities under the direction of an articulate modern conscience, but with problems, irrelevant to the matter of poetry, of choice of individual mode of employing the traditional resources of poetry for psychological purposes. I shall treat of exemplifications, among modern poets, of this tendency to the conversion of the practice of poetry into a form of behavior, offered as having contemporary significance as expressive of types of modern personality-predicaments. I shall bring into comparison attitudes of poets of other times to the poetic rôle, and to poetry.

As to the relation of what I shall present to the scholarship of poetic criticism of the time: I shall explore my view that its values of judgement are not in relation to standards appropriate to the traditional actuality, poetry, but to philosophic revisions of the conception of it, redefinitions that relieve it of its historic identity, bestow upon it an identity of a rhetoric of opinion that is both personally and philosophically synthetic. (For, as I see this, there is no force of contemporary philosophy, there are no contemporary philosophies: the generalizing intellectual operations of the time are like psychological experiments in thinking. There is no connection between thinking and belief. I think it is not mere coincidence that modern conceptions of the nature of poetry and the nature of truth have both become so confused that confusion of definition of them seems authentic modern revelation.)

I see the crux of the exercise of modern sensibilities with regard to the fate of poetry, and the rescue of the belief in truth as the speakable reality of the sanely thinkable, in the arrival at enlarged, intensified consciousness of the potentiality, for all who have language, of eloquent truthfulness of word fulfilling the ideal that was long nurtured, with certain unconquerable limitations in the conception of poetry, in its practice. I mean to cover, besides various aspects of the problem of poetry, historical, critical, moral, matters of compositional peculiarity, such as the prominent part assigned to metaphor in poetry, by craft convention. The matter of language, the linguistic failure of poetry, the theme of the human natural in linguistic success, will figure in appropriate connections.

Robert Fitzgerald's words of 1939 on my poems suggest the motif of language-concern underlying my earlier and later views of poetry, and this project: ". . . these poems should one day be a kind of *Principia*" [if "the dignity of truth telling, lost by poetry to science," were regained]. "They argue that the art of language is the most fitting instrument with which to press upon full reality and make it known."[1]

[From a grant application, 1973.] I have left little room for describing the other project to which I have referred, a book, quite long ago planned, called *The Failure of Poetry*, which I might be able to assemble from accumulated writings and notes in a general state of working ease—but the work on language has prior claim with me, as to this, and everything else. In this book concerned with poetry, I should treat of the good hope it raises, the stasis to which it brings poet, reader, at its best; treat of poetry in the past, and the present; and of my own poems; of the criticism of poetry; of—in the words of the title of one of my essays—"What, If Not A Poem, Poems?"[2] That question is about the general spiritual efficaciousness of language.

---

1. [*Kenyon Review* 1, no. 2 (1939): 342.]

2. [*The Laura (Riding) Jackson Reader*, ed. Elizabeth Friedmann (New York: Persea Books, 2005), 239ff.]

# I

# Truth Begins Where
# Poetry Ends

# Introduction for a Broadcast;
## Continued for *Chelsea*

For many years I have discountenanced attention to my poems, of which there are none of later making than those contained in my *Collected Poems,* published in 1938. The final poems of that work concluded a long exploration of the possibility of using words in poetry with the true voice and the true mind of oneself. I had fervently believed that in poetry the way so to use words might be found—which had nowhere, yet, been found, completely. But after 1938 I began to see poetry differently, even to see it as a harmful ingredient of our linguistic life. My view of poetry, which led me to suppress my poems, has not changed. But I feel that it may now have matured to a point at which it can usefully illuminate, and be usefully illuminated by, my poems. This feeling is my reason for co-operating in this broadcast.

As I reflected on my past poetic activity, I perceived that, in casting my voice and my mind in the poetic mold of speech, I had shut out the realization of the very thing I sought. The equivalence between poetry and truth that I had tried to establish was inconsistent with the relation they have to each other as—the one—*art* and—the other—*the reality.* I came close to achieving, in my poems, trueness of intonation and direct presence of mind in word. But, what I achieved in this direction was ever sucked into the whorl of poetic artifice, with its overpowering necessities of patterned rhythm and harmonic sound-play, which work distortions upon the natural proprieties of tone and word.

My poems have a strong attraction for some, which proceeds, I think, from their appealing both to the innate desire for the true in the use of words and to the cultivated appetite for the poetic in their use, and their seeming thus to offer two kinds of satisfaction at once. Because they are poems, they can provide only one kind of satisfaction, poetical satisfaction. But the very evocation of the other kind provides something extra, a bonus. To many, however, this bonus is an annoyance. For a number of poets, my work has been as a new primer of poetic linguistics. For me, it is poetry *in extremis,* poetry caught in and confronted with its factitious nature as a mode of linguistic expression.

How did I make the mistake of assuming that, from the art of poetry, the reality of live, personal truth could be precipitated? The time had come for someone to make the mistake. Poetry gradually appropriated the house—the haunted but never occupied house—that language had built for the speech of truth: the time had come for someone to put the occupancy to the test by treating it in good faith as legitimate. Through my mistake, I have learned things that I could not have learned, or learned so well, otherwise. I have not learned them just for myself. I see them as part of the equipment needed for our giving ourselves a new linguistic dispensation.

I have learned, for instance, that poets, to be poets, must function as if they were people who were on the inside track of linguistic expression, people endowed with the highest language powers; that, in functioning so, they not only block the discovery that everyone is on this inside track, but confuse themselves and others as to the value of their linguistic performance; that the novelties of expression achieved in poetry leave ordinary speech, and its literary counterpart, prose, sunk in their essential monotony and unaspiringness; that there is no vital connection between the verbal successes of poetry and our actual speaking needs—they are no more than dramatic effects produced with words. I have learned that language does not lend itself naturally to the poetic style, but is warped in being fitted into it; that the only style that can yield a natural and happy use of words is the style of truth, a rule of trueness of voice and mind sustained in every morsel of one's speech; that, for the practice of the style of truth to become a thing of the present, poetry must become a thing of the past.

It has been hard for me to learn such things, and harder still to reconceive my working course in the light of them; and even harder to communicate what I have learned. Among my problems, when I endeavor to recount my findings, that of offence raises its head menacingly. I am aware that my animadversions on poetry will excite not only disagreement where there is esteem of poetry, but personal resentment besides, since esteem of poetry and self-esteem tend to become intertwined—as I have reason to know. I take this problem seriously: any offence felt can be presumed a thing I would have averted, could I have done so.

### Continued for *Chelsea*

In the foregoing statement I presented my thought on poetry in cross-section; here I present extents of the general view of which it is part. There I reported on a break with an established set of values; here I give some of my new orientation-points. The possibilities of what-more-to-say, beyond what I have said, are numerous. I shall apply myself here to two themes, both of which have to do with the question of seriousness. I know that to some my position seems over-serious.[1] So, I should like to speak of the part poetry has in human life, and, then, of the self that uses words—and may looks-askance at my seriousness dissolve, as I do.

The most serious character poetry bears is that of being a mode of expressing what would be otherwise inexpressible, and of constituting, thus, an area of spiritual exercise and experience. This character confers a spiritual distinction on poets, of which their audiences partake. But the poetic area of expression and experience, while inviting the soul, is not habitable by it. It is a small, socially hallowed enclosure in civilization wherein recognition is given to the immediate need of people to speak from all their soul—which the religions do not fill. Poets perform there; their audiences flock there, as to a spiritual theatre

---

1. [Stanley Kunitz had in 1955 expressed such a view; see Elizabeth Friedmann, *A Mannered Grace: The Life of Laura (Riding) Jackson* (New York: Persea Books, 2005), 394. Perhaps L(R)J was also recalling Yeats's notorious description of her "school" as "too thoughtful, reasonable & truthful." *Letters on Poetry from W. B. Yeats to Dorothy Wellesley* (London: Oxford University Press, 1940), 69. See also note 1 on "Then, And Now."]

or fairground. Then, it is over, and the lights go out. The poets withdraw to their feelings of satisfaction or dissatisfaction, centered in the poem. If they have produced good poems, they have done their professional duty, and are entitled to a reward from society. But, for poems, "good" is a complexly qualified standard.

Historically, a poem is a ritualistic arrangement of words designed to work a spell of ephemeral exaltation, and remains this within its artistic envelope. Properly, poetry does not belong to letters—there is too much of the nature of incantation in it, it is too weak intellectually, too wild emotionally, the poet is too much the shaman. The "good" poem is a linguistic feat, but not a solid literary feat; it is a fictive spiritual feat, a beguilement of the soul. Nor is it a solid linguistic feat. The words are only part of the poetic formula: the rest is ritual, and the reason in *them* must contend with the mechanics of magic-making in *it*—and must not win. A poem must always stay within the given social limits of seriousness. It can achieve an immortality there as social property—to share in which is the poet's reward. But there is no way to convert the poetic occasion into a real spiritual opportunity. Nothing can occur within the bounds of that occasion but the operation and the enjoyment of contrivance. The final value of poetry is *play*—not purposively, but by organic deficiency of seriousness.

Poetry has developed from the medicine-man mysticism of charm-speaking through leaping stages of sophistication. But sophistication must bring us closer and closer to awareness of its incapability of doing more than produce word-charms, and while away the idle spiritual hour. Because there is no social provision for immediacies of open-souled speaking, and truth thus becomes formalized into a religious or moral or other categorical specialty, some go to poetry to try to work salvations of the truth-instinct under its gilded sign: they go to it because there is nowhere else to go for this—and are trapped in a nowhere. The place for this must be created new—anywhere, everywhere.

There is much genuine pathos of person in the effort of poetry. But there is also much astute professionalism—more and more as the traditional importance of poetry seems in danger of diminishment. Accommodations have been made; the elevation has been brought lower, made more realistic; indeed, in the close past, the poem, by an inversion of its magic, was put into service as an elegant depressant. Yet the trend of internal decline has little effect: poetry is sustained from without, by a fostering social possessiveness. Its passing will come only by sheer renunciation, the resolve to end all dalliance with word-ritual and language-art—and learn what soul-honor can teach of fair ways to speak.

Now I turn to my second theme. My phrase "with the true voice and the true mind of oneself" may seem to indicate that I believe "self-expression" to be the ideal object of the use of words, the ultimate linguistic good. I do not so believe. Nor do I subscribe to a canon of impersonality, in imitation of that one proposed for poets in their word-craft, a time ago, as the proved rule of artistic excellence the past bequeathes. The good use of words I take to consist in perfect fidelity to oneself (in a single management of intonation and thought) in their use—irre-spectively of the speaking-circumstances. But implicit in this no-tion is the notion that the very use of words transmutes the self-hood by individuality into a representative selfhood—if self be truly subjected to the conditions of language. I stress the per-sonal factor in the use of words; I reject "self-expression" as the fulfilment of the function of language.

Poetry depends too much on powers of enlarging upon and exploiting the physical features of words to allow of fulfilment of the function of language as I conceive language. Poetry is lin-guistically freakish; and it is not, in its freakishness, the natural spiritual speech of human beings—there is more animal mag-netism in it than spiritual intensity. It does not, actually, trans-mute our private, bodily selfhood, but borrows language-graces for it from the soul. It leaves one as one was, knowing even less how to speak from one's soul.

I conceive language to be the peculiar equipment of beings for whom being is an indivisible experience—a resource issuing from their nature as beings of such a kind. I see every languaged being as centered to a principle of unity of being, which is no mere social postulate or religious generalization but is the in-ternal fact of human life; I see every language as concentric with every other (whatever its indigenous idiosyncrasies) in its being a manifestation of human identity. I see human identity as ap-prehended, and exercised, through language.

Human identity comes—to carry my theme a little further—of being more than oneself, more than one is within the restriction of individuality. Human nature provides extensity of being; and language answers to this extensity. Where in the use of words a purity of human personality is maintained, the speaking expresses not just the forces and qualities of individual being, but those of being in the whole. Where such a purity is not maintained, the speaking is impure, is "selfish." The poetic standard of purity is a standard exclusively of art. The speaking of poetry has all the sublimated selfishness of art in it; sensuous satisfaction in the words is the given, imposed, first interest.

The apparent contradiction between the concept of self as the animate essence of individuality and the concept of self as the spirit of responsibility, or soul, dwelling in individual being and making it act with supra-individual reference is a reflection of a false dilemma. There is not real duality of selfhood, only a difference between limited seriousness and whole seriousness of being. The world of the former is full of things that make it seem sufficiency, themselves insufficient; if we move our selves into the world of whole seriousness of being, we shall lose merely what is humanly insufficient. But great is the sway over us of the superior things of that inferior world! Poetry is one of them. The practice of what I have called the style of truth is not.

# The Failure of Poetry

1.

This essay takes its title from an essay I wrote eight years ago—
from April to June 1965. That time was itself about twenty-five
years after my renunciation of poetry, my discontinuance of
being a poet because of coming into a changed view of poetry.
I began writing definitively on this changed view a few years
earlier, and I have written on it a good deal since. But there is
a broadness in the explanations of that essay that makes them
permanently serviceable. I shall quote extensively from it, and
reproduce passages from it in revision, and combine these extracts with new commentary suggesting itself as I proceed.
What comes directly from that former essay I shall distinguish
by quotation-marks.

Before getting this essay underway I ought to comment on
my names of "Laura Riding" and "Laura (Riding) Jackson." It is
by the first that I am known as a poet. When I renounced poetry
I ceased to use "Riding" as my surname; but I have retained it,
parenthesized, for continuity of authorial identity, in the authorial name I have used for all my writing since my marriage.

As to my renouncing poetry, I present a very brief introductory summary: I renounced it "as disappointing the hopes it excites as seemingly the way of perfect human utterance, or articulate truth."

It would not take me very long to expound my view that *poetry fails*. But I am concerned here with more than a mere ex-
pounding of my view. I want to communicate not only my view
but my personal thought-experience through the years in which
I have looked at poetry, and poets, and poems, and attitudes to
poetry, with the eyes of one who had been and was no longer a

poet. And I hope that my report will not be classified as literary criticism. My interest in composing it, and the story I have to tell, pass over the boundaries of literary criticism.

Perhaps I can give some helpful indication at the start of the kind of ground—extra-literary ground—on which readers will very frequently find themselves here. They will, for instance, meet with a rejection of the authoritative character automatically attaching to the poet-rôle as that of persons gifted with special powers fitting them to be representative spokesman for the rest of humanity as unequal in capability to the finest forms of human expressiveness. Some human beings do seem to incline naturally to the rôle of poet, and there is requisite for the rôle a skill of language that relatively few human beings have at ready state in them. But I think that the call to the rôle that strikes upon people and reverberates in their responsive breasts is, in its primary nature, its humanly serious nature, a call to their natural human inclination to rejoice in the powers of language, reinforced by the appeal of the prospect of exercising the powers of poetry. There is, beyond question, in that appeal, the attraction of opportunities for the exercise of personal powers. But I leave this analysis, for the present, at any rate. What I particularly want to establish here is that there are critical observations to be made about things classifiable as literary subjects from a viewing-point that does not itself lie within the professional domain of literature—that has its station on the general human ground of evaluation. Such observations I term "human criticism." (I use the term in the preface to *Rational Meaning: A New Foundation For The Definition Of Words*,[1] the book on language of my husband's and my collaborative writing, in conjunction with the term "linguistic criticism.")

Somewhere in the course of this essay, I intend to cite a picturing by Yvor Winters of the personal powers of poets, which, though naïvely theatrical in conception, illustrates the tendency in poets to associate the rôle of poet with the exercise of personal powers. I am moved to add here immediately to what I have said as to the departmentalistic character of literary criti-

---

1. [Edited by William Harmon; introduction by Charles Bernstein (Charlottesville: University Press of Virginia, 1997), 22.]

cism that the subject, in literary criticism, is always literature judged with reference to other literature: all judgement, in literary criticism, is relative to literature which, supposedly, is relative to human life. Literary criticism may be said to divide human life into literary and non-literary aspects, with its reality reduced to half in the division—the "real" half regarded as not fully real except as the literary half defines its reality.

## 2.

"Human beings have had in poetry a course of action in which experimental attempts at remedying certain deficiencies in their ordinary life could be made, the poets making these attempts on behalf of all, theoretically at least, with general encouragement. Poetry still has the status of something human beings can do, or have done for them, about something in which they ordinarily suffer lack, or disappointment, that may remove the lack, or nullify the disappointment, or, if it will not do this much, will afford the pleasure of imagining the possibility of it. It is with the story there is to tell about the part of poetry in human life—its commitment to a beneficent part in it—that I am mainly concerned in this essay. What I think of poetry is of value only as my judgement follows the lines of actuality that can be traced in that story.

"I do not mean to present a historical account of poetry. My story will have to do with the activity of poetry as a historical continuity, the human purposes from which the invention and cultivation of the activity of poetry have issued, and the elevation of it to one of prime spiritual importance, and with the advantages attributed to the general presence of poetry in the human envisionment, and the rewards associated with particular engagement in the activity, and with the particular devotion to its products. I shall try to bring under one light, hold within one story-frame, the nature of poetry and human nature, as a crowning grace of which poetry has long ranked.

"It will be helpful for an understanding of the point of view from which I tell the story of poetry I have to tell if I distinguish at the earliest here between the two categories of consideration into which, as I know poetry, everything pertaining to it falls.

These categories I call *craft* and *creed*. In every poem there is—its being a poem requires that there be—unremitting attention to craft. As a piece of work of words-combination, a poem *is* craft, and to an extent, or rather, in a way, impossible with a piece of work of words-combination of the prose order. The words have had to be fitted together into a compact, unalterable unity. It is a poem just because it must not be—is not meant to be—taken mentally apart, as can be done with a prose passage of words-combination without damage to its effect: a poem is supposed to be apprehended from one word to another in continuous instantaneity, as a perfect whole. In the aspect a poem has as craft it offers itself as perfect in verbal workmanship. This, of course, is not all that makes a poem. But where another would say, there is the emotional circumstance, or the poetic scheme of associations, or simply, the poetic subject, I say, there is, besides the *craft,* the *creed.* What I call the creed is not the subject or the reason of the poem, but the reason why the poet makes a poem rather than writing in another way—why the poet is a poet.

"Creed in poetry is the belief that there is an ideal condition of the human personality characterized by complete awareness, complete articulateness, completely intelligent liberation of spirit from the gross physical preoccupations incidental to human existence, and that the condition is realizable in poems as nowhere else—anything close to it seeming realized elsewhere being called 'poetic.' The effects of the realized condition, for the poet and the participant audience, constitute, by the creed, a peculiar state of being, in which there is suspension of the pettier life-values, and a grand sense of things, a sense of a grand scope of existence, suffuses the being, and moves the understanding. Implicit in the creed is the importance of words in the fulfilment of the potentiality of attaining to, and existing for a time timelessly in, this state. This poetic state is conceived to be at a height of removal from the ordinary mixed condition of the human personality at which the emotions become purified, the thinking-energies harmonized, and the whole being, transformed into a vibrantly articulate intelligence, is vested in words of an eternal truth-value.

"Without the element of creed, which has never been succinctly defined, but which, simply, inhabits the area of human life that has been reserved for poetry, filling it like an atmosphere, there could be no poetry, no poets. The consciousness of poets is infused with it even if they do not seriously subscribe to it. All have to subscribe to it formally, ritualistically; not to do so would make *craft* inane, motivationless—except as child's play or superstitious word-medicine. Profession of creed is implicit in the assumption of poet-identity; creed accompanies poetry as a matter of natural historical course—creed has been the propulsive force by which poetry has lasted through, and outlasted, ages.

"The reason why there has been this combination of a purely spiritual intention with a literary objective is that the intention has never yet had a natural home in customary human behavior, and has taken what home it could get—its having an official home in poetry is the closest it has come to having a natural home. Supposedly, in poetry, human beings—poets, and others with them—*succeed* spiritually, succeed for the while of the poem; they enjoy sensations of knowing perfection in a unity of perfect feeling and perfect thought in perfect word, the poetic experience seeming to raise the self not out of itself, as the pattern of religious experience promotes, but to a final fullness of human personality. Everywhere else, the human being seems, in the final sense, to fail personally. In poetry there is at least an immediate imagination of the task of personal attainment to highest spiritual success. The odor of poetry suggests an aroma of immortal truth humanly spoken, it excites a feel of the ultimate virtue throbbing in the words. Such, all in one, is the conventional character, the literary pattern, the spiritual theory, of poetry."

### 3.

I have spoken of the attraction that the poet-rôle holds of opportunities for the exercise of personal powers. This goes beyond the simple dramatic appeal of the literary rôle generally, that of binding the reading or listening audience in a spell of rhetorically compelled attention. It concerns a more than temporary effect, an influence more potent than that of excitation of mind and feeling for the time-being. Poets *can*, by the allowances of poetic craft, exert fascinations upon the aural and visual imaginations of readers, listeners, that transfix them permanently in certain orders of ideas and emotions. Generations of readers, nations in their centuries, can be held fixed by the potency of the verbal arts of poets exuberant in the poetic leave given them (or that they take to be given) to work with words as physically wieldable tools *upon* others. In exerting such influence, poets exaggerate the weaknesses of poetry: they become locked in impotent acceptance of a relationship to the others (the readers, etc) that makes the others slavish attendants, where their rôle is theoretically that of vigorously responsive participants in the poetic act of utterance. The exaggeration is a vulgarization of the weaknesses, but the exaggerative force employed can make the qualities of the results seem qualities of poetic strength.

"The presence of a publicist forcefulness in poetic writing can far outweigh, with a poetry-public, a want of courage in poets to expose to it their moral predicament of consciousness of rhetorical temptations difficult to resist. The public and its poems-providers tend to strike a tacit bargain by which they, as in mutual courtesy, ignore what is reciprocally demeaning in their relationship. There are many examples of this indulgence of poets, under the sanction of emotional custom, in hypnotic verbalistic power-play—and there is much variety in the examples. A very respectable general example is, that of Shakespeare."

**4.**

"Poetry allows—or seems to allow—of a temporary exercise of the spiritually essential human faculties—those in which the personal nature of the human being is concentrated. Yet, in its literary aspect, in its technical character, it is, besides being linguistic structure contrived for the entertainment of the mind, according to the motivating principle of all literary production, a practice in which canons of verbal sensuosity are substituted for the ordinary literary canons of 'style.' What by human tradition properly makes an appeal of a most elevated spiritual kind, by literary convention properly makes, first of all, a sensuous appeal. The words 'must,' through a craft of utilizing the physical properties and physical associations, maintain a continuous effect, upon the sensibilities, of utter attention-engrossment; the poem-audience 'must' be contained within an area of sought compulsive receptivity. The conditions of personal relationship between poets and readers, in poems, are on a different level from that of their spiritual functionality, which they have by the creed implicit in the fact of their being poems.

"There is a contradictoriness of levels in poetry from which there is no escape: between the level of sensuous susceptibility on which the physical word-enchantment is worked and the level of spiritual liberation, which the very words that make the enchantment are in *meaning* supposed to realize. In offering a refuge to human beings where they can put off the narrow identity of physical being, and classified identity of social being, and assume the broad and open identity of the state of being where the person is the soul, poetry is spiritually anomalous in that its major ministrations are to the physical person. The spiritual person is indeed only symbolically provided for in poetry, through the physical person as representing it. The fact that poetry does not concern itself with the social person (at least, not theoretically, and usually not overtly, when it actually does) contributes to the effect that its direct address to the sensibilities of the physical person has of, seemingly, an evocation of the spiritual person: its literary simplicity seems to attest to the reality of the spiritual level to which it invites ascent. But the two levels are not in reality encompassed in poetry. The upper level is a receding area in poetry, disappearing as it is approached, within poetry by implication and beyond poetry when the implication of it is pursued; and poetry, having itself the character of a beyond-place for which room was long ago found on literary terrain, has no occupiable beyond.

"The spiritual intention of bringing within the range of living experience accession to a finally articulate condition of human personality has had a foster-home in poetry. But poetry itself has no home but an intruder's enclave in literature. Were it not for poetic creed, from which comes the elevatedness of poetry, this intention could not be domicilable in poetry. For the craft of poetry is—contrarily to the general impression of it—of a *linguistic* quality more uneven, unsteady, intellectually crude, than that of any stylistic procedure of ordinary literature: verbally, poetry has certain irremediable inferiorities to ordinary literature, even to ordinary speaking, which the grandeur of creed and the influencive sensuosities of craft (the sound-play, and rhythm-play, and play upon the physical associations excitable with words) obscure.

"The idiosyncratic nature of poetry manifests itself in everything pertaining to it. The pursuit of poetry as a career is socially honored, in principle very highly so, yet it has no clear functional identity, occupying nervously a position of religious dignity while having only literary status, officially. The part of creed in poetry makes devotion to it as devotion to a cause. But it has no continuity except in subscription to creed: there is, has been, no development in it of achievement on the basis of creed. It amounts *practically* to nothing more than a cultural activity, that is, a token activity in which certain faculties are exercised, but not fulfilled. These are faculties of sensitivity to the possibility harbored in words of realizing in them the ultimate spiritually complete articulateness. Poetic creed makes the possibility the atmosphere of poetic utterance. But poetic craft stops in the excitation of expectancies of spiritual events, in the form of word-utterances; actually, the words cultivate sensations of expectancy rather than precipitate, themselves become, spiritual events. Thus it happens that the *summum bonum* of the poetic creed resolves itself, in experience, into a satisfaction of equating sensuously pleasurable word-effects with actualities of successful spiritual articulateness."

5.

"There is, besides the confused issue of poetic experience that has been described, a by-product that has a large attraction for people of more than average linguistic literateness. Since much sheer linguistic knowledge and skill can be spent in the management of the verbal sensuosities of poetry, poetry serves as a field of linguistic connoisseurship, and is comparable, in the room it holds for educated appreciation of linguistic expertness, to the arts that make direct appeal to the senses and yet swell into large fields for connoisseurship on an elevated intellectual plane. But this aspect of the experience of poetry is a vague literary enlargement of it, concerned less with what the poets do as poets in their poems than with what is secreted in the poems of linguistic versedness. It is a parasitic form of appreciation, having no relation to poetry as it organically and idiosyncratically is, only to poetry as literature *par excellence*, which is something not poetry at all, a backwater in which inertly lurk all the things adumbrated but not expressed in it, the stuff of failure and not of excellence, the area of the poet's linguistically self-conscious surrender to the restrictions poetic procedure imposes on articulateness.

"Almost all professional poetry-criticism has its seat in the field of literary connoisseurship, and is mainly not the criticism of poetry itself but mainly the criticism of the peculiar linguistic sophistication of poets that crowds ghostlily round their poems and works its way mutely into every emptiness in them in which, under the name of artistic discretion, the continual failure-to-say of poetry hides itself. Not only has there been no tradition of evaluating poetry according to how poets adjudicate in their poems between the demands of creed and those of craft, and how, generally, they fulfil the spiritual function that poetry is committed to fulfil: the very writing of poetry has been to a very large extent orientated to the values of such critical connoisseurship. Indeed, there are poets who write their poems from within this connoisseur-field, sitting even in the seat of its literary criticism of poetry—and, sometime[s], combining there the office of poet and that of critic, and turning from one to the other with little alteration of mental focus. T. S. Eliot was entirely an inhabitant of the connoisseurship-realm, as critic and poet both.

"Poets who take their orientation from the viewpoint of literary connoisseurship of poetry are substituting literary creed for poetic creed. The effect of doing this can seem admirably, finally, satisfactory: there are no loose ends in sight to justify suspicions that what poetry in faith aims at it cannot possibly in practice achieve. Poets under the literary aegis have their poetic legs drawn in neatly under them; they squat in the general complacency of the literary mood, with the comfortable sitz of people whose function is socially cut for them.

"The difference between the poet who does service to poetry incidentally to doing service to literature, and the poet having a direct allegiance to poetry, is in the matter of ingenuousness. The former is consciously disingenuous, professionally sincere because consciously so: the trimming of poetic creed to the limitations of literary interest is done under auspices having a piety of [their] own, that of contributing to public sophistication. On the other hand, poets who try to be loyal to the creed are bound to be martyrs to their ingenuousness—martyrs to the extent to which they succeed in being, in remaining, ingenuous. For the truer they are to the poetic function, the bigger failures they will be, by the measure of the inspiring poetic creed. The creed itself dooms them to failure, since it confines spiritual success of word—success of soul in success of word—to an artificially created, artfully induced, addendum to ordinary verbal experience. The creed of poetry is, in fact, inseparable from poetic craft, is conditioned by it, as poetic craft is reciprocally conditioned by the spiritual insufficiency of poetic creed, which, clinging to craft as its supporter, strengthens it in the very things that render it a mockery of a spiritually successful mode of expression. At any rate, the more ingenuously *poet* poets are, the more at a disadvantage they will be, with the critical connoisseurship, and with the public that takes its cues from the critical connoisseurship, and, most of all, with themselves: they will not be satisfied, ever, with themselves as poets."

## 6.

"The general tendency with poets has been to strike compromises between the poetic ingenuous and the literary disingenuous, or to mingle them carefully; but there is great variation in the ratio of one to the other among them. Very few, if any, have been able to maintain a stand of unmixed poetic ingenuousness. One may get a sense of relative difference, in how poets vary in the degree to which one or the other disposition predominates in them, from viewing Wordsworth and Coleridge side by side: though Coleridge was much more professionally active than Wordsworth as critic, and might thus be thought to have functioned as a poet with greater sensitiveness than Wordsworth to the canons of literary connoisseurship, he was the stronger in poetic ingenuousness, Wordsworth much more self-conscious literarily. And quite naturally, it is Coleridge who stands out as being at a disadvantage—the disadvantage of having taken poetry the more seriously. Wordsworth lent towards the literary definition of creed. Coleridge lent in the other direction—which is a main reason for his intense preoccupation, in relation to poetry, with matters philosophical and religious."

The distinction I have drawn between the Wordsworthian and the Coleridgean disposition to poetry inheres in a difference of view as to of what order are the values fundamental to poetry. For Wordsworth, they are values of compositional excellence of a loftiest literary order. For Coleridge, they are values of linguistic virtue of a most serious spiritual order. The crucial weakness in the spiritual basis of poetry is the compound nature of its linguistic principles. They are of the purest ideally, as principles of *poetry*, while being overridden, for the actual construction of *poems*, by a governing premise that construes the ideal in linguistic performance to be not practically realizable. Hence, the linguistic predicament of poetry, treated as having a certain potentiality of successful linguistic performability, has been continually perpetuated by the pursuit of verbal practicalities that reaffirm the linguistic ideal while putting it at eloquent removes of impossibility.

Poetry, from its beginnings, has suffered from endowment with the status of a function of elevation of the human personality to a level of *some* practical success for human beings, in the enjoyment of the character of higher beings. The success, its practicality, is qualified. Poetry is intended to be, for the poets and for its audiences, an actual occupation of a plane of sensibility and intelligence above the human commonplace for the period of its spoken duration. The poetic experience is, by the prescription of general human custom, a temporal remission from ordinary experience: the prescription by which it is an established, privileged, esteemed, form of deliberately constituted experience limits it in time. The attainment of a spiritually energetic, verbally intense, articulation of human consciousness in poetry, which is designed for this, is not meant, by the design, not expected, to extend itself practically from the poem-time into the ordinary temporal continuity of human life. There is thus left unresolved the spiritual aspiration to which poetry ministers, yet within limits that must be described as literary.

If readers of this essay will turn at this point to my *Collected Poems*, they will meet, in its preface, with my quarrel with the confinement of poetry to the temporal limits of literaryism.[2] I was defending poetry against the imposition of temporal restrictions upon its spiritual force, the literary necessity of this. But in treating poetry as being thus defensible, I was actually quarrelling with the unacknowledged flaw in its nature.

Critics of the practical-minded order have become increasingly sensitive to the danger of being pressed, by the devoutly serious nature of poetic spirituality, into the area of religious emotionalism. Modern literary (poetic) criticism is self-consciously jealous of its sensibleness. The very nerve, in poetry, of quickness to the dilemma of its having a definable literary function and a literarily unplaceable human commitment to spiritual purification of motive and end, in the personally expressive use of words, is deliberately deadened in the devoutly humanistic scrupulosity of the doctors of modern literary criticism who would cure poetry's ailments—fundamental in its constitution—by treating them as conditions natural to it as a *human* enterprise. The trend, in the contemporary criticism of poetry, is towards a realistic conception of the spiritual plane of poetic activity: it must not be religious in degree of poetic intensity—although it may be religiose in extent of use of religious imagery for dramatic enlivenment of poetry as a stage for linguistic performance. Critical tolerance of themes religious and irreligious, and verbal style adapted to their respective different emotional postures, is contemporarily of the broadest, indiscriminately so, with a generally

---

2. ["To the Reader," *Collected Poems* (London: Cassell; New York: Random House, 1938), xvff.; *The Poems of Laura Riding: A New Edition of the 1938 Collection* (Manchester: Carcanet; New York: Persea Books, 1980), 406ff.; *The Poems of Laura Riding: A Newly Revised Edition of the 1938/1980 Collection* (New York: Persea, 2001), 482ff.

governing reservation: the intellectual level must not be other than "human," that is, realistically human—it must be a literary level, in a best, "human," sense of "literary."

To myself, that criticism of poetry which does not face the necessity of answering questions, or at least posing questions, as questions of prime difficulty, on the kinship of poetry and religion, as verging upon each other in an identity of *intellectual* location, is a disprizer of the spiritual intention animating both poetry and religion in their aspects of intellectual sincerity. Both issue from human thought at the same point, and both round back to that point, poetry taking an experimental path of personal responsibility for truth, religion taking a path of reliance for truth on *chosen* authority. Both call for treatment as intellectual alternatives in spiritual experiment.

But I must slacken the flow of my later commentary on the long-obscured character of poetry, and the peculiar problems with which the obscuring of its character enlarged the general problem, of human beings, of forming understandings matching their capabilities of comprehensive intelligence centered in self-intelligence. My earlier commentary moves at a rate I do not wish to outspeed.

## 7.

"It could well be asked: what could the criticism of poetry be, other than literary criticism? There are two kinds of criticism that fit the idiosyncratic character of poetry, and that, joined, would be, truly, poetic criticism and not literary criticism: these are, spiritual criticism, and verbal criticism. I shall speak first of the spiritual criticism.

"The spiritual criticism of poetry would have to concern itself with the degree to which poets accepted and attempted to fulfil the poetic creed, or to which they avoided putting themselves and their work to the test of it by making qualifications of it in their interpretation of it. The trend of my own critical writing on poetry was towards such criticism; and, in the closing years of my functioning as a poet, I approached its borderlands—in my writing in the critical miscellany of my editorship called *Epilogue*, in my preface to my *Collected Poems,* and in a book called *The Left Heresy* [1939], to which I contributed much as a collaborator of Mr. Harry Kemp, its first author. But one would have to know that poetry had to fail spiritually, for a certainty, to be able to sustain an accurate spiritual criticism of it; and this I could not know while I was pressing to its ultimate reach my faith in the ultimate achievability in poetry of the ultimate spoken human perfection.

"My commitment to the poetic creed became more and more intense even as I became aware, in the maturing of my sense of the comprehensiveness of the human speaking-potential, and increasingly so, of barriers in poetry to the perfect realization of the potential, not yet thrust aside. Seeing poetry as necessarily the initiating ground of such realization, and the realization as implicit in human existence, I imagined no other course, no other hope, than that of pressing upon the potential of poetry itself. My guiding concept of poetry was unblemished with the sophistications of literary connoisseurship (by which poetry is a socially licensed, or 'cultural,' pursuit rather than a self-responsible spiritual activity); I looked to an entire revision of the standing concept of literature. For if one puts so much faith in poetry that one divests it of its idiosyncratic character, in one's notion of it, it will fill up with the light of intelligent hope that attends the expectation of the perfect in words; and this light will shine embracingly upon literature, which leases to poetry a precinct of its worldly terrain, and lend it potentialities of fostering a spiritually successful poetry.

"I believed in an ideal literature, spiritually kindred with poetry, believed in by me as the ideal experience of articulate humanness. Literature as well as poetry, by the measure of my ingenuous longing for evident fruition of human potentialities of soul, had a *destined*—if not immediate actual—goodness. My criticism of literature may be said to have been an extension to literature of a poetic criticism—a criticism concerned with making direct spiritual evaluations, rather than the usual judgements by the book of literary professionalism, in which the Good is an ideal of cultural sophistication merely. But this criticism of mine, in its application to both poetry and literature, fell short of the final mark of spiritual wisdom because its uncompromisingness towards the spiritually devious attitudes of literary connoisseurship had the internal weakness of compromise with poetry in its yet unproved capability of opening the way (seeming barred everywhere else) to full exercise by human beings of their truth-function.

"A spiritual criticism of poetry that goes all the way in judgement, unstayed by nostalgic favoritism towards it, must have the company of a completely unbiased verbal criticism of it. However, the verbal criticism of poetry, given that it be made from a position of critical judgement in which there is total resolution against indulgence of linguistically insufficient or unfaithful word-use, cannot go very far without leading to a crisis of choice between the necessities of poetic craft and the requirements of poetic creed, with the code of truth of word implicit in it to its core. And so long as commitment to creed holds, even the most ingenuous of poets will strain their ingenuousness to the breaking-point of disingenuousness to justify to their spiritual conscience the shadings in their linguistic sense of honor that the very exercise of the craft, with its relentless insistence on physical potency of word, imposes. In fact, we cannot have perfectly enlightened verbal criticism of poetry except where commitment to creed has finally taken the poet outside of poetry— commitment to that end of pure speaking (and therefore of pure being) that has worn the accoutrements of poetry in order to win itself a place in the human world.

"Those who have been poets can show the true verbal nature of poetry. The critics of poetry who are not poets cannot be expected to tear themselves away from the gratifications of association with it, and the same holds for the whole body of the poetic connoisseurship: so long as poetry exists, it will have its cultural consumers, there will be cultural demand for it. It will take the poets themselves, the producers, to rid human life of this anomalous feature of its conscious activity and experience.

"To speak of myself. . . . First, I stopped writing poems, because I felt I had completed a span taking me to the very shore on which the pure and full speaking I had sought in and through poetry would become a pure and full reality, instead of being an always partial achievement, with all the light of reality engendered by the words making, always, a shadow larger than the achievement. And I thought that it might be that I would not write poems for a while, until the difference between partial and full achievement was a fact of my existence on the new shore, until full truth of word was my poetic habit. But, with the stopping, and very rapidly, there came retrospective revelation— after-revelation—of the uncomfortable verbal part one must play in being a poet: one must follow a pattern of word-sound, word-association, word-arrangement, compelled by what seem laws of physical inevitability (but are only dictates of chance, of which one's verbal experiencedness becomes the agent-will), and *at the same time* be in all honor persuaded that one is in every word abiding by the prescriptions of the poetic creed, and that every word not only rings physically, feels sensuously, right, but is spiritually right. Only when I had stopped did I know the fundamental irrelevancy to each other of the commitment to the creed and the inseparable commitment to the craft. There is only the straining honor of the poet in the effort to reconcile them that holds them together in decent alliance.

"The scales of tolerance of the ruses of poetic craft, seen as honorable service in the cause of the creed, fell from my eyes when I knew, in the lull of poetic inactivity, that nothing called poetry or that could be called poetry could be the fulfiller of the cause that poetry had made its creed."

## 8.

"Verbal criticism of poetry that does not pay regard to the sacrifices of linguistic principle exacted by the craft (of poets, and their readers also) disregards the poem's nature as a linguistic actuality. There has been hardly any recognition in the verbal criticism of poetry of the straining of the poet to be linguistically honorable as something falling outside of the limits of the craft aspect of poetry. What is linguistically best in a poem and what is verbally suitable to the fact that it is a poem face in different directions, the one towards creed, the other towards craft. It is critically customary to subsume everything pertaining to the use of words in a poem in its poetic verbal mode, its verbal poeticism; but the linguistic struggle, the struggle which is also a spiritual struggle, for truth—as distinct from verbal suitability to the forms of poetry—does not, in a final sense, fall even within the frame of the creed aspect of poetry.

"There is an element of manifest effort in some poems, that is, which is dedicated not to poetry but directly to truth (I do not say, which is of the order of truth). Yet the words of poems are critically evaluated, almost invariably, as if they constituted a solid block as it were of craft—of speaking-work in the poetic verbal mode. They are this only in amateur poems, poems in which an ever-amplified craft partners unlaboriously with an oversimplified creed. In the main, the word-substance of poems consists of that which is there in consequence of poetic craft and that which is there in consequence of that straining honor of the poet of which I have spoken, the effort to apply the test of truth to the capricious pulse-beat of the craft-flow of the words. The word-substance of the poems, that is, is an uneven mixture of these two elements, the proportion varying generally from poet to poet according to personal character, and from poem to poem according to what the subject-material and the chosen craft-design allow, apart from personal variations in the sense of linguistic honor (dependent on the degree of creed-seriousness of the individual poet). I have referred to that invisible factor of unspoken overflow from what is said in a poem which to the critical sophisticates of the connoisseurship is the most precious element of the poem—and is actually the very stuff of the poem's failure (a failure unavoidable, because it is a poem) to be a linguistically whole, and spiritually sound, speaking-accomplishment. This stands with them instead of that in the poem which is done for honor rather than craft.

"The hardest straining to make the words of a poem both right in truth and right in verbal art cannot produce continuous identity. The poem is in a constant state of having to be kept from coming apart, and repaired and patched—the amount of such labor depending on the extent to which the poet is of ingenuous conscience in the poet-rôle. I am speaking of poems in which there is some happy animation with creed, and solemn concern with integrity of statement for honor above the mere professional honor of craft, more sensitive to standards of verbal seemliness than to those of linguistic probity. How little and how much of such animation and concern there can be in a poem it is very difficult to know in the terms of the familiar critical values (those of the 'connoisseurship'), in which there is implicit professionally disingenuous trimming-down of creed towards a literary norm of the Good. The values of connoisseurship intervene between the word-appreciating eye and the words of the poem, making a film through which the actual linguistic operations of which it consists are not visible in perfect distinctness.

"I believe that I came to know in and through my own writing of poems the limit of linguistic integrity to which it was possible to go in a poem. I did not know that it was a limit of that kind until after I had stopped writing poems. I knew it simply as a limit in *quantity* to what could be said. The poem seemed to invite one's saying all, faithfully, yet there was as it were a devil in every poem opposing one's saying of one's all, with which one had to struggle. But the very besting of the devil stole something of one's all-expressive force, so that the victory over it was, always, not that one said one's all but said nearly one's all, knowing that one was saying somewhat less than it, and holding on to the undelivered remainder in one's treasury of good-faith. Trust in the poetic possibility of saying more than just very nearly one's all kept me from knowing the quantitative limit as an index of incomplete linguistic integrity. It cannot be truth not to say one's all. But to a person who applied the test of truth unceasingly to the verbal make-up of her poems, as I did, and was at the same time committed in belief to a complete potentiality of truth in poetry, the margin between complete and short-of-complete linguistic integrity was not definitively drawn in any particular poem: the individual poem was viewed as part of the process of effort to realize in poetry the full perfection of truth promised in its creed. In each poem I experienced the failure of poetry, but it counted with me only as the saying-nearly-but-not-quite-all of the particular poem, not as a general defect in poetry's capability of linguistic integrity.

"How little care for linguistic integrity there can be in a poem without its validity as a poem becoming suspect may be understood by considering the character a poem has as something falling under the government of the values of the literary connoisseurship, something confined under the aegis of the connoisseurship—as is the case to a large extent in the making of poems. The literary norm of the Good to which a poem must conform, to fulfil the prescriptions of creed that the connoisseurship imposes, always takes in less—and generally much less—than does the ingenuous commitment to the creed of poetry in its entirety as a creed of aspiration. But that modified Good has in it the compensation, for attenuated emphasis on the ideal of truth and its implicit corollary of linguistic integrity, of special emphasis on an ideal of literary excellence, and an implicit corollary of literary integrity, which is always undergoing redefinition from critic to critic and poet to poet, among critics and poets, as they are orientated to the connoisseurship.

"It is a curiosity of the history of poetry—which, however, because of the ineradicable self-contradictoriness of poetry, is bound to be full of curiosities—that the most barren notion, the most constricted interpretation, of literary excellence as the poetic ideal comprises—just because of being concentratedly 'literary'—a dedication to linguistic respectability. And this dedication, this acknowledgement of a poetic responsibility in regard to language, ensures observance of the *forms* of linguistic integrity. The poetic literature of the connoisseurship—poetry not as an area of spiritual endeavor, but as the material cultural inheritance of poems—becomes endowed with hierarchical significances of value, to which poets attune themselves in making their poems, conceived as additions to the literary cultural poetry-mass. The newcomer poets present themselves as dedicated to the sustaining of the linguistic commitments embodied in the historical quantity poetry, while ringing, to the confusion of general perception of what these were, confusions of changes on the established standards of the linguistic superior as exemplifiable in poetry."

The straining of poets and the literary connoisseurship's sponsors of poetry to support poetry's antique prestige as the site of attainment to virtuously valuable elegance of language has been steadily diminishing as a self-cohering element in the contemporary production of poetic literature—poetry-criticism included. It may be said with a reasonable effect of historical accuracy, I think, that it is only, now, the *effete* literary linguistic educatedness of a pseudo-aristocracy of practising poets, combined with the energetic professional purposiveness of the remnants of a once substantial body of critical connoisseurs, that keeps poetry existent in a state of formal honoredness. Some poets adopt at least a posture of treasuring language, manifest an urbane self-consciousness in the employment of it as the professional instrument of poets; and the poem-texts of these will show at least the trappings of linguistic sagacity—their linguistic behavior will be within the bounds of literary-critical conceptions of poetic linguistic decorum. I wrote as follows, further, in the initial draft of this essay.

"The struggle between the requirements of creed and those of craft will cease to reflect the fated struggle of poetry between the discipline of truth and the technique of verbal sensuosity {it has already ceased to do this} and become {it has already become} a struggle between a technique of experiment in the poetic representation of the intellectually plausible and the strictures of a discreetly relaxed craft-technique. That is, creed has come to consist in but the precautions of a freely vague literary honesty, in the connoisseurship-province of poetry, the effect being a vestigial respect-paying to it as the crux of the existence of poetry. And craft-pressure has been modified to allow of shifts from meeting exigencies of verbal artistry to the functioning of poetic craft as general management of poetic linguistic style. That is, the struggle between the requirements of creed and those of craft has degenerated into a literary fiction. It is to a blank conventional pattern of poetry, as a perennial actuality that lost its survival-vitality in the first half of the century, that poets and critics conform, in their endeavors to identify themselves with the historic dignity of poetry as a literary profession."

{Unfinished}

# Then, And Now

*[Introduction to a projected selection
of Laura Riding's poems]*

## 1.

The usual ritual for the reintroduction to the public of out-of-print poetic work is to engage a poet or critic whose recommendation currently carries weight in the councils where the fate of books is decided, to bow in the dead or nearly dead, or forgotten or nearly forgotten, author. There are a number of reasons why this ritual does not fit the present case, of which I shall set forth a few.

A little over thirty years ago, not long after the publication of my *Collected Poems*, I experienced a dissatisfaction with poetry of a final order (on which I shall be here saying something), in consequence of which I suppressed my poetic work, withholding my poems, as I could, from anthologies and all other forms of reproduction. I did this not because I found fault with my poems, as poetry, but because I found fault, and major fault, with poetry. My new-found adverse view of poetry did not weaken, after that first comprehensive experience of dissatisfaction; it strengthened, and it has grown into an extensive criticism, making matter for an eventual book, to which I have given the title, in advance of completion, of *The Failure of Poetry*. This attitude, of which I eventually made public explanation, has been sloppily misinterpreted, so that I have been here and there described as having found my poems in particular not to be truth, or as having, categorically, rejected *my* poetry. It has also been derided from various points of view. "Oh, so serious!" was the mocking comment of the editor of a book of literary annals on my report, made for it, on my renunciation of poetry—himself a poet of ambition to whom, presumably, abandonment of the emoluments of poetic distinction could not be credited with sufficient sincerity to be taken seriously.[1]

I do not, then, offer these poems in the simple capacity of a poet making a return appearance; I do not desire merely to put another book of poems on the shelves of contemporary poetry-lovers. While not denying importance to my poetic work, as an example of what can be done in words within the limits of poetry, I view the conditions of word-use imposed by poetry as obstacles to what I regard as the most important human performance: so to use words that they are truth. As a poet I believed that words spoken under poetic conditions could be truth as words spoken under other conditions could not. But I have learned that the conditions of word-use conducing to an immediacy of truth in words do not obtain either on poetic or on ordinary speaking-ground, and are, indeed, hindered from developing on ordinary speaking-ground by the assumption that the peculiar beauties of poetic utterance come closer to being truth than words can elsewhere come, and as close as words can be expected to come. The importance of my poetic work will be justly estimated only if its relevance to the historic character of poetry as the furthest fulfilment of human linguistic capabilities is brought into consideration, and its qualities are examined in the light of the question later raised by me, whether the poetic furthest in language is, rather than a veritable fulfilment of these capabilities, a makeshift with which human beings may beautifully deceive themselves. This question simmered in my poems, although it did not boil up out of them (but, out of me—eventually): they were written with sensitivity to the necessity of putting poetry to the proof as a real attainment, an uttering of real words outstripping the mingled true-false-clear-dim of usual talk. There is a putting of poetry to such proof in all my poems—the conclusion being always loyally deferred.

For a long time I suppressed my poetic work without reservations or exceptions: and for the most part, in this time, I kept

---

1. [The editor was Stanley Kunitz. See also note on "Introduction for a Broadcast."]

silent on the personally decisive judgement I had formed that poetry is inadequate to the human speaking-needs to which it undertakes to minister—needs that are, in common recognition, of a prime order of importance in the general scale of human needs. When I felt that my thinking on this inadequacy, and the environing subjects, had reached the maturity point, I modified my policy of total suppression, and stood ready to permit reproduction of my poems where place was made for an accompanying statement by me of my later view of poetry. The first instance of this procedure was a BBC presentation of some of my poems in 1962: this was preceded by a summary of my later stand on poetry ["Introduction for a Broadcast"]. There has been a little disregarding of my stipulation, which I regret.[2] There have been exclusions of my poetic work from collections by editors, who sought to have it represented in them but were either unwilling to make prefatory reference to my present view of poetry, or prepared prefatory remarks on it that were unacceptable. (One, for example, insisted on a prefatory reference that had me, simply, renouncing *my* poetry; the reference remained, I withdrew.) I did not actively consider the question of a reissue of my poems until several years ago. My rule as to an accompanying statement of my present view of poetry must apply, of course, no less to the reproduction of my poetic work in the large than to the use here and there of pieces of it. This, also, has made difficulties.

The likeliest plan of a publisher who favored the reissuing of my poems would be to procure a preface-writer with authority to argue my "meriting a chance" and award me special commendations for my contribution to contemporary "poetics," and—into the bargain—to make a selection from the whole on the basis of "contemporary relevance and appeal"; a bone could be thrown in of allowing me to contribute a brief preliminary note that would formally meet my rule—but not seriously distract readers from what the preface-writer conjured up, to meet other rules. Publishers, of course, have to mean business. But I mean business in my later view of poetry, and no less certainly, where my poems are concerned, than in other connections. I can hope the

2. [See "What, If Not A Poem, Poems?," *Reader*, 240.]

two businesses are reconcilable, for I believe that a reissuance of my poems accompanied by an undoctored account of myself as poet and as poet-no-more would be more useful, to the public, and interesting, than an introduction in which I was handled as a pawn in the competitive game of poetic culture.

Besides to the general public, I feel an obligation to that scattered handful of a public that retains some consciousness of the existence of my poems, which I have had to leave for a long time in bewilderment as to what had happened with me as a poet, that I should have stopped being one in the midst of going full steam ahead. Such ones know me as one who identified poetry with certain objectives high in the scale of ideals: it has been owed to them to have it made plain that there is a vital kinship of ideals between my past positions as a poet, and my present position, as one who has renounced poetry—and the debt extends to the poems themselves, which were wrought in the service of those ideals (as ideals deemed realizable in poetry).

In the circumstance of a publisher's having enthusiasm for the combined presentation of poems of mine and an exposition of my adverse view of poetry, I should in principle not object to someone else's assuming the task of selecting the poems and composing the exposition of my view—and providing an appropriate quantity of critical and personal data. But not only are none of the relatively small number of those who chance to be acquainted with my view deeply grounded in it, but a desire to become so for the sake of just and competent reporting on it is not presumable in anyone of the poet-ranks or critic-ranks—not yet. The problems I raise are troubling ones even for those who perceive that I have some right on my side; they have much touchiness to get over in the matter of my view. Most, whether having advance acquaintance with it or not, would be rendered powerless to deal with it with even superficial accuracy by the absence in the parlance of literary politics, which the parlance of literary criticism so much is, of stereotypes to fit it. As to the ability to make informative critical comment on my poetic work as a whole, I think the stereotypes of critical expression limit it; and rare and fleeting have been the comments on it the terms of which referred to it directly. As to the selection of the poems by someone other than myself, I think there is a connection between an ability to understand my later view of poetry and an ability to make a representative selection. I mean by representative, representative of the character of my poems in the whole; and I doubt that this is successfully graspable without consultation of my later view of poetry. In the ordinary way of things, the Collected Poems of a poet of the age of thirty-seven would, over the next twenty-five to thirty years (given life-continuance), acquire a rather large sequel. There being, however, no sequel to the collective volume published in 1938, the fact and the why of my ceasing to write poems have to be added, as the sequel. Only if this is done will the trend-marks of my poetic work be clearly apparent.

As to the supplying of pertinent personal data, I believe no one could so well as myself trace the line of personal life in relation to the line of my working life as a poet, and beyond poetbeing. Others would very likely lose it at various points, and seek it a distance from the working-life line, among what would surely be irrelevances. The two lines have been, ever, a unity; I doubt that another could make a comprehensible characterization of that unity within the limits of abbreviated personal commentary—as I shall endeavor to do. There is further reason for my making such commentary myself in the fact that in so far as my life-course has come within the knowledge of others, it has been a good deal known through mispainted pictures. These could make no problem of research for me.

It is, probably, not going to be easy for any kind of reader to accompany me in my explanations of my views and experience as a poet and as, then, one who was and is poet no more, and in the personal delineation I give of myself. Some will be antagonistically disposed at the start—as soon, at any rate, as they comprehend, as they must *very* soon, that, while presenting my poems, I am at the same time presenting a case *against* poetry. Among these will be poetry-orientated readers (poets, critics, professors of, appreciators of poetry) who, having unbent over the years to the extent of deciding to be inclined to think well of my poems, feel ill-rewarded on discovering that I have strong criticism to make of them because they are poems. Starting in this discomfiture, such readers as these will perhaps mistake their discomfiture for confusion—and remain confused. For other poetry-orientated readers, the experience of accompanying me in my discoursing, here, will seem to involve too much work; and they will perhaps feel that what I have to say of poetry on the adverse side can have nothing to do with them, in their security of involvement in it. In the words of one poet who commented to me on some published expression of my later views on poets and poetry, they may "not get the involvement," and leave it at that. I urge every reader, whatever be the kind, to contemplate awhile before going any further the legend that appears on the opening page of this section of the book:

Truth begins where poetry ends.

I am going to try to show, on the basis of my own experience, where, how, why, poetry carries its end—its destinedness to amount ever to Nought—within it; and I shall set against this seeming tragedy the prospect of a sequel of truth uncompromised by verbal side-effects, such as compromise the poetry. The reader may anticipate difficulties; but what I present concerns serious difficulties we are all in, whether we are poets, or persons otherwise orientated to poetry, or persons to whom poetry is just something "*there*." The total import of what I have to say is a happy one. It is, that truth—the speech of truth—is a real and immediate possibility. But the poetic shadows that veil it must be torn away before it can be seen to be so.

## 2.

I want, in presenting these poems, to point to things I consider of large importance for the future (and present) of *speaking*—to talk not just about poetry, but about speaking. This could seem an exploitation of the occasion, and of my poems themselves, for the purposes of philosophic propaganda, and as such a victimization of readers who have a straight interest in poetry, and poems. But I think it is a natural concomitant of an interest in poetry and poems to be concerned with the matter of speaking: concern with it is properly basic to the making of poems, and the reading of them. In mingling the matters, I feel myself to be doing nothing other than rendering a stock-taking report of a kind long overdue from poets to their, and the, public. My relating poetry to the matter of speaking is practical, not philosophic.

Poetry has been, is of its nature, an ambitious experiment in speaking, a grand attempt at a perfect way of speaking. However, the implicit objective of finding a perfect way of speaking has, on the whole, been ever kept theoretical by poets; they have, generally, made it subsidiary to an immediate objective of pleasurable speaking having the temporary worth of *seeming* to be perfection. I myself was literal in my adoption of the implicit objective of poetry; the accomplishing of it was for me a real, not a theoretical, end. And so there is observable in my poems, I believe, some direct action in pursuit of an objective usually only theoretically pursued in poems—though it is the given, the traditional, the only seriously justifiable, poetic objective. At any rate, this past endeavor enables me to comment with a certain degree of confidence on the practical possibilities afforded in poems of achieving perfection of articulate utterance—that general human hope, which poetry has been upholding like a prating Atlas.

I digress a little here to give a warning that may be useful to readers. My being prompted to do so I owe to the pious disgust felt towards my terms of discussion by one who, priding himself on being the salt of modern poetic criticism, was put by chance into contact with some of my unpublished writing on poetry, and could not resist casting progressivist scorn on my thought, as of antediluvian date-quality. Particularly, among my terms of discussion, did the word "spiritual" excite froth of repugnance in his critical mouth. Therefore I say to readers, Be prepared to find that word here! May the warning forestall the shock the word apparently produces in the Darwinian sensibilities (which I had thought had become somewhat antediluvian themselves). For, in the case of the person in question, the shock caused so much confusion, in conjunction with others produced in other sets of educated sensibilities by such words as "truth," "perfection," "goodness," that *what* I said with these and other (not *yet* obsolete) despised words apparently swam like a scene seen through sea-sickness before his eyes: he read nothing straight. Perhaps readers, forewarned, will bear with me better in my use of old-timer words. Looming up immediately, additional to those already mentioned, is "ideal."

The implicit objective of poetry, that of forming a perfect way of speaking, becomes its ideal objective in *not* being practically pursued. This ideal objective is split into a theoretical objective on the one hand and a practical objective of pleasurable speaking on the other hand, which is sentimentally equated with the ideal objective. In this splitting of the objective of poetry, and identification of its pleasure-aspects with an ideal of perfection of word involving the very fulfilment of human nature, truth (surely, perfect speaking in all the senses of perfection) is split into an abstraction Truth, a legendary deity of poetry, and an aesthetic earthly twin, beauty, conceived of as the concrete representative of truth abstract. The split, become normal in poetry, perpetually defers the tests of actual truth, which is a complete standard, and admits of no separate standard "beauty."

This truth-beauty pairing is no mere philosophic cliché in poetry, but a condition of its life, favorable to its continued existence; though the twinned terms become unfashionable, critically, the notions persist, in various disguises—that of beauty a standard for the poem in its physical reality, that of truth a standard for it as meaning, to which it is supposed to conform sufficiently in conforming to the first. The term "beauty" can be dispensed with in the criticism of poetry as emotional styles change and the name of what pleases the emotional taste changes with them. But no term makes a critically convenient substitute for "truth," which designates values of care for scrupulosities of meaning that constitute poetry's code of honor: they are a constant, the principle of the ideal which poems are supposed to exemplify. No actual tests of truth are made, in the criticism of poetry, but conventions of judgement are observed that appear to be tests of truth—and poets, however much they lie, and love lying, must make some sort of subscription, be it contorted, dishonorable, to what "truth" ordains.

The matter of truth is central in poetry's *raison d'être*, and yet through the ages poets have been viewed as dealing in something less than truth—while being given sentimental credit for dealing in something assumed, vaguely, to be more. However much revered what poets say may be, as spoken under the inspiration of awarenesses exceeding the ordinary, it does not rank as truth, practically, it is not expected to be truth, precisely. It is not thought of as having *that* kind of seriousness. Plotinus long, long ago, putting aside what Empedocles said on certain themes as not having the requisite validity, pronounced a judgement that fits the common attitude to poets in any age: "he speaks as a poet."[3] The attitude exists irrespectively of prejudice, merely by force of the traditional dispensation poetry enjoys of freedom from need of passing the tests of truth. Though not required to prove itself, poetry is ceremonially accorded as much dignity as what passed the tests of truth would naturally possess. This arrangement between poets and their public, and the critics, has seemed to work to everybody's benefit.

The case is, as to poetry and truth, that poetry's *raison d'être* would dissolve if poems had to justify their existence by meeting the requirements of truth—actual truth, not the abstract truth of poetic apologetics. The words of a poem do not go as far as the suggested sense; there is an overreaching in a poem that is supposed to be a reaching in which something is touched, but strokes the air only. The words are used in a manner designed to make them succeed in doing what words do not ordinarily do; but the success is a failure, for the difference is too little. The words of a poem cannot be taken out of the poem: nothing is changed because of them, in living fact. The poem raises the hope of truth, but is not of itself true.

### 3.

Since the tests of truth are not applied to poetry, there is no evidence—no tradition of evidence, no collated knowledge—to the effect that poetry could not withstand them. Poets, of course, better than any, could know this; a self-protective instinct urges them to leave well-enough alone, and their public, and their patrons the poetry-critics, do not ask otherwise. I was not content to leave well-enough alone. But, far from being prepared for

3. [Plotinus, *The Enneads,* IV.8.1, trans. Stephen MacKenna (London: Faber, 1969), 357.]

an accumulative discovery of an inherent obstructiveness in poetry to the achievement of truth (actual truth), I remained confident to the end—not knowing it was an end when I came to it—that poetry could ultimately satisfy (be, with combined faith in it and in the possibility of perfect speaking, made to satisfy) all the tests of truth that might be applied to it.

The applying of truth-tests can be perceived in my poems, and with this an effort to eliminate the truth-beauty twinship from my poetic thinking and method, and have in its place a single concept of the poetic good—the poetic good as identical with the linguistic good in all its perfection. That is, what I am saying here introductorily ought to make these things perceptible. These and some other things I say here of my poems did not become early or all at once all-clear to me myself; certain of them I either did not fully perceive or did not fully comprehend until after I had ceased to write poems.

The notion of poetry held, and the motivation felt, by a poet are necessarily of one quality. Where the poetic good and the linguistic good are identified, as they were in my notion of poetry, the line drawn between poetry and the ordinary way of speaking ascribes no special professional motivation to poetry, by virtue of which poets develop special professional graces, but only a line between mixed and pure motivation in speaking. Everything in poetry written with a sense of practising a special verbal art must have some taint of verbal foppery in it. Yet poetry is by its nature incapable of consummating, in the speaking ways possible within its limits, the pure linguistic motivation: it is impossible to be a poet and maintain pure linguistic motivation at every verbal turn. As for myself as a poet, the reason of being that, for me, was to speak, and, speaking, to take speaking to the full of its potentialities; however much being a poet frustrated the reason of being that, and prompted digressions not recognized as such, I kept returning to the reason, within the poem, in the next poem—and when, in my experience, poetry dissolved, the reason why I had been a poet did not. One might well call this reason, the sense of the responsibility to learn the laws of the harmony of words, which in practice is truth.

I think my poems will be seen to be, very much, things made of *words*. How much poetry consists of "poetry," verbal matter aestheticized, is not generally detected. This character of my poems, of being, very much, things made of words, has not been specifically identified by anyone, but it has had effects, conducing to some increase in word-consciousness in poets—who so readily treat words as if they were an incidental or extraneous quantity in poetry. My stress on words, in and out of poetry, has been variously adopted, but nowhere grasped in its large simplicity. In the case of poetry, I thought and I think that we have something that must be judged finally as speaking, if the use of words in it is not to be dismissed as professional mummery (a use of them in which they mask an actual saying-nothing). In the case of every use of words, in all the courses of speaking (voiced speaking, written speaking, thought speaking), human being itself is put to the tests of reality, and in these tests spiritually verified or discredited—out of one's own mouth, as it were: thus I thought and I think. (I mean, with "spiritually," to relate reality and spirit, yes!)

I endeavored strenuously in other years to impress on every worker in the fields of words with whom I had some close acquaintance the importance of attending to words as *words*—not as things that, of malleable material, are shaped into what one wills. In a letter written by me over thirty years ago to a young poet who had the common view that words of their nature were often defalcators, or traitors, I wrote as follows (the letter has chanced to come my way again):

> Words are instruments of truth. That people attempt to use them for other purposes doesn't make them—words—{something else}. . . . When they are not used to tell truth they somehow escape, leaving only husks in the hands of the fools and the liars—remaining themselves intact, not really *used*. . . . Indeed it matters that you don't distinguish between the various uses and meanings of words—it (such distinction) matters more than anything else in the world.[4]

---

4. [To James Reeves, 1934. L(R)J's 1974 transcription of the letter is part of "Advice to a Young Poet," Berg. See also *Rational Meaning* 578, and "A Commentary on a collection of letters written to James Reeves . . . ," Cornell.]

But I made no spiritually deep impression on poets with my view of words, as it was exemplified in my poems or directly communicated; where I made some impression, with it, I excited more appetite for, more ambition of, verbal virtuosity, than pure linguistic passion. But I do not attribute this poor success just to my fallacious belief that my view of words could be *totally* put into practice in poetry. The idea that words have any intrinsic authenticity is a stranger both in and out of poetry; to this must be added the lamentable fact that poets are so much affected, congenitally, by the paradoxical principles of poetry that words can be of even less worth to them than to others, the special preciousness attributed to words as the stuff of which poems are made being for them a property mystically acquired by them in poetic use.

It is a defect of the poetic condition of mind (a term I think preferable to the grandiose "the poetic mind") to be crucially sensitive to everything about words except what it is crucially important to be crucially sensitive about in their use—given an intention to use them honorably. In these later years, in which I have been free of indulgent assumptions as to the potential capability of poets to show the way to the use of words for life-fulfilling speaking, I have been able to see how culpably lenient poets are with themselves in their use of words. The leniency is an addiction, the drug being confidence in themselves as poets to make the poem come out right. They think of the poem, under the influence of this confidence, not as words but as an aesthetic structure of which words are not the exclusive component: it is presumed by them that the words will come out right in consequence of the poem's coming out right.

As a poet believing that words must be used as words, and as closely as possible to the full of their capacity as such, and especially by poets, I worked with other poets to help them make their poems better poems by making them better linguistically; and I deceived myself into thinking that in their idea of improvement they counted poetic and linguistic improvement as one. I now know that in the satisfaction they felt there was little main linguistic interest. The linguistic improvement was, for the most part, additive, for them, not integral; there was hardly anything fundamental involved, for them, in questions of linguistic right-and-wrong—there was hardly, indeed, any such thing as linguistic right-and-wrong. In such improvement there is no future. I cannot regard my experience with poets as a special case. Poetry (poetry in the quantitative sense) provides little evidence of radical efforts to improve it linguistically; attention to words as words has always been subdued by the demands of the poem. Dedicated to a happy perfection in the use of words, poets cannot *work* at it to the last: the poem is the beguiling way-station offering so much apparent advance-success in the use of words as to make it seem unnecessary to go to the end.

The futility of laboring to win poets to unreserved concern with determining what is linguistically right—that is, *true*—has been very clear to me in my later converse with poets, as one who came to know the basic futility of trying to make poems fulfil in their actual words the requirements of actual truth, without any pinching or slanting of utterance. There have been some poets who have seen so much reason in what I now point to in poetry—the impossibility, lodged in its nature, of its succeeding in the function of affording self-eloquent truth to which it is by its nature committed—that they were stopped; and I have felt uneasy, exerting influence where it might only produce total inaction, tortured, self-righteous. But, little by little, the cloud under which the poetic habit had lain dissipated, even while they held to their persuasion of the correctness of my findings about poetry: they emerged from the crisis stimulated to try to beat the impossibility inherent in poetry with poetry! I had caught them in the never altogether unconscious apprehension poets have of being found wanting, and for good cause; but, exposing their vulnerability, I made it look to them (after some moral exercise on their part of candor with themselves) a far less serious thing than they had suspected it of being before I opened their eyes. For, after all, it was, by my showing, nothing more formidable than *a matter of words*. All poets, until they reach the inward extreme where a final choice must be made between poetry and truth, think they can fix *that*.

I believe that I have no illusions to soften my sense of the difficulties my later view of poetry has to face in finding understanding. I have seen how my stated reasons for ceasing to write poems can be lauded as a manifesto liberating the poet as man from the poetic bind—though my concern is not for the psychological happiness of the individual poet, man or woman, but for the good fate of speaking, the happiness of all in their speaking. I have seen my notions identified with a poet's murky reflections as to poets and virtue—the poet righteously feeding my notions to, and losing them in, his own. I expect massive incomprehension of my "position" (I have already encountered incomprehension of it of sizeable proportions) before it is just a little perceived that what I call in question is the functional character of poetry, the generic combination of things that has the name of poetry—what makes poetry, poetry . . . and that in calling this into question I am calling into question the entire trend of human disposition to words that has given us poetry for the very best we can do with them.

I have had some expectation that what I had newly to present regarding poetry would meet with responsive understanding sooner among American than among English poets—presumed a likelihood of there being in them more residue than in others of hope of final goodness of word, from the cynicism of accommodation to the obstacles to it to which the circumstance of poetry exposes all poets. But the record of responses is so far scanty, and unclear. Several English poets with whom I came into correspondence on the subject of my later view of poetry showed agreement with it, but this by subsequent proof was too much tinged with literary opportunism to be of significance for the record. The two persons most intimately acquainted with my view, both of whom have had the experience of being poets, are Americans;[5] but their support figures in a different record. I have given some public expression to my later thinking on poetry in America, but there was no substantial response to it. The rather spacious expression of it that this introduction, (and the autobiographical epilogue here included, to fill it out),[6] constitutes, has been inspected by a number of persons accounted authorities on poetry, the while the script of this book made sojourn with an American publishing institution desirous of pub-

---

5. [Schuyler Jackson and (probably) Sonia Raziss.]
6. ["An Autobiographical Summary," *P. N. Review* 97 (May–June 1994), was to have followed "Then, And Now," as part II of the introduction.]

lishing the poems; but it elicited from there, I have been told, only a profession of confusion (they were described to me as having been more confused at the end than they had been to begin with)—it was described to me, at least, in terms of confusion. By prognosticative instinct I still tend to think that Americans before others will recognize that my findings about poetry have radical importance for the practical fulfilment of the human ideal, pointing to the possibility of a practical identity between the human and the linguistic ideal—something that poetry thwarts. But, truly, I have no preferences as to just where, and how, the log-jams of difficulties with poets, critics, publishers and people in which my message seems bound to be involved shall be broken. Broken it shall be, for the message has a momentum of its own which ensures its eventual delivery.

Developments in my knowledge of the nature of poetry have gone apace with and been of one learning experience with developments in my thought on other things. What I tell of my new thinking here is but a portion of the story of it having special relevance to a new publication of my poems—which were written before my present view of poetry was born. To tell less than this would be to subordinate to the poems what has happened since, in my laboring with the problem of being and the problem of whole utterance, and falsely assign to the later, further stage of my intelligence-journey a minor importance. But on the other hand, I mean to make no division between the poems, presented here, and the non-poetic elements of the book. There is a bond between them of underlying purpose and ultimate aim maintained in an unbroken continuity. Readers can best unify the contents of the book for themselves by reading it to the extent possible in their capacity as inhabitants of the world of us all, of which those who are categorically literary readers must be at least part-time inhabitants, and making reference to the innate awareness they have as such of there being no other serious function of words than the truth-function. This book is centered in the inevitable question that, curiously, has been ever evaded, "Can poetry, nurtured over the human centuries, as the extreme of what can be done by human beings in words, be a serious enough way of using words to give entire fulfilment (which elsewhere seems only ever part-possible) to their truth-function?"

The poems are a long-prolonged action of faith in that possibility. The rest is a Report on the choice between poetry and the hope of truth to which this faith led. None in their natural human senses (which the literary sensibilities can perplex but scarcely except in special cases paralyse) is without desire to discover how to make truth all-actual in words, if it can be done without folly—or, in a deepest recess of desire, a yearning to achieve this, be it accounted folly—to know how to measure shortage of truth in their words and those of others, test whether the filling sound and impression of meaning come of a fullness of it. This accounting folly the total truth-objective is one of the causes of its having had relegated to it a refuge (a place of exile) in poetry, that puts a veil over it the folds of which fall into ever-changing alternating forms of folly and wisdom. My poems try to treat that ambiguity. My Report from Later tells of the treating—which required a break with poetry itself. This folly-wisdom veil poetry casts between the achievement and the desire is but a thin one, but as impassable, ultimately, as other barriers between us and truth of our speaking. And I think it likely the others will not be seen wholly for what they are until poetry is—in which is concealed so much the difference between truth and less. . . . I bring before readers no mere tale of an insane sudden walking away from a poet's career in its live midst, or of a cowardly flight from poetry in foresight of a prospect of exhaustion of power, or of anything of still sorrier sort; and may none let their readers' innocence be spoiled by certain vilely false explanations peddled about of the reasons why I renounced poetry. What I did in renouncing poetry is what we all have to do—and it can be pictured entirely in plain terms of common human need without resort to literary paint of any color. Historically dedicated, all, to versions of the courage for truth below the human capability of it, we have to leave the inadequate dedications, give our full.

4.

In withdrawing from poetry, I did not change my objective, which was a mode of speaking that would be perfect in being truth, and truth in being perfect, but, rather, moved in its direction out of a path that could never bring me—or anyone else—into practical proximity to it. I could no longer compress the objective within the poetic vision of things. Far from putting *finis* to my dedication to it, I redeemed my dedication to it from the doom that all hope of final goodness of word that harbors itself in poetry faces. My renunciation of poetry involved a more exacting application to the problem of how to succeed in our use of words to the point of making them *true* than had my commitment to poetry: it made me free to apply myself to the problem in ways in which one cannot function freely as a poet. I "took on," of labor in the cause of the enlargement and fulfilment of the potentialities of human utterance, greatly more than I gave up.

It has been suggested to me that there is some resemblance between Rimbaud's severance of himself from poetry, and the literary life generally, and what I have done.[7] There was finality in both actions, but they differ extremely. I had the advantage of eighteen years more of experience in the specialized field of utterance that is poetry, and the stability of a devotee of poetry to whom the happiness of the adventure was in seeking achievement inseparable from the words themselves; I had a structure of hope, built in the terms of faith in the Good as ultimate necessity, for support, for shelter, whatever happened in the adventure; and my inspiration came from everywhere. For Rimbaud, the essence of the adventure was outside the words, outside words—he was impatient to be off from them even as he was uttering them. He tried to distil from the words the elixir that would empower him (and all of like self, perhaps) to make happiness out of unhappiness; he had no hope, no support, no shelter; his own desperation was his inspiration, and as he flung it out, wide, it narrowed back faster and faster to himself—and would have destroyed him, in the end, had he not run away from it, far. . . . Since I renounced poetry, nothing has changed for me but my judgement as to the field in which human utterance can best find its perfections. That, through its consequences, was a large change, but no retreat.

---

7. [Some of the material in this paragraph was used, reworked, in the preface to *Selected Poems: In Five Sets* (London: Faber, 1970; New York: Norton, 1973; New York: Persea, 1993), 15; *Reader,* 233.]

Before I reached the point of cessation as a poet—which was not for me a death-end but a point of turning—I had long anticipated a margin in speaking-achievement to be crossed; and I thought it would be crossed *in* poetry, and the new step on the other side be taken in the poetic course of speaking. There was adumbrated in my poems themselves a breakdown of a wall dividing the formalized intensity of poetic utterance from a natural intensity of utterance, that would require no artifice of perfection, but generate its own form, at once natural and perfect. Indeed, as I approached the climacteric of poetic maturity, I saw ahead the possibility of a pause in my personal poetic course, after which, in the renewed speaking, there would be new increase in immediacy of truth, as a quality of the words, a new reality of truth encompassed within the words. I trusted poetry, I knew that I myself came as a poet close to showing that quality in my words, to bringing that reality to have presence in them; but I also knew that, while nothing of the like could be achieved in the ordinary manner of speaking, in poetry it was, still, hardly more than an ideal invoked—realized, if at all, only in momentary portions of the entire event a poem constituted, these so difficult to keep alive beyond their moment that one could wonder whether anything had happened at all.

If poetry was to justify the assurance it gave of being able to yield something better in human utterance than the ordinary speaking-mode yielded, something in a final and total sense truer to the human speaking-capability, its way with words would have to have more sureness in it, more of everything proper to the pursuit of perfection of utterance: this was to me imperative—for poetry as the utmost in words. . . .

In thinking that in poetry the speaking-urgencies that work in human beings could be satisfied to their utmost with an expressive utmost in words, I viewed my personal career as a poet as effort partaking of the identity-at-large of those urgencies; I viewed those urgencies as a single moving destiny, beneficent in its direction, all-involving, all-affecting. I was indeed going my way, but my way was a seeking to go the way—a seeking to find the way—of that destiny. *Somehow*, speaking must wholly tell its burdens: somehow, there must be made to be speaking that so does. I had accepted poetry at the hands of history as the Somehow that would rescue words and their speakers from the ever-insufficient speaking of impermanent time-cramped life—as all poets who take the name not from self-concerned ambition must in their dedicatory spirit accept it; in pressing upon the poetic possibilities of utterance for evidence of the actual feasibility of saying poetically what appears to be otherwise not entirely sayable, I was doing no more than what poetry—as a pursuit of genuine high human purpose—has always called poets to do. My initial attitude to poetry and my subsequent experience as a poet, and, then, a renouncer of poetry, cannot be laid to eccentricity unless fullness of commitment to the ideal round which the poetic tradition has formed itself is judged to be eccentricity in a poet.

But, to tell what happened, at the point of change, where I parted from poetry: to tell what I now know to have happened. . . . I suddenly found myself on new ground. I had been catapulted there by the accumulated force of the intensity of speaking-preoccupation that had had to be kept unloosed within the poetic limits of utterance. The new ground was not merely other-than-poetic ground. Here was everything on account of which poetry claims consideration as an activity of the first order of seriousness. This everything consists of three things, and poetry is traditionally supposed to concentrate them in itself in indissoluble harmonic combination; and they are, the essential graces of language, which are rightnesses, the essential clarities of truth, which are goodnesses, and the motion of spirit at its intelligent promptest. All this—the reality implicit in words, and dependent on words for its living embodiment—was present here as the complete subject of one's desire: the desire underwent no change, it remained wholly fixed upon the subject. But, where the envisioned happy threefold excellence of utterance was in the poetic setting seen as a single pinpoint on the horizon of desire, on the new ground it was seen larger, closer, and, as it were, disassembled, so that one comprehended better of what it was made—what one had to do to realize it. The vista of potential perfection of utterance became clearer, broader— even, it became boundless. And there was no poetry.

Nothing had happened to me except that my concern with perfection of utterance, which had been one in its progress with my commitment to poetry, had carried me beyond the confines of poetry. I had "done" nothing; and on the new ground I was not preoccupied with something different from that with which I had been preoccupied on the old ground. My objectives remained the same, though I could no longer subsume them in the name "poetry." I am only formally exact in saying that I renounced poetry: I overpassed it, beyond going back. I had pressed on along the path of poetry towards a destination to which I believed the path must lead. I learned in retrospective examination of my experience that, not only did poetry not take as far as that destination, but that, if adhered to, it took only around and back to its beginning-point, and round and back again, and again, denying full possession to language of its graces, to truth of its natural clarities, and to spirit of its generosities—while seeming to confer this. There is, apparently, a point of involuntary escape from this circular route if the momentum of one's single devotion to the three linked classes of excellence exceeds the momentum of the devotion to them to which the path of poetry can give accommodation. At any rate, it befell me to travel unawares, before my fortieth year, out from the locked circuit of poetry, upon a tangent of delivery.

To discover what there was to do on the new ground, and what could be done, was a slow work of years. My findings are, still, in terms of perfection of utterance. But this perfection differs from the poetic ultimate of utterance in that, while requiring more of the utterer, it is pursuable on the new ground with an ease of heart and conscience, and a firmness of intellectual footing, impossible in the pursuit of the poetic ultimate on poetry's own self-hospitable ground. It belongs to a kind of utterance in which the rightness and goodness and quickness of word supposed to be found in poetry, but existing there only in experimental interplay, adapted to the exigencies of the poetic occasion, are *functionally* unified—are not countable as rightness and goodness and quickness of word unless they are all that, and in a single immediacy of excellence. Further, this kind of utterance, envisageable on this new ground, has a practicality exceeding the professional literary limits of poetry; it is, without the mediation of literary conditions of utterance, anybody's practicality. The purpose of it is not merely to explore tentatively what might be done in utterance in a state of fully conscious being, but to give fully conscious being pure existence by the cleanly substance of ourselves taking cleanly form! The difference between the two kinds of utterance is that between personal utterance attaining to speaking perfection in the live moments of speaking and formal utterance, imaginatively anticipated in attunement to an imagined effective presentation. Always a poet must speak in theatrical advance of a naturally perfect speaking-performance, a normal event on the possibility of which the poem itself throws doubt.

Intrinsically beautiful, linguistically, is this other utterance, not beautiful by the measure of its external effects; the words in their individual meanings will serve, each one to its full, the total meaning, without divagatory exception for rhythmic or tonal side-experiences. And it is not, as poetic utterance so much is, a prize-package holding surprises of truth among the patterned verbal felicities: it is, if it is at all, complete with truth—is completely truth, its size and shape and content determined by what is sufficient for its being completely and uniformly truth. And it is inwardly all-moved with the force of the sayer all-moved with the force of spirit, and not, as with poetic utterance, with the composite influence of mind, flesh and feeling, spirit present to the utterance only as a guest. (And what is this thing "spirit" I speak of? How is one sensibly to construe this word I use with an accent of specific identification? It is the action in us of the being we have, which when known within us by us, imparts its powers: it is the action of universal being in particular being enlarging it with its origins. I think we could not speak our all without the word, by such a meaning.)

Poets work divided between the personally idiosyncratic workings of mind and flesh and feeling and the workings of spirit known as something outside themselves by the indulgence of which they have a (presumed) magical capability of being exaltedly superior to themselves. But on this ground of which I tell there are no poets. There are only speaking beings who have such a motive of truth of word, and are aware that powers of executing the Good in words must, necessarily, accompany the motive: . . . and seek the powers within themselves. I say elsewhere, in an essay entitled "Poetry and the Good" (so far only part-published—in the magazine *Chelsea*, issue 14 [January 1964]),[8] that "There are poets of ingenuous breed who *are* poets because of an original motive of truth of word. . . ." But, to come here, poets must save the motive, and the powers that accompany it, from the hope-exhausting tortuosities of poetic verbal procedure, in which the lure of success in wielding the potencies of verbal effects gradually replaces hope of success in executing the Good in words: they must declassify themselves!

The speaking being who *here* attains to the perfection-mark is anyone who fulfils the natural implications of the speaking-capability to the natural utmost. There is no division, on this ground, between a higher and a lower self, and between an ordinary and an extraordinary speaking-moment. There is, here, the spiritual self for a one and only self, the constant self of the being only. The multiple creature of differing kinds of moments scatters to the four corners of nothingness on this ground where Continuity is not a ring of poetic moments or a continuum formed of disjointed moment-sequences tied together as "ordinary" speaking-time, but the uninterruptibility of being perfectly speaking being . . . of being become perfectly speakable.

On the ground where grace of word and goodness of word, and spiritual quickness of word, are not merely poetic approximations to the reality, one knows language itself differently. One does not stop here at using language curiously well, time and again, as one puts a tool to work in this or that fine fashioning of something, but uses it in all one's speaking to the full, as one can, with its full the measure of one's own full—and will more and more so use it as the ground becomes more and more familiar to one's nature as a speaking being than any other. Here, between language and ourselves becomes possible the perfect equalness there ought to be between ourselves as spiritual beings and language as the intelligence we have, as such, reasoned into speakableness. But to know language thus one must relearn one's words . . . learn them as a child first learns words, in the innocence of having nothing prepared to say with them. What one

---

8. [The whole essay was published in *P. N. Review* 84 (March–April 1992), and *Reader,* 208ff.]

speaks—will speak—on this ground is the new. To try to speak the new on poetic ground is to try to speak the new with the old.

## 5.

There are to be heard, these days, pronouncements, by people professionally associated with poetry, suggestive of new attitudes of scepticism towards it not unlike the new scepticism that has become a sanctified ingredient of the new theology. Such pronouncements can have had their origin in an embarrassed consciousness of vulnerabilities in poetry as seen in the (near-blindingly) harsh light of contemporary philosophic realism; some of them, certainly, have been formed under stimulation of acquaintance with my later evaluation of poetry, which many years ago I began, sparingly, to make known, and in more recent years have expatiated upon publicly and treated of freely in various correspondences with people of poetic "connections." One of these pronouncements, of a catchy simplicity of phrase, lingers with me: it is to the effect that we must not expect "to be saved by poetry." An explanation of what I thought and think about being "saved" may be helpful, here.[9]

I had not, before I turned away from poetry, thought of it as harboring a saving deity, but as being where language could come into its own, and the speakers of words with it: such only was my poetic religiosity. Language is as the net of reason thrown over the universal spread by the force of that all-touching spirit of being which it is human to be all-moved by, so that we are as ones having the net in our hands. Then do we but keep the net clean, whole, well-mended, losing nothing caught within it, ordering everything in our mind's safe-keeping, knowing well what we have in each word (for *word* is the form of that which we catch in the net), we shall fulfil the sense of the net, of the spread over which it is spread, of the spirit that attends the spread and casts the net and gathers in ourselves, and the sense

9. ["Salvation" had been a topic of discussion in her correspondence with Martin Seymour-Smith in October 1964; see Friedmann, *A Mannered Grace*, 403.]

of ourselves. This was and is my faith in Good Possibility, my notion of Good Possibility: I believed, I believe, that with words we can make utterance of such rightness—itself harmonious with itself and with that of which it is the report, the breathed witnessing thought—that a binding-together of the sprawling actuality of the World can come about, by this as by nothing else.

When I found that the promise poetry gave of affording place for an occurrence in which words, World, and ourselves came, through words, under the saving principle of truth was but an invitation to act out—with the happiness of art—the tragedy of the Impossibility of such Good, poetry itself became Impossibility to me. And so it ought to be for anyone who accepted its hospitality in true hope of more than the satisfactions, for poet and for reader, hearer, of poems, of tasting Impossibility made sweet with art. And anyone who accepts it without true hope of more, or, having had the hope, loses it and yet stays on that ground, assassinates Possibility. So much for salvation.

I bring together here many threads. Some are pertinent to my poetic work itself, some to my earlier, some to my later, view of poetry, some to my view of language and my attitude to words, some to a related happy significance I read in human existence itself, some to the view others have of poetry, and to the impact of my own upon others. Then, there are threads pertinent to my laboring, in earlier years, to instil in others the values of a linguistic scrupulosity carrying commitment to that literal spirit of words which is truth. And to these should be joined threads pertinent to a mode of general evaluation, of a new order, that I instituted, which put a mark of finality between the human existence of history and a human immediacy that stays, and rendered the Past understandable in terms *of not just itself.* This was the general-values background to the linguistic values I tried to make loved. The general thinking manifested itself in my poetic work in a search for a way to realize such post-historical immediacy in the uttered word. I took this effort, there, to where the realization of it was as only a paper-thin breadth beyond my words' reach (though never to the point of actual realization because, as I later learned, this was poetry, but poetry), and, in what I did in trying to help other poets advance their words closer, closer, to the truth-mark, my effort was as intense as that which I exerted for my own words' sake—I wished nothing for myself that I did not wish for others.

I developed the structure of my evaluative thought towards a practical universality of coverage, in non-poetic work, from the model of the truth-process I formed in my poetic work to the measurements of poetic vision—which, crowded within the limits imposed by the verbal artifice of poetry, can only apprehend the nature of the truth-process in the scantiness of miniature. My teachings in matters of words had behind them, thus, a broad intellectual experience, and were fired with urgent feeling on large human issues: what I made available to those who came into fellow-poet association with me went far beyond the bounds of the professionally topical. The work of general thought I describe had some public expression—for example, in the literary-intellectual movement I endeavoured to foster in the three critical volumes of *Epilogue* (in which, besides being editor, and a ubiquitous contributor besides, I was an invisible co-author in nearly all the contributions of others), and in the publicistic *The World and Ourselves*. But a large part of this thought-action had expression in the private forms of personal communication, and of application to the thought-problems of others, especially those affecting their work. My donations of this sort of concern to the work of others, mingled with donations of direct linguistic concern, exceeded the bounds implied by the term "influence." However, the term has been found convenient by critics, as one employable without laborious fact-finding; and for the beneficiary it has the convenience of seeming just while sparing laborious fact-furnishing.

Among the many subject-threads here brought together, those falling under the subject-heading "influence" need some careful differentiation. For the term has been put to much slap-dash use in my regard; much of that to which it has been applied would be better described if described otherwise. As one who worked with others on behalf of their work, with eyes trained on the good of the text, for object, I made little accounting of the difference between mine and thine; and, generally, I kept no jealous watch anywhere, in the time of my being a poet, for indications of "influence." For instance, in the case of W. H. Auden's assimilations of my poetic procedures (extraordinary in their bulk), I was the last to become aware of the phenomenon: the attention of my friends (and that of his friends also, apparently) was engaged by it long before mine was. I shall return shortly to the question of my influence on Mr. Auden, to complete my comment on it briefly.

I have become aware of there having been, generally, a great deal of imitative attention paid by poets to linguistic features of my poetic work, and of the kind of emotional and mental pulsations that attend them there. The whole, in my work, could be characterized as an aliveness that believed in itself as containable in words, entirely, believing in words at the same time as perfectly capable of containing it. Nothing like this had ever happened in poetry; the suggestions emanating from it of an alliance between the total being and the total language excited, then, a hardly understood linguistic self-consciousness. And, since my work was not stamped all over with personalistic quirks, poets responded to its stimulating impacts as to signatureless products of natural origins. If I had not been so good a poet, what was adopted from me would have been perforce specifically associated with its source to a greater extent than has been: the quirks provide a sort of copyright protection.

It has, surely, been felt about my work by poets in the past (and poets in the immediate too), here is a great new area of poetic address opened up. Yet what is it but the area of insistent articulateness, that recognizes no limit: this is no personal preserve. And they have been right. Right likewise as to the new poetic facility that I revealed, which was nothing other than the total language: *that* can have no identity of personal ownership. Still, I was able to introduce into poetry this confidence in speech of the speaking being, and in the possession of language enough to justify [it], only because I began further back and went further ahead in my vision of being than had anyone before, within the frame of poetic vision. The real reason why my poetic work has been so much treated as an open public quarry for linguistic stripping has been the indolent disregard to which its visionary content has been subjected: the surface's authorlessness for poet-readers had its start in their self-indulgent failure to make personal acquaintance with its depths. The use that, under the name of "influence," has been made by other poets of my linguistic habitudes, regarded as things-in-them-selves, which they are not, is, essentially, a crass one; and the crassness of it is intensified, not diminished, by their having used them to produce for their poems a patina of intellectual dignity and finesse, an all-over effect of distinctions of verbal touch—something which is very much lacking naturally in the poetic matter of this era (in which the difference between distinction of verbal touch and distinction of literary touch has widened into wastes of linguistic helplessness).

The discrepancy between the small extent of the distribution of my poems in the time of their availability, together with the subsequent tightening of their availability that resulted from my changed view of poetry, and the rather extensive but private familiarity of poets with them, very little expressed publicly, is to be accounted for in large part by the use to which they have been put by poets as nameless stuff in their private poetic cupboards, very good for deficiencies of linguistic good-taste. (I borrow that term from Mr. Auden, who once deprecated my being left out of somebody's anthology as a failure of good taste, in communicating with me about an anthology of his own.) This stuff has been gathered up as a top layer of something deposited on the poetic scene that has been assumed to have no other use or interest because the handling of it calls for more *thinking* than poets could consider it within their dignity to soil their minds with.

The 1942 edition of *Twentieth Century Authors* provided an elegant description of the kind of anonymity that my work has enjoyed. After a non-committal reference to it as a subject of dispute, comes the assertion there that "what cannot be disputed is that it is the work of a serious, precise intelligence and that its qualities of bite, dryness and abstraction are in process of being absorbed into the tradition of modern poetry." The author is got out of the way with an expeditious bow, as if to be a serious, precise intelligence was to exist in a personal vacuum; the poems, presumably partaking of the unreality of the author (oh, the deadly touch of a serious, precise intelligence!), are hardly existent either. Only the absorbable qualities have reality. As to these—they imply a disagreeable nicety of word and bareness of sense productive of poetic pleasure in others' management, though not in my own. The term "abstraction," intended to cover all the absorbable virtue of my work that "bite" and "dryness" do not, is the most flagrantly perfunctory. The tag "abstract," and "philosophical" with it, have been attached to my work as critical devices for evading the responsibility of identifying the subject-content of the poems—what this serious-precise intelligence concerns itself with. Such shiftlessness of critical procedure, which leaves the poems not otherwise classified than as words, the stuff of language, has contributed to the absorption of their qualities.

To speak, now, of the second component of my "influence." . . .[10] It has become a convenient critical cliché of historical reference to have me in the character of a period-influence on this one and that one, causing divergence from a natural personal path into one given over, by my lead, to "abstract" and "philosophic" poetic antics. First, it should be said, in this connection, that, since after the thirties I ceased to write poems and withdrew my poetic work and myself from literary availability for a very long time, there had been had by anyone who wanted it all the influence there was to be had (for a very long time)—to the quantity desired, be it for short or long. For the rest, I dispute the attribution of influence upon the kind of poetry written by poets whom my poetic work and thinking touched. In so far as I tried to exert influence, my concern was for poems' having all possible genuineness as things made of words: a more honest speaking than the ordinary, even because this was poetry, not a less honest, was the theme of all my counsel to poets. And there were evidences at least of experimental attempts by some to abide by literal standards of word-value in the poetic use of words, as I urged, and seek to speak truth as much as to make a poem. "Too thoughtful, reasonable and truthful," W. B. Yeats pronounced what he called my "school"—proper poets being, by his poetic lack-faith, "good liars."[11] Indeed, I was against lies in poems, and poems that were lies. But I do not accept that that, or failure to exercise restraint in setting standards

10. [It is unclear from the heavily revised manuscript whether the following four paragraphs were to be excised or retained; and, if retained, where they were to come.]
11. [See note on "Introduction for a Broadcast," 25.]

of thoughtfulness and reasonableness and truthfulness for poetry, made me a beguiler of poets into the domain of the abstract and philosophical. I was not myself—whatever say the
stereotypes, however go the clichés—a poet in that genre.
In part, I think, the use of the terms "abstract" and "philosophical" of my poetic work originates in lazy funk; it seems
safer to critics who are not sure of their critical feel (and, the
more authority they acquire, the more they tend to a policy of
unsureness where special courage would be needed for independent judgement) to spray one or the other or both of these
in the direction of my poetic work, and escape before the mist
clears and some people, as it might happen, begin asking intelligent questions about my poems and expecting intelligent answers. Thus, in an account provided in a recently published literary register, my poetic work is described as consisting of
philosophic chunks; and it is there set against the inability
evinced to speak definitely of my poems that the jacket of the
book in which they were collectedly presented did not itself
supply any hints as to what they were all-about.
In a commentary on my poems published several years ago (a
revision of one that formed part of an early book of hers), Miss
Sonia Raiziss said, refuting with gentle justice what the ticket "abstract" insinuates: "It's unfair to infer that this passionately stark
poetry is without tints other than cerebral shadings."[12] The ticket
"philosophical" clinches the unfairness—to use Miss Raiziss'
kind word. My poetic work was not in the philosophical field; it
is critical vulgarity to make such an ascription. The tenor of the
thought, the temper of the emotionality, in the background of
my poems are not categorically philosophical. There was an elas-
ticity of subject, in my poems, between the small and the large of
things; but that is not the nature of philosophy. In treating my
subjects, I dealt with them within the possibilities of poetry as a
field of endeavor to make certain prime human functions of sensibility and intelligence work better within the peculiarly restricted verbal method of poetry than they otherwise do; I dealt
with them straight, as poetic subjects, and by the verbal method
of poetry, not obliquely—I dealt with them personally and not

---

12. ["An Appreciation," *Chelsea* 12 (September 1962): 28.]

philosophically. (I mean no derogation here of philosophy; I hold philosophy in some honor—where it has not become science's servant—as a church to those who try to make doubt into a form of belief.)

My poetic way with words can seem to poets who have difficulty in maintaining a consistent personal style amidst a confusion of contradictory pulls, to which they feel obliged to expose themselves in proof of modernity, a way to hold one's poetic own no matter *what* one says. Without fear of poetic malapropism, I introduced a spaciousness into the narrow frame of the verbal method of poetry by using words in extensive variety and intensively varied combinations and with a promptitude of sense that kept them from getting in one another's way—endeavoring always to make the word be itself, literally a word, to the exact compass of its sense, and, very often, coming close enough to doing so to brush the actuality. This could present, where a problem of stylistic character existed, vistas of unlimited textual coherence, vigorous, serious, unponderous: right possibilities of word, phrase, rhythmic advance and cycling, and of intonating attunement of the outer and inner part of utterance, could seem to lie within the sufficiently bold imaginative reach.

There has been, then, a selective effect of my poems on other poets, a professional sensitivity in them to the verbal impact of the poems as something separable from their total impact, coupled with an insensitivity—an irresponsible indifference—to their nature. This effect, a widely distributed one, has worked its way down through the years into the present, with the identity-marks of its source becoming fainter and fainter in the process—till the notion that anything has been transferred from my work into the body poetic can seem a critical hallucination or (should the notion be mine) a neurotic obsession. Where a poet has made concentrated use of my poetic work as a course of instruction in linguistics-for-poets, the poet's work itself may become an active distributor of my "influence" without anyone's being aware of it—even the poet being vague-minded as to the fact. W. H. Auden's poetic work waxed so potent itself in influence that by this means alone hundreds and hundreds of possible and actual poets have unwittingly had echoic experience of salient aspects of my poetic way with words. Some direct resort to my poetic work by poets, of educative value, has continued—now and then I come upon evidence of this—in the work of some younger poet with whom I have had no personal contact whatever, or in the form of private acknowledgements from poets whose work I have not even seen. (One younger poet unknown to me, writing to me with desire to come to see me, expressed the relationship in these perfectly unembarrassed terms: "You stand on the perimeter of my work.") Sometimes the evidence of what might be called my influence exerted *in absentia*, as distinguished from that which I delivered in person, has in it ghostly suggestions of personal qualities of my mode of poetic utterance—as if the poet had sought to derive from my poems, besides verbal skill, traces of their psychic reality for the artistic authentication of the skill. This complex sort of "influence" almost eludes description. I should classify that which W. H. Auden helped himself to as being somewhat of this sort, with a difference resulting from his having received inordinately much. What was taken in grew into him, becoming an integral part of his poetic talent. The psychic something-more taken in along with the linguistic lessoning was used, rather than to substantiate it artistically, to lend an appearance of philosophical unity of person to the expansive confusion created by the exercise of new verbal powers without matching new things to say. It could be that it was Mr. Auden's guilty sense of shreds of another mind ingested along with the word-way which prompted him to call me, as he once did, "the only living philosophical poet."

A few words more on the subject of my influence on Mr. Auden, and I shall have done with it. I should not be treating of it to the extent to which I am if [it had been] treated of by anyone with something other than cursory sloppiness.

Mr. Stephen Spender, in an article in the *Saturday Review*, April 23, 1966, described Mr. Auden as "much influenced in his early work by Eliot and a bit later by Laura Riding; but influenced also by Owen and Edward Thomas." Just twenty-seven years before, Mr. Spender had written in *The London Mercury* of Mr. Auden: "Every kind of influence from Anglo-Saxon to Bing Crosby, including Byron, Burns, Tennyson, Eliot, Robert Graves, Laura Riding, and Rhyming Slang (to mention those that immediately spring to my mind) pours into his verse." Perhaps Mr.

Spender stood too close to Mr. Auden at the earlier time to estimate the degree of any particular influence pouring into his work, and became able only after many years had passed to single out the degree as "much." In the article he wrote on myself in *The Concise Encyclopaedia of English & American Poets and Poetry* [1963] (a careless article, on which only a petty amount of work was done), he represented me as having influenced Mr. Auden and Mr. Robert Graves for a period. I was no period-influence in either case. For one thing, I am not that kind of influence; and, for another, what Mr. Auden took in he took into the back room where things stay. Some observers were aware of the taking-in long before 1939. The English poet Herbert Palmer in *Post-Victorian Poetry* (1938) recorded the results of an assiduous investigation of the use by poets of other poets' work (which he disliked). Wrote a reviewer of the book: "His work as a literary detective, spotting Laura Riding in W. H. Auden, Charles Kingsley in A. E. Housman, Francis Thompson in Gerard Hopkins, and Housman in Sir Henry Newbolt, is especially interesting and convincing. . . ."[13]

I am aware that "borrowing" has respectable status in the literary world, and is very often treated critically, under the name of "influence," as conferring distinction on influencer and influencee. I myself, as a poet and one no more a poet, make little allowance for appropriative activity as a right ingredient of poetry. Poets tend to become verbally hypersensitive, and, reading much in other poets, they are in difficulties between the scrupulosities of loyalty to their poetic individuality and sympathetic reverberations in their ears and the rest of their nervous system of the poetic say of other poets. But where, in this problem of the impact of poets on one another, can a line be drawn between learning from one another what is general to the nature of language, and to that of poetry, and *borrowing*? My principle for this matter concerns the place from which the poet speaks. Genuine learning (involving attention to the general proprieties of language and poetry) would not interfere with a poet's speaking from the heart of the poetic page; and what would have been

---

13. [Herbert Palmer makes the Riding-Auden connection on p. 349 of *Post-Victorian Poetry* (London: J. M. Dent and Sons, 1938).]

learned would be only present as strength gained. The rest, the assimilation of personal word-ways of other poets and adaptation of actual matter of theirs to one's poet-advantage, is something done from the margins of the poetic page. Yes, I think it is possible to draw the line between learning and borrowing: watch where a poet's speaking comes from, where there is an appearance of fullness, and you will soon know how much comes from the page's heart, and how much from the margins—how much consists of veritable personal presence in the page-heart, how much of acquired tricks of the trade. Under such a test, what has been absorbed, assimilated, adapted, from the work of others would, though personalized or transmogrified to the point of complete unidentifiability, show in the marginal area of speaking and the true emptinesses of the page in the space of the poem proper. My principle differs altogether from that which T. S. Eliot called "economy of effort," and enthusiastically advanced as one calculated to make minor poets thrive; this other principle posits a common source of equipment in what has been already "done," from which poets may legitimately draw to achieve distinction that they would not achieve by their single effort. His encouragement was hardly needed; but it has sped along the diminution of the size-standard of poetic effort, and the declining sense of responsibility in poets to do with words their own and the words' utmost. (Poetry has been, in this spirit, made so easy that the deficiencies in what is produced cease to be noticeable. . . . How, then, is it to be perceived that there is basic fault in poetry itself?)

My feelings about "influence" merge with my feelings about "borrowing," for I see little in what is called influence that is not borrowing, and nothing in what is called borrowing that is not taking. The key to this matter is in the motivation of the person's attachment to the texts of another: there is no honorable motivation except concern with *learning*.

But how to determine what is genuine learning? The key to *that* is love. Only where the object of attachment is loved is the motivation unquestionable. The difference between larceny and love in the attitude to the object of attachment is discernible in the extent to which inspiring texts (their author's labor of love) are not separated from their identity, in the process of "influence." As one who has been a rather free-flowing source of "influence," not only through published texts, but through personal impartments in profusion, by spoken and written communication, I have had special opportunities of observing the behavior of the influenced. I have seen general and particular learning from my poetic work that springs from no more than covetous appreciation—borrowing executed with unfeeling professional selfishness—and I have seen little else (and that "little else" is said for human loyalty's sake to allow for the possibility of something lovely, yet unknown to me, to contradict the ugly picture). I have seen what I have personally given out, of my thought's labor, greedily put away by others into their mind-pouches, and converted there into coin of their literary realm. Nowhere, so far, where I have encountered evidence in the work of others of impressions made by my work or my confided thinking on them, have I been moved to satisfaction or, at the least, to respect for what I found; I hope some will believe me in my saying that the reason is always, first, the emptiness of virtue of the uses made, and only second the essential heartlessness of the being-influenced procedure.

Within the last few days (as I write) I came accidentally upon two unmarked reflections of my "influence," in casual reading in a literary magazine. One was the employment in a review of a book, there, of a term of my formulation, important in the general course of my thought, which I used with serious point in a letter a number of years ago to the reviewer, in an account of ideas of mine bearing on some of the material of our correspondence; the correspondence has since lapsed, and I have since used the term in a piece of published writing, with serious emphasis. This very term was employed by the reviewer at the close of his review, for a touch of stylistic pomp, with its content largely leaked away along with all regard for the term's origin. The other instance of "influence," come upon, in a scanning of some pages of literary journalism, was in a little essay on style: "As Robert Graves says 'the writing of good English is thus a moral matter.'" Mr. Graves is, of course, a very special case, in the history of my influence. For a period of about thirteen years of personal association, he, a man of limited, and largely derivative, literary skill, and constricted intellectual outlook, but of an audacious ambition, suggesting, by its very audacity, intents and virtues beyond the ordinary, had all he could use of my influence. The influence presented itself in the form of intensive grounding in the values of linguistic good as a moral discipline of the mind and a spiritual discipline of the sensibilities, and in the form, also, of extensive direct contributions to actual writing, in the cause of virtue of style and sense; all this, together with the general store of my thought-experience, emerged from its service as influence with its identity thoroughly masticated. The notion that the writing of good English is a moral matter has run down into a pietistic cliché from the original thought-and-study operation—though prompting in me a start of recognition.

I think it likely that, if my influence, in and out of poetry, had been met, where it acted, with a seriousness matching that of the thought and practice from which it issued, there would have been far less mere absorption of the things of my work and far more *true*—useful, not prostitute—use of them. But I think, also, that my influence was fated, in the main, to follow the course it did, even because my thought and practice were centered in poetry as an area of human life where the human reality (a phrase by which I denominate the whole actuality of human existence, with all that it comports universally), might fully speak itself; not only can poetry not contain all the seriousness it invites of its practitioners (so much that is done on its ground is excess, and doomed to be waste), but the poets have latterly been reducing the scope of the poetic ground to fit the narrowed scope of the modern imagination, in which the human reality is shrunk to the proportions of psychological realism. I could not, out of my present knowledge, name anyone whom I had affected, in some form and degree, in the sense of influence, who had not failed by want of seriousness in imagination to learn from me what might have given spirit more breadth, in the poem, and word, there, a finer concentratedness of sense. Among those who have had large suffusions of it, none has benefited in the essentials—the substance. One who was keenly sensitive to the original verbal niceties of my poetic practice, which were the flowers of poetic dedication to truth, has no compunction, in identifying himself as a crusader for the idea of poetry for beauty's, not truth's, sake. The procedure of close linguistic scrutiny of poems-texts as a new method of general critical evaluation, which I early elaborated, has by various channels of influence done service belying implicit principles inspiring it.

What I have here written on the subject of influence may help new and old readers of my poems, alike, to dissociate them from literary environments with which they might seem, for one reason or another, to have some connection, and encounter them in the native atmosphere of their qualities. And let readers not be induced by what I have said on the limits poetry puts on seriousness to think that they ought be read with qualified seriousness. On the contrary, they ought to have the benefit of all the seriousness with which readers can receive them: however short the poems fall of the truth-reach because they are poetry, the reach itself can be felt in them—learned from them—foresense acquired of what the full measure of seriousness might be, lived in spoken word. Can poetry exist, then, only as the full of truth is not yet realized? Does it, existing, prevent the realization of it by ever futurizing it, with itself?—my poems may help readers to answer such questions.

But what were my poems "about"? This is a thread that might better be left not drawn into the nexus of summary, for it is hardly a true subject-in-itself. But I shall try to single it out; the question implies a mysteriousness in the matter of my poems, and I feel a responsibility to counter a description of the actuality to the impression. I must proceed somewhat slowly here.

I was, as a poet, an inveterate propounder of a necessity of non-distinction between person and poet. Verily pursued, that non-distinction makes ultimately one: *the person.* Professionally pursued, it makes repeatedly one: *the poet.* I place myself, as a practiser of my principle, as one who aimed at a unity of person and poet in the person. The action of making poems, of forming utterances in the poetic way, was for me of a piece with my general personal motivation in utterance, and choice of manner of utterance (as inclusive of the mode of sensibility and intelligence from which utterance flows). I took the rôle of poet for what it had, in the allowances and commitments of its peculiar poetic manner of utterance, that matched my natural proclivities of utterance. As a person—not only the kind of person I was, but the very person I was—I was moved to try to form utterances towards a certain kind of object of utterance; and, after I became a poet, I gave myself over *all I could* to the poetic manner of utterance because it came, in vital respects, closer to my natural proclivities than any other distinct manner of utterance of established serious use.

Where an attempted unity of person and poet issues in the single repetitive identity of poet, rather than in a continuing identity of person, with the poet-identity continually subsumed in the continuity of the person, the poet-identity is actually a discontinuous theatric identity of the person, the natural person becoming more and more, between the acts, the ape of the other. With these two poles fixed, of attitude-to-being-a-poet, one could lay out all the zones of poet-behavior. But my concern here is to speak—with some effect of general characterization—on what my poems were about.

As a person who was a poet in the course of being the person I was, I was as a poet identical with myself as a person—so far as poetry can be made a personally natural manner of utterance. My being a poet was for me instrumental—and in that sense incidental—to my fulfilling my natural potential of utterance as a person, insistent within me. So, what I had to say as a poet I had to say not because I was a poet but because I was a person. But let it not be thought that this described relationship between person and poet is but a formula of poetic subjectivism. A "person" is to me no mere dryad of a tree of private-life. I view the person anyone is as, by natural propriety, an active agent of entire-being. In every person, the full reality, being, that which manifests itself in the varied sequences and conjunctions of this universe of effort, narrows to a head of utterance: if all goes well in a person, there will be one who speaks out of the entire range of being, uniting the personal locale of life and its great setting. So do I see. The process of re-integration—re-integration great and fine following upon dispersion great and fine—that is the universe works in its final stages in and through persons; and it (its successes, its failures, the vision of it, its plainness, its obscureness) is what everything is "about."

Universal re-integration is the general context of language—the context into which language puts all experience. It is what poetry is "about," in so far as poetry can be taken at the value of its creed, which, like a sacred torch, poets have passed on from generation to generation of themselves. Here in poetry, goes the creed, by resort to a special verbal craft through which what is to be said is isolated from the impure demands of ordinary manners of utterance, everything to be said can be said in accordance with truth's proportions—truth, here, seems to have on its side a perfected harmonic ritual, that excludes what would profane it. If one wholly accepts the creed of poetry, as I did, one's poems will be about anything language makes a possible subject of utterance, for one will feel freed of the limitations that ordinary manners of utterance put upon what one talks about, as well as of those that they put upon how one talks about what one talks about; accepting the craft along with the creed, wholly, one will trust to it to mediate between the difficulties of speaking with the pulse of the World the tempering measure of one's words and the necessities under which one speaks as oneself. One sees no barriers ahead blocking the way to certain subject-regions: one can set out for anywhere, and one envisages one's reaching, by one's poet-craft, points of complete utterance—and drawing from this confirmation of self strength of hope with which to attempt ever more. (I am not accounting for poets who plan their poet-travels to subject-regions on literary maps, and always reach their destinations—old places to which they give new names.)

But the poet-craft is a trap. It is a mistake of ages to think that the utmost in saying can be achieved with the aid of simplifying devices that affect only the surface problems of saying. One cannot know till later how much vanity has gone into the unfortunate human heritage of skill in mustering words in the curious patterns of poems. . . . Later, if one keeps pressing the creed, as a person who is a poet because of it, the craft will evaporate; and one will not miss it, although one has loved it along with the creed, perceiving that in itself it was indeed nothing—a cult-worship of verbal accident, its fond rites filled out with the natural good of language. And the poet one has been will be absorbed in the person one was while one was a poet, and one will be, no more a poet, one's continuing self, as before. And the reality of poetry, though not that of the creed of which it has been the foster-home, will dissolve as one discovers that the words of one's poems, even because they are the words of poems, cannot live a whole day through as visitors on truth's ground: both dark and bright, there, frighten the timid creatures back into their poetic day, a length of half-light. . . . Yet, I think, I made the half-light glow frequently, in my poems; sometimes it is possible to see by them a faint point of demarcation, not quite out of sight, where poetry ends and truth begins—or, at least, can begin. To the extent that this is so, my poems were about the creed of poetry—minus the craft, which thus was put to the service of the creed with poignant directness.

And now I leave this theme of what my poems were about, having followed the thread of it from one end to the other. May the readers of those that are here presented find themselves more interested in what the person who spoke in them was saying to the same effect in all than in what their poet-author had for different subject in each. My poems were a book new-begun in each, new-completed in each; they shared one story—I meant to tell but one.

## 6.

My *Collected Poems* (after the publication of which—in 1938—I came to know that poetry provided no solution for the main crises of human utterance, as it can seem beautifully fitted to do) was introduced by a preface by myself telling of the faith in which the poems composing the volume were written. This faith was two faiths joined. One was, that perfect truth of utterance linked with perfect goodness of being was the destined culmination of human existence. The other was, that by the perfection of utterance it exacted, poetry could unite the two potentialities in one fulfilment. Against the appearance of foolish extremist ingenuousness that such faiths, whether individually or coupledly held, can surely have, I set merely the record of human aspiration. The furthest objects of human effort have been to know rightly enough to speak rightly of the Whole in which one is, and in that speaking to straighten out of the self the twists of self-separation (which twist the sense of the Whole). There is no other full reach of human aspiration—all other objects of human effort fractionize it; and I stand by this total idealism, though the appearance of folly may be at present indissociable from it in the minds of many. Likewise as to the view of poetry I had as a poet: I regard that view as the only view honorably congruous with the choice of the career of poet. I loved what I have called the "creed" of poetry, the doctrine implicit in it—stripped of which it is but something that borrows its name; and I loved what I have called "the craft" for its sake.

I hold it to be not literary naïveté to take the tradition of poetry—the entire activity, poetry, from its beginnings in civilized society as an alternative, in its immediacy, to the futurized fulfilments of religion—at its spiritual word. Anyone who, as a poet, does otherwise engages in literary opportunism, using the traditional spiritual credit of the name "poet" while forswearing the traditional responsibility of the poet to try to discover, in the revered poetic quarter of human performance, how to press the universal essence of human personality into words—so that in utterance all things may have their shape of truth. We do not need Aristotle, that philosopher of the obvious, to point out that poetry deals with "the universal consideration," to know that by its traditional pretensions, at least, poetry is where the Whole and the parts are supposed to make peace in the final reconcilements of true words. I have never thought that I put a faith in poetry that exaggerated its traditional pretensions, or that I mistook its identity; nor did I ever view it by the light of Matthew Arnold's elevated humanism, as a cultural corrective of religious engrossment with the supernatural—something I should not have thought required saying had not someone a critic by calling, publicly active as such, not long ago privately explained my thinking on poetry to me thus. I accepted poetry at the full value of its creed of fulfilment of being in perfect utterance, which is its spiritual justification; I renounced it as doomed by its craft-character to frustrate the hope its creed excites. There has been a good deal of whittling down of that value, to mere cultural proportions. But poetry's given spiritual proportions are of the largest. To be a poet and treat them as other than so is to make a puppet-show of the trials of human beings as beings who are true speakers of their own meanings only in being true speakers of the universe's.

Thus, it can be seen, I am, I was, "a believer"; I believe, I believed, in the possibility of so using words that in the telling of the story one has to tell—the story each human being has to tell of self in the World—the entire sense of Existence will glow in the words, and selves be ardent with an eternized humanness. And I *was* a believer at once in poetry as the way of this human truth that will prove identical with the truth of the World (I use "World" as the human name of the universe). I went as far in poetry with the story I had to tell as the linguistic conditions of poetry allowed me to take it.

Poetry has been the vessel, in human society, of the objective of spiritual articulateness; and the vessel was not adequate to the pursuit of the objective. Why poetry, then? Why so many devotees of it, on and on through the varying times? Why, if it was inadequate, was it not abandoned and replaced by something better? Human beings face crises of utterance they cannot avoid without denial of their nature: they have a final sort of speaking to do, and poetry conventionalizes the necessity, frames in the crises in a manner that seems to put the solution of them within safe reach. There is that in human society which seeks to capture and contain the real within the boundaries of the conventional; it is the male instinct to try to control the extent of human traffic with reality even in the quest of it, and poetry bears in it deep—and, as I think, ineradicable—traces of that instinct in its make-up. All human beings, male and female, have given of their personal substance to fill out the conventional forms in which they have lived their lives as social beings; and, more than any other of those forms, poetry has been vibrant with sensitivity to the aspect of reality it has the assigned function of bringing within the compass of socialized experience as part of its continual content—the articulate relation of human beings to the universe as the speaking selves of its Self. Human society as we have it could not have been a society that felt itself human, without poetry. However, because of that male instinct that insists upon both identification with the real and self-reservation from it, at will, poetry, along with every other institution of human society and not less so than any other, has in it an opposing limit to its capability of making the particular experience of reality it typifies come wholly to life within its frame. This limit is not in the creed of poetry, but is fundamental to its craft, which, amalgamated with the creed, has made place in human society for it under the institutional name "poetry."

The question of the inherent masculine temper of poetic conventionalism—the very conventionalism by which poetry as an activity having spiritual ends has been able to form part of the social synthesis of institutions—is a new one in critical thinking, I am aware. I do not mean to explore it here; I raise it because it has general relevance to the subject of poetry, though one can go far in describing the nature of poetry without touching on this factor of a sexual order, and also because it has relevance to myself as a poet. Since all devoted poets expect to transcend in poetry the limitations of ordinary utterance, the limitations of poetic conventionalism itself are viewed by them as instruments of this transcendence, and the possibility of seeing them otherwise is not one they could take into their minds except at an extreme of consciousness of what they are doing. Those who are men feel, undoubtedly, a special naturalness in the conventional characteristics of poetry. But the fewer who are women can also feel at home in them, by the rule of self-lending to the institutional formalities of society that gives them human breath and makes them emblems of humanness to their followers. The same rule must, indeed, bind men who are devotedly poets to the poetic formalities—bind them as human beings honoring a social institution that is a patron of precious human aspirations, apart from their instinctive acceptance of these formalities as echoic of masculinity.

All poets, be they men or women, are confronted as human beings with an opposition in poetic conventionalism to the necessarily natural quality of utterance to which poetry, as a creed of faith in a spiritual fulfilment achievable through words, is committed: how they deal with this opposition must be, if their dedication is true, a matter of *human* temperament. Yet a poet's being a man or being a woman makes inevitable differences (with unlimited possibilities of individual variation) in the character of the attempt poetry calls for to combine its conventional apparatus and its principle of spiritual perfectionism (as a principle of utterance) in a humanly harmonious manner. I think that in my own case my being a woman caused me to be tolerant of the apparatus to a degree almost inconsistent with the intensity of my pursuit of perfection of utterance as a realizable ideal within the utterance-scope of the apparatus; and I also think that my being a woman contributed to the literalness of my pursuit of the poetic ideal as a general human ideal, and, beyond that, to my ability to know when I had reached the point of impossibility—had come where further employment of the apparatus as the intimate instrument of the realization of the ideal would consume the power to move into the area of the reality.

So long as poets are conscious of a necessity of laboring with the contradiction between the requirements of poetry as utterance that must proceed under conditions of natural freedom of word and its requirements as utterance that must keep itself within certain formal bounds of restraint, they can move in an atmosphere of crisis, in their poems; and the crises with which they deal in their poems can seem to reproduce exactly the crises of utterance that wait upon all human tongues to be solved. All the virtue that poetry has had inheres in the capability poets maintained of recognizing the *oddity* of trying for so much, in utterance, with the scrimped means of poetry's conventional instrumentalities, and struggling in the circumstance of oddity to give to what is said the value of the natural. The struggle has seemed to poets to contain the entire conflict between the grand objective of perfect saying and all the opposing impediments; and it is this earnestness with which they have met the difficulties of poetry—endowing its freedom-obstructive instrumentalities with a crucial dramatic importance—that has raised their utterance-efforts to levels of achievement at which all that is said both celebrates truth and simulates truth, in one rapture of utterance.

Poetry has endured because of the poets who have innocently accepted the curiosity of the poet's given situation, and gone to work in it as if, for all its curiosity, the potentialities and obstacles peculiar to it constituted an essence of the human situation—the predicament of the human person, whose powers of speech are imprisoned in constraints of human nature they alone can break. The triumphs of freedom, the elevations of poetic word-flight, have no higher range than that of illusion. But there is a poet's innocence (and I think this became for the most part, in our age, a lost innocence) that redeems the poetic illusion (of true success of word) from the impurities in the aspiring vision that bears it up on high. Poets are prone to self-flattery, attributing to themselves a privileged nature, by reason of which they can make up with themselves for general human failures of vision and word. Of course, they cannot, though others encourage the persuasion, taking the "pleasurable excitement" supplied by the "picturesque and vivifying language" of not ordinary speaking-occurrences to be their human due of complete human articulateness they cannot give themselves: the mutually flattering "well-understood, though tacit, compact" between the poet eager to provide the excitement and the reader eager to receive it is not a healthy one, there is no possible mutual fulfilment, only a varying private illusion of it—the poet's own having no more validity as truth than any reader's. And yet there's room for innocence here! In feeling caught between the large purposes of poetry and the constrictions of its conventionalities, poets may fight to resolve the opposition with fierceness, and know a sense of sacrifice, though it is not an opposition that brings forces of matching importance into engagement. They can be poets with a generous conception of their rôle; and generosity is the substance of innocence.

The phrases "pleasurable excitement," "picturesque and vivifying language," "well-understood, though tacit, compact," belong to Coleridge, whom I judge to have had poet-innocence in decent provision.[14] He dug himself into the problem of reconciling the contradictory elements of poetry as into a grave from which he must resurrect himself as a matter of poetic honor. He placed the natural element in the realm of "passion" and the restrictive element in the realm of will, and blessed "this salutary antagonism" into a union from which the elements, interpenetrated, issue as delight-giving words. The justification of the oddity of the poetic process is desperate, loyal, fanatically sincere in depth of effort to prove the compromise between the spiritual mood of poetry and the canny technical management to be of a nobility perfectly practical and a practicality perfectly

---

14. [*Biographia Literaria*, vol. 2, chap. 18, Everyman's Library (London: J. M. Dent, 1967), 206.]

noble; he strains himself (does so generally, indeed) to make his conscience and his devotion to poetry come to honorable terms. It is such moral restiveness in poetry about poetry that distinguishes the workers within its interior contradictory conditions and the parasitic dwellers upon its long-lived body. The difference between the kinds can pass undetected, for both kinds can be ardent on behalf of poetry. To my feel of things poetic, poetry began a while ago in time to retreat to its place in history, by the natural rhythm of living actuality (the waning away of the workers, the rising of the human need of word-goodness to crisis-heights beside which poetry's are the miniature-crests of a dwarf-model of the need); among the remnant poets-throng there is much calling this-and-that, of their poetic Day, "new," but I can see there neither old innocence nor new. Their ardor on behalf of it is more and more a narcissistic enthusiasm (where there is ardor)—loving preoccupation with it, in them, is more and more with the naked fact of being-a-poet.

Let it not be thought that I am a poets-whipper. I honor what is virtuous in the poetic legacy, the fervor of the struggle to wrest something that might be *the right words* from the operation of the laws of poetic craft, mistakenly viewed as an action of judgement in which the possibility of rightness of word is put to the proper extreme proof. I believe that there have been many poets who were poets because they took poetry to be the ground on which solutions of a final order to the perennial crises of human utterance could be achieved, rather than because they found themselves able, in the rôle of poet, to convert themselves into utterers-at-large and walk as ones word-gifted among the mute. I think that the generously-moved have preponderated over the greedily-moved, those whose conception of poet-being is self-generous and whose conception of poetry is correspondingly meagre in respect to its relation to the total case of human utterance. I cannot make fond generalizations about poets of the present, or fond particularizations, either, but I do not keep a grim watch on them, condemning all to an incapability of pleasing me. No poets of any time please me, truly; poem-speaking, in any time, is fated to belie its best intentions, I have come to know, so that the very idea of a "good" poem is a tragic fallacy.

Contemporary poetry has long been suffering from a condition peculiarly its own, resulting from a change in the identity of the poet borrowed from the dominant philosophic mood of the time: poets shifted from the identity of *spiritual individual,* which is indispensable to the practice of poetry as a devotional career, one centered to a career, to the identity of *psychological individual.* Poetry has become centered in this time, instead of to a creed, to a programme, the guiding plan of which is Egoism—Egoism increased with the arguments of Art. And so, while being shrunk from its characteristic scope to small-time proportions, poetry—the contemporary activity that has the name "poetry"—flares with all the psychological importances that can be aesthetically extracted from Egoism. The variety it offers, whether in historical cross-section or on the top-layer of the moment, keeps receding back to its essentially monotonous source, a subjectivism that seeks its law in itself: it is a variety without natural human significance, not a "found" one, in which some natural unities might be read, but one artificially created out of the chaotic psychological raw-material that is in philosophic fashion as the substance of human individuality.

There can be no adumbration, even, of fundamental crises of human utterance in contemporary poetry—not to speak of the solution of them. The utterance-crises on account of which it exists are self-originated, their reference-points are all subjectivist, and they can have nothing in common but a concern with craft; and neither the differences nor the resemblances in craft-procedures have any significance except within a precinct of critical journalism in which poets and critics mingledly keep tabs on one another. In this poetic regime little has been left to talk about besides the things of craft, which, severed from vital attachment to creed, have been inflated in importance beyond their capacity for importance, and are ballooned about in the cross-currents of literary shop-jargon in new patterns of absurdity or speciosity. The egoism-factor in contemporary poetry is something it was never in times preceding. Before, it was the vice that being a poet either tamed or inflamed, but a vice that intruded itself uninvited onto the poetic stage, having no part written for it; now, it has all the parts, and there is neither vice nor virtue, only manifold psychological adventure, appropriating the poetic stage.

The entire plant of poetry is taken over, and the reason for its existence forgotten. The new users are too much at their ease in the use of it. The difficulties of perfection of word that poetry failed spiritually to meet must haunt us all—they have no right to their ease. . . .

Ultimately, the crises that poems may seem to solve, the crises of utterance for which there has seemed to be no other solving-ground than poetry, can be brought to truthful height and a livingly occupiable level of settlement only through the maintenance of direct relation between the person and language, without the intermediation of any aesthetic simplification of the difficulties of perfect utterance. The weakness of poetry is in its offering for problems of utterance solutions that are apparently all-linguistic, but actually in part sub-linguistic: poetry offers linguistically incomplete solutions the incompleteness of which can be concealed in sensory supplements without there being observant consciousness in reader or poet of any linguistic deficiency or misfunctioning.

Poets can feel very brave, "going" to poetry as men "go" to war. Cowardice of word seems an impossibility, just as to the soldier it can seem that bravery is assured, on the road to war. But both poetry and war provide many opportunities for cowardice; and poetry also provides many opportunities for wasted bravery, for in it peace has to be made before the battle-test is reached, there being no real enemy. Poets are dedicated, in being poets, to overcoming obstacles to finally adequate, happily articulate, utterance presumed to inhere in the ordinary linguistic course of things, irremovably. These are fictive obstacles, however—as one will find if one persists in seeking out the reputed cause of them, human nature and language's nature in alliance. I began to do this in the midst of my poet's bravery (and cowardice) without special poetic zeal, in instinctive respect for the quality of this alliance. I became a close student of the general proprieties of word-meaning and word-use of the English language from the point of view of a desideratum of general human linguistic happiness; and there was increasingly with me the sense of all persons in their crisis-relation to language, and of a necessary equivalence between the general human linguistic "situation" and the special linguistic situation of the poet, in so far as the poetic search for solutions for problems of utterance could claim general human relevance. The more one studies the words, the plainer is it that what is thought of as the ordinary course of things linguistic is not ordinary at all, but a course of almost infinite mindless deviation from what ought to obtain between a language and its speakers: the nature of the speaking person and that of the language so match each other, in the whole and in the minutiae, that all the greatly less than perfect utterance called ordinary would be better called humanly and linguistically grotesque.

But where, then, does poetry come in, if perfection is encompassable in the (unabnormal) ordinary? . . . But one does not come to ask that question—the character of the (unabnormal) ordinary course of things linguistic does not become so plain that one cannot but ask it—until one has broken loose from the hold of poetic hope, and then one answers it as one asks it: poetry was an effort to create linguistic happiness along the rim of the vast linguistic wretchedness that our speaking life still is. Its creations, though standing like forms of hope on the horizons of the wretchedness, wrought no change in it.

I went on exploring the possibilities of perfect utterance that the language itself allowed of, without any resorting to special conditions of use, after I had ceased to try out the possibilities of this under the auspices of poetry. The exploration has been a work of long thought-experience; my husband, himself a study-er of words, joined me in it, and there is a product on the way that ought, completed at last, to contribute considerably to a general improvement in linguistic self-consciousness, and sensitivity to word-meaning values [*Rational Meaning*]. I speak of this to fortify the idea I present that where poetry fails—fails to transcend linguistic difficulties *linguistically*—the normal linguistic means can succeed by pointing to the substantial actuality, a language, *language*, ever responsively at mind's call, and the more so the better known. Poetry itself, existing against a background of assumptions about language in which its potentialities are made inseparable from limitations, becomes an absolute limitation to the realizing of language's potentialities to the expressive full of human utterance, which is truth. Accepted as the territory of the verbal Beyond, where only few can penetrate, and speak, it precludes there being anything beyond itself, and, with this, the keeping of that final appointment of human beings with language in which they meet with it as their own reason articulated into utterable forms, and all can begin to be spoken.

## 7.

To postulate a point at which poetry ends and truth begins is to give poetry a crucial place in the development of the human capability of truth. But I do not mean this in the sense that poetry is a natural stage along the way to truth—that truth would be impossible without the antecedence of poetry. Poetry is "there" to human beings as it is, a chorus of voices heaved up out of the bosom of common human hope yet seeming to have come from a charmed unknown and using the accent of the Strange, because truth has been envisaged only with the eyes of historical vision, which ever sees what is by the light of what has been: poetry is, actually, story-telling having the theme of truth, but with what is told cast in the realm of the imaginary. The provided-for story-telling procedures of poetry are especially adapted to the production of *effects* of truth; and, this achieved, poetry has reached its limit. But no one ever thought of going any further in utterance, and the most have never thought of going that far, not, at least, by the energy of their own words. With poetry, humanity has drawn a band, a border of inviting word-sound, round its speaking life, and here the compulsion to truth vents itself to extremes of eloquent helplessness; and, indirectly or in the person of the poets, humanity feels itself purged of the compulsion and assumes that it is sufficiently satisfied in the feeling—for the present, and the present, the story of which, and the story of which, however, continue to make not truth, but only history (and little more than literary history, at that).

I think that without the breaking of this band of poetic speaking-life that encircles us all in our existence as speaking beings (though many are hardly aware of its being there) we shall not know how to form the sense or strike the tones of truth. This border-life where words seem to free us from ourselves is *an inertia*:

it is where words are stopped short of being truth by a spiritual reservation pinning humanity down like a ball and chain it attaches to itself for its own supposed good and then forgets about, so that it enjoys both the sense of the possibility of freedom of word and the sense of security from the possibility. A balm, poetry has been, to the embarrassment and pain of human reluctance to face in actuality the full potential of truth implicit in words—and in the human speaking-capability. The reluctance is comparable to the attitude to death: who would not dream favorably of deathlessness, but who wakefully would turn countenance to it favorably and fearlessly as a state immediately enterable upon, without the assistance of death? . . . Poetry has in it the great deathliness of ages of mere human dreaming of truth.

Could not the band of poetic truth-suspension round our speaking-life be left to disintegrate as poetry deteriorated in its passing from poet-hands to poet-hands, each little poets-era more indifferent in the handling of poetry to its historical relation to the total human problem of truth? (I mean, not the problem of "finding truth" but of making it, so that utterance *is* it, is *all* it—this "finding truth" I think mocks truth, which does not lie abroad unfound but exists only by and in our speaking.) . . . If we left our problem of truth to be resolved by the mere disappearance of poetry, when it was quite gone there would still be a band there between us and our self-fulfilment as speaking beings, and one the faster-binding by the gradual replacement of the afflatus of hope with which poetry enlarged the reach of utterance with the afflatus of cynicism with which poetry in deterioration would have maintained the conventional apparatus of verbal transcendence. We need to move in our beings from where we have been pinned in our speaking, and so cease to be self-condemned to reach with words towards truth's fullness as towards outlying possibility: the band to be broken is at once the poetic band and our historical human lesserness to what we are humanly by the ultimate sense we have restrained our words from making. When we live where the band was, there will be no band—it is but a ring of failure where there is no excuse for failure except its offering refuge in time from what can, as the whole nature of things human attests, be done.

The poems that follow are presented for the view they may afford of how much identity may be effected between the problems of poetry and the crucial—the truth-involving—problems of human utterance. I believe, as I have endeavored to make comprehensible, that dedication to poetry in human good-faith (in something more than professional literary loyalty) not only obligates the attempt to effect perfect identity between the poetic and the universal utterance-problems but enjoins confidence in the possibility of the happy resolution of the latter in the other, in poems, under one identity. I have chosen poems for this book with a desire to show (knowing what is there to be seen) to what improved proximities the poetic and the natural necessities of utterance can be brought (I think I narrowed the distances between the two to the last degree short of self-evident irreconcilability) without more union than a flare of sparks between—signs of the poet's effort to make the poem real utterance, the brightness obscuring how much it is not. (What I cannot show by poems is the consequence for the poet of holding thought, sensibility, knowledge, being itself, arrested in the hope of giving to utterance within poems a sure value of truth it is wanting in everywhere outside them; but the arrestation reflects a general human condition, describable as helplessness endured as the helper of hope.)

The poems presented here constitute an epitome of the total effort and success-in-failure and failure-in-success of my total poetic work—according to my reviewing judgement, which I have tried to steer clean between self-indulgence on the one side and self-unsympatheticness on the other. They are arranged in what seems to me the most communicative order, not in simple time-sequence. I shall be making further reference to my poems at the back of the book, in some further commentary, more autobiographical and personal in tenor than this introductory talk.[15]

---

15. [See note 6, p. 62.]

# The Otherwise of Words

*A Little Essay Written Especially for the*
*1972 Harvard Reading*

Poetry being, as I believe, faulty, and just because it *is* poetry, something made up, a representation of the human best in the utterance of words rather than an actuality of speaking circumstance dedicated to such a best, what is there to suggest that poetry can be transcended?

In a little work called *The Telling* I attempted to open to the imagination of possibility a scene of speaking wherein what is said is said *to one another.* A communicating is envisaged here of that which each has to tell, of what we all have to tell in the expertness of being we have in being human—tell one another. But do I do more in that work than show the possibility of conceiving of speaking in which there is address to one another, dedicated address? How can I know that what I say in it will reach humanly open ears and earn the company of other saying, offerings of other tongues to the proposed actuality of our being a unity of audience and address? Until such unity is achieved, can any single saying be all-delivered, be a full saying, or we be fully actual, as those formed to speak to one another: the human?

Let us think what can be learned by examining the pattern of perfection to which poetry conforms. Where is the faultiness? It is, that the perfection is the perfection of a pattern. The address of poetry is closed-circuit: it returns to itself, it plays the part of both address and audience. Much is written on the function of the poem of producing effects on the reader or listener as its audience; but the reader or listener is drawn into the closed-circuit, loses existence in the poem's identification of address and audience. The only element in this pattern that can countervail the magnetic attraction of it to itself is the generosity in the poem laboring outwards towards the reader or listener that the poem is drawing inwards into its circuit of address. This element gives to poems a virtue above their perfection as patterned utterance, causes something of human perfection to be present in the poem. The addition, which is almost secretly made, cannot break the humanly faulty enclosedness of the poem in itself; but what brave touches of perfection a poem may have are the gift of this element. Nor easily does the gift make itself at home there.

Neither poets nor critics nor readers, listeners, have any distinct consciousness of what I have described, and it would be very difficult to identify instances of this other kind of goodness of utterance as departures from the norm of poetic utterance. While I have this tenuous matter in momentary grasp, let me attempt a practical characterisation of this good in words that can be found mingled in poetry with *its* kind of good, but as something else, something more, and yet is swallowed up in the poetic. It is a speaking that sends words out, not to stop till they reach another. Words so sent in poems do not get out; but it is possible in some places, in some poems, to feel the force of the sending, to recognise the sent words. When sent words actually travel, the private occasion of utterance evaporates. Poetry's faultiness is such that poems remain spoken within the poet's private occasion of utterance. They are by their nature a less than perfectly human speaking.

What is then the sounding they make among us as of a perfect speaking? It is an invented speaking that puts us behind ourselves in an immediacy lying between non-human fore-time and human now. It is a queer purchase of a nondescript immediacy in utterance at the price of the possibility of a perfectly human articulate immediacy. The price is paid in the coin of doubt of the possibility, though the character of the money is not generally comprehended.

At stake is the effort to do otherwise with words than what can be done within the range of the respectable or the accepted in imperfection. The relation between doing such an otherwise with words and an imperfection-surmounting otherwise with ourselves, human, is functionally of the closest. The confusions attending what we try to do, and do, linguistically and humanly are of the same moral kind. I might be charged with having added to these confusions by devoutly serving poetry and then solemnly renouncing it. I wish I could have moved faster in the effort to find the otherwise of words, could have outgrown sooner the innocence that makes poetry seem to be the place in which to look for it. I at least discovered that that otherwise is at the remove from how we ordinarily do with words at which poetry is while being, yet, not that otherwise. It is a remove of chosen delay in having that otherwise come next. Poetry is an interposition between this next and ourselves, the ones of the nature to speak to one another and be our all in saying our all.

The name of poetry is kind. But it cannot make the deflected good in words, the perfection of less than all spoken as if all might be hidden within it, into outright address, cannot make it otherwise.

# [From] Story, and Story-Style

I have pronounced poetry to have failed. By my account of the history of story, has not story failed? In the case of poetry, my view is, there has been an ultimate of failure implicit in its nature from the beginning of its development as a form of expression in which the potentialities of language were elevated to a level of explicit truth far above the expressive potentialities of language in its "ordinary" courses of employment. While this creed, attached to poetry, has had associated with it the highest human aspirations in the use of words, the hope of achieving perfections of expressiveness in it of a final value, that is, the perfection of truth, the functional actuality, in poetry, binds it to oratory formalities of utterance in which the concern with truth of utterance must be continually, sustainedly, painstakingly, qualified by concern with effective delivery of the to-be-uttered words. This peculiarity of poetry as a higher form, an aspiring effort, in the employment of language introduces into it a factor of power of utterer, over the witnessing audience of the words, of a physically persuasive sort. Poetry has, thus, a congenital defect of postulating a limitation for truth, as humanly achievable, of eccentricity, achievability under special, forcibly created, conditions, by which poetry is both a technique of stimulation to acceptance of uttered words as truth and an actuality of truth delivered. Story has no such confusion, such self-contradiction, within the corpus of its organic constitution, and, therefore, no inevitable destinedness to functional failure [. . . .]

# [From] Some Notes on Poetry and Poets in This Century, and My Influence

[. . .] *To a degree—to some degree*: herein is the crux of the question of the title of poetry to high placement in general human regard. So long as there is an intuition of an unresolved problem in the attitude of poets themselves to this matter of *degree* in the achievable in poetic word-use, so long as the sense of a constant of partialness in success in the poetically achievable does not assume significance of adequacy of a kind—so long as the ground of poetry is occupied as one that borders distantly on the realm of the possible perfect in the putting into words of what has not ever yet been gathered into distinct sayability. So long as inaccomplishment of what must be eventually accomplished with words, if the human capacity is not unequal to the human store of words (if human nature does not fail to be true to itself), lies in naked view, sight of a realm of the unspoken beyond, not veiled off from the poetic borderland, delight-giving as where words take meaning to wakeful day-ends of the mind, and thought's further, language's more of place for thought's travel in itself, is but a brief night away, a sleep's, a dream's, length of time-lost ceasing to count.

So long as poetry was in heart a rite of loving obeisance to a belief that words could be used with a success of saying all, the rite being the proving that telling true was possible *to some degree*, in patches of most watchful utterance in trial of ways of truth-devoted expression, in forms enmeshing words, by sympathies of sound and utterance-movement, in harmonies of truth-likeness with one another: so long, there was no lie in it, though no sheer actuality of realized truth. And where else was there no lying, words confessing themselves to be at best no more than *to some degree* true-telling? This was an acknowledgement of what might be *done*, though it was not, in the use of words.

Poetry was the host of acknowledgement of a natural will, in the human mind, to transmute the experiences of consciousness, and the determinations of thought formed upon the ground of consciousness-experience, into an overt self-revealing reality of speaking being. Poetry has fulfilled the necessity of humanity's posing this objective to itself, as ideal, to make good its right of identifying itself as human. That poetry should be treated as a final perpetuity becomes, at a certain point in the human course, sacrilege against the verities of which it was a rite of faith. At this point (*which has been passed*), poetry begins to be perverted into a rite of acknowledgement of the desirability of *some degree* of tribute-paying to an objective of perfect articulateness of word, as a useful stimulant to human self-esteem. More and more, the criss-crossing and chaotically directionless tracks of word-skill vanity obscure the old paths in poetic *endeavor*, which were intended to be in *some degree* in the direction of truth[. . . .]

# From a Notebook of Essays-In-Little

*(Entries of Many Years)*

### 1.

The demands of the practice of poetry on the sensitivity of the poet to the effects of words are so elaborate—so much more varied and, in their unremitting insistence, more severe than what the nicest prose-composition would require—that poets are generally assumed to be linguistic perfectionists, uncompromising devotees, by intention at least, of linguistic excellence. However, if these demands of poetry are "broken down," they will be seen to enforce, *and to allow for*, only a partial preoccupation—and, moreover, a subsidiary one—with linguistic excellence. Poets must be vigilantly sensitive to the physical effects of words—to their effects as successive masses of voiced sounds. This preoccupation is a predetermined one, existing apart from preoccupation with sense and sense-development, and competing with it, and overbearing it in the course of composition to an extent that is never taken into measured account—either in the criticism of poetry, or in readers' consciousness of the poem-composing poet.

The effectively invisible proportion between word-physicality, in poetry, and word-intellectuality produces the suggestion of mystery as an element of the poetic process. There is, however, no third element in poetry, additional to that of meaning-stress and stress of the vocal, tonal, enunciative, components of utterance. The only third factor in an analysis of what "makes" a poem is the tendency of word-physicality to be preponderant. That this should be so is an oddity where the matter of meaning, of word-intellectuality, is supposed to be treated with an intensity of preoccupation presumed to be either not linguistically possible, or not conventionally provided for, in ordinary word-using procedures. The oddity is deepened by the confusion of the care for physical effects with the care for special pressing upon word-capability of delivering *meaning*. The progress of meaning from word to word in intellectual patterns of delicate coherence and the course of utterance in physical patterns of sound and movement, more forceful in impression, more attention-compelling, than the physicalities of other modes of verbal utterance, run into each other. The nature of what is going on is obscure. This obscurity is treated as the nature of poetry itself—a unity of not distinctly identifiable parts. But when poetry is perceived to be a *compound,* the obscurity explains itself. There is no real unknown in the make-up of poetry.

## 2.

A poem has something of the character of a toy, a verbal toy made for the spirit. The spirit, fondling it as if it were a live actuality, and one perfect in the qualities of truth (the speaker faithful to the words, the words faithful to the speaker), scarcely knows that it is a toy.

## 3.

There is self-contradiction in poetry in the emotional heightening of attention-to-things that becomes inextricable from it—more with some poets than others—as a traditionally ordained part of the psychological conditions of poetic composition. In the poetic area the emotional intensity is also supposed to be, traditionally, concentrated in the verbal circumstance—the words are supposed to compress all that arises for expression into their meaning-mould. But the psychological ordinance divides the emotional consciences of the poet. Attention splits. The poetic subjects draw off some, the verbal process pulls the other way. There results a strained double intensity—an over-emotionalized "natural," raw-experience emotion (as to the subjects), an over-emotionalized poetic emotion (as to the verbal embracing of experience of the subjects).

## 4.

The high points in [poetic] wisdom take on the character of formulas, essences. They have the beauty of formulation that is both strict and simple. They press up towards being wisdom of complete thought that is at once complete sensibility. And these finest gems seem to constitute a poetic wisdom above wisdom. But, though poetry suggests the presence in it everywhere of such wisdom-potential, and the actuality seems to be of a happy—though tremulous—frequency, the wisdom-aspect of poetry is, truly, a small portion of the total delivery. It is the counterpart to the pleasure-element of poetry—and, supposedly, the two intertwine into a unity of the wise and the lovely. But the wisdom-product of poetry is a thing-in-itself of fine fragments that suspend themselves to a height in the poetic atmosphere, and then drop to its general level of elevated mood, not much of it lastingly distinct as other than "poetry." Wisdom in poetry is also of slight substance as compared with the total potential wisdom-product of human utterance, reckoned according to the actual, existing, human wisdom-heritage. Poetry's apparent susceptibility of wisdom of a rare quality of excellence is not all illusion. But the rating issues, largely, from a comparison of poetry with itself, a self-comparison that continually takes place in it, as if automatically: the general ground of poetry is one of expectation of incidents of wisdom-utterance, and when they occur they have a prepared noteworthiness in the poetic atmosphere, or scene.

## 5.

There is a curious exchange made by the poet. The escape from the limitations of ordinary modes of expression is to a different set of limitations, working by which you are confined within a single operation of isolation of imposing the non-constricted kind of say as say of yours. The emphasis on self is enormous. A stage is seized for self-presentation, for the ridding oneself of built-up impatiences to exercise verbal intensities of utterance—to release all that you find to say in *poetic* time. However long the poem, it is always in time seized out of time. And the audience's part? The wistful admiration that seems love? The audience feels: this is what I should like to have said. A vicarious release-sense is enjoyed, from which comes the odious vice of quotation, the absorption of poetic saying into a common domain of linguistic mediocrity.

Nowhere else has there been, in activity supposedly of an intellectual purity, moral trustworthiness, so intense an emphasis on the self. Poetry is the haunt of "loners." In it the self will not find a true other to itself. One's soul-self cannot live extendedly in poetry. One is alone in that realm.

This view of the personal dilemma of the poet as locked in a circumstance of saying a whole say that cannot be more than something said *to* oneself and for oneself, however much one might wish and conceive it to be otherwise, brings into its focus the music-element secreted in poetry, the "body-talk" component of it—which can say nothing, can only dumbly express the unspeaking movements of the physical imagination. This element, in its very active presence in the poetic occasion, converts the so-much-not-actually-said into what seems determinate, distinct, precise, eloquent; but it is an ensconcement of the said in the privacy of that humanly vague existence-unto-oneself which is the life-area of the physical. The poem, for both poet and reader, can intensify self-confinement in, rather than provide openings out of, this area.

## 6.

In the literary use of words, and especially so in the poetic use of them, the contemporarily irreverent mood towards words, and the reconstructed, scientific wisdom of words that goes with it, as an improvement on the natural human word-wisdom, acquire the dignity of linguistic sophistication. Professional writers, and poets especially, put in place of the traditional concept of "mastery of the medium," which is mastery in the sense of a mastering of the requirements that language, of its nature, poses for the use of words, a concept of speaker-autocracy, by which the word-user is the master of the words, making them do whatever is wanted of them, and the individual field of literary or poetic operation is the personal theatre of its master's voice.

## 7.

There are at least two words "poetry," one meaning linguistic activity of a certain kind, the other meaning verbal matter produced by such activity. I speak in this little essay of what it is that poets are doing and what their activity amounts to in the scales of human behavior, rather than of poetry the verbal matter—although I may be drawn into making incidental references to it. Another way of describing my point of view, here, is to say that I am trying, here, to function in the field of human criticism rather than in that of literary criticism. (In my fundamental attitude to poetry as a poet, my conception of poetry was not a categorically literary one.)

During my career as a poet I became increasingly an advocate of poetry. In the final stages of that career I claimed, I think, more than anyone has ever claimed for it. I believed that it was the way of truth, and to truth, the "of" and the "to" being mingled in my mind in a fond hope that somewhere along the way approach would turn into arrival. Lest my use of "truth" in the preceding sentence throw a religiose mist over my meaning, let me recast my phrasing: I believed that it was the way of speaking true and the way to speaking true, both path of the ideal in language and place of its realization. This double focus was the result of my not having a categorically literary conception of poetry.

I came, eventually, to believe there to be something ineradicably wrong with the activity poetry—and that this was reflected in poetry the matter. I arrived at this belief not from disapproval of the cultivation of extraordinary linguistic powers, to which poets are professionally dedicated—not with any priggish bias towards the plain-ordinary verbal level—but in the persuasion that poetry involves a distortion of a natural human ambition of linguistic self-fulfilment, and that poets delude themselves in feeling that they attain a verbal serene above the murk of commonplace articulateness, and that they obstruct the general vision of human linguistic potentialities with the appearance of doing so. In the ordinary way of speaking, and the ordinary way of writing, called "prose," which is modelled on it, there are obvious murkinesses; the "good" speaker or prose-writer is one who is able to keep their number low. In the poetic way of writing, which is at once a non-ordinary way of speaking, there is no escape from murkinesses, but they are concealable there; the "good" poet is one who keeps them so inconspicuous that they make no overt problem for his or her or anybody else's intelligence. Much of the magical effect that poetry gives of rendering everything it touches pellucid comes from the necessity of compression that it imposes. The impossibility of pausing in poetry as long as may be needed to make sense clear causes many a set of words actually deficient in linguistic workmanship to pass for an eloquent brevity.

The obscurity, often called "difficulty," that is charged against "advanced" modern poetry, and against the charge of which it has found more and more defenders, is real, but is something apart from the ingenerate poetic defect of which I have just spoken, something additional to it. It originates in a general progressive weakening, in modern time, of the seatedness of human minds in language, a loosening of the hold on them of formalistic ideas of the coherences of language without the correction of an enlarged view of the nature of those coherences and their importance. People generally are divided between world-weariness and innate passion to make words mean aright for them, and are all linguistically at odds with one another. Poetry still holds aloft, above this scene of disorder, its emblem of relief from the stale and sordid in language, but poets themselves are enveloped in the disorder. Freer rein is given in modern poetry to mental and verbal idiosyncracy; there is a sharp decrease in the amount of common intellectual ground occupied by poets through the use of a common language. Poets more and more speak their own different languages—their personal versions of the language they use: this is what lies at the root of modern poetic obscurity, "difficulty." I myself came under attack as guilty of one or the other offence in my career as a poet, but I believe my case to be a different one. I labored to discover the obscured coherences of the common language: from that came my linguistic strangeness as a poet, not from my speaking, after the manner of my fellow-modernists, a language of my own—and came also my having an influence on the word-craft of many poets.

My word-ways seemed to extract more "poetry" from language. But I only extracted more language from language. The "influenced" poeticized my enlargement of the linguistic compass of poetry. None who have drawn upon my poems for advantage to their own have comprehended and acted upon (made intelligent application of), in so doing, the broadening and strengthening of the intellectual function of poetry that was the basis of, the governing reason of, my enlargement of its linguistic compass. Those I helped directly, and those who took help from me in the form of "influence," remained insensitive to the line of connection in my poetic principles, and my poetic work, from the spiritual aim of making poetry truly real, a believable mode of truth, to the intellectual pursuance of the ideal, the treatment of it as within the reach of rational practicality, and from this to the linguistic honesty of a spacious exactitude, the attempt to justify the poetic use of words as naturally "right" by attempting to round, in it, the linguistic natural to a full, a perfect, expressiveness. Every poet who has been affected by my poems or my help, has converted what they, or I, have given, into mere *behavior*, an additive to their work of spiritual, intellectual, linguistic superiority to itself that leaves behind the spiritual, intellectual, linguistic point of the source-material from which it has been derived.

## 8.

Poetry has been, and still is somewhat, an object of worship, an idol. The tutelary spirit of language seems to dwell in it; it has the appearance of an emblem of Purity. However, the intellectual harmonies of language are sacrificed to it, rather than exalted in it. The hybrid objective of physical and intellectual pleasure, from what is done in poems with words, makes an impossible linguistic ideal; the intellectual pleasure falls ever into second place.

Poetry is a substitute, for linguistically sensitive people, for being of full human linguistic age, which no one can isolatedly be, and the human generality is not yet. It is an enactment by poets of a drama of accession to a state of final knowledge of the secrets of words. The poet dramatizes the common dream of the loosened tongue: the poet's audience delights—or is supposed to delight—in the performance as a reality in its own right, an end in itself. Thus poetry charms the lovers of words into forgetfulness of the reason of their being lovable, which is their holding a promise of perfect, whole, self-delivering utterance for human beings.

Between the poet as language-priest and the reading congregation there is an unwittingly unholy covenant to evade the intellectual, and therefore linguistic, final difficulties, and yet by exploiting a certain "way with words"—the poet leading, the congregation following—to transcend them, dissolve them, soar past them. There is a diabolical side to poetry, which adds overtones of angelic beauty to the din of ordinary parlance. This is its futility, its ministering to the vanities rather than to the needs of human beings in their dependence on words, its raising them to heights of illusion of linguistic felicity only to let them drop down to real speaking ground with no increase of capacity to make—or rather, let—words carry full burden of meaning. Ultimately, in the human production and enjoyment of poetry, poetry proves good only for itself. It provides something to admire—to do which may be argued to be useful and also argued to be an empty justification for its existence.

### 9.

Poetry involves an attempt to fulfil natural linguistic impulses more successfully than they are fulfilled by ordinary speaking-means with the aid of artifice. Poetry—what poets do—is, therefore, a self-contradictory performance. And general attitudes to poetry are self-contradictory in relation to this peculiarity of it, and the poets' own attitudes to it, likewise: it is viewed as providing experience of a character that is outside the norm of ordinary human experience, and yet touches the very heart of human existence, and speaks the intimate language of its meaning. If it did this in real effect, it would obliterate the difference between ordinary and super-ordinary, dissolve the self-contradiction in itself, and solve the painfully haunting problem of human uncertainty as to what the human "real" is.

## 10.

The rhythmic pattern of the poem, which forces continuity of attention—incites a pleasurable compulsion to "follow"—is either a tried metrical suasion-contrivance or a specially invented pattern of physical insistences, equally, if not more, binding in its effect on the reader. From a straight linguistic point of view, there is room for wonder if there is not latent vice in this environment in which pleasurable physically compelled responses, produced by incidents of poetic utterance, are identified with the Good.

It is very difficult to judge of the poet Wordsworth without clearing from the scales a heavy suspicion that one's moral instinct places in them in spontaneous innocence of prejudice. The natural impressions that his performances from early to late make of a calculating mind and personality clothed in literary piety, and the unavoidable deduction of a secretive heart, from Coleridge's generosities of unreserve of himself and restless strivings of spirit and intelligence in special relation to Wordsworth, besides in his general activity and disposition, and what the course of Wordsworth's work in particular respect to Coleridge's generosities suggests, could discourage a view of Wordsworth as a man of sensitive conscience, with energy of conscience penetrating from the personal into the literary life. But there is some circumstantial basis for deducing that a sense of personal guilt was not unfamiliar to him. And there is an odd quality of guilt virtually felt—a sort of literary guilt doing token service for conscience—in Wordsworth's expressed uneasiness over the metrical features of poetry, and his offering an elaborate apology for this aspect of poetry. The uniqueness of such position-taking, whatever the key to the question of sincerity in Wordsworth's regard, gives the position an importance of an absolute degree: the position, put on record, is in itself a respectable one.

There are other effects associated with the excitation of responses of certain kinds besides those produced by the material features and rhythmic patterns of poems. Wordsworth's identifying as a function of poems the evocation of experienced emotion irked the sensibility of T. S. Eliot as a literary vulgarism. His own conception of the part of emotion in poem-making was a subtilized one. Emotion, with him, was attenuated in processes of critical theorizing that actually entered into his poem-making; it was not for him a determinate element in a poem, as emotion is, in and out of poems, but one that waited upon the indeterminate intellectual element of the poem (always an indeterminate one in his own poems) to arrive at a full determination of its indeterminateness: emotion became emotion about itself in this intricate literary circumstance. Wordsworth faced the technical deviosity of poem make-up in a professional manner perhaps intended to be disarming, communicating as it were the poet's awareness of a rôle in tradition's and the public's eyes of producing some emotional effects. Eliot was for playing down this rôle: he made the emotional element as a private factor in the poet's experience of composing a poem. Readers could be sensitive to it, but they were on their own, there was no overt courting of their emotional interest.

Wordsworth's position as to the poet's relation to his public seems also oddly forthright. He treats the problem with practical simplicity as a professional one, from the point of view of the poet estimating just what it is his business to attempt: there is the job of producing poems, there is the public, and there is himself who has got to stand in the poem and out of it, both making it and intermediating between it and himself and it and the public. The Wordsworthian posture is not likeable but it is respectable. Eliot's posture, in his construing the nature of the poem and the poetic act, takes the entire situation out of the workaday literary world and plants it in a world of literary criticism in which all problems are in terms of the troubles of self-evaluation of the poet as an irresolute mind partly accepting this as proper to the times in which he lives; the poet's mind is assumed to be, humanly, of psychological and all other kinds of irresolution, and for the rest one that must steel itself to the professional requirements of poet-identity by forming a competitive self-consciousness keyed to the most intellectually respectable poetic competencies of the past and to the most intellectually innovational poetic trends of the present. The posture is of so elaborately professional a cast of self-centered preoccupation as to invite, to have invited, highest respect, literary, academic and popular, as a paradigm of the predicament-of-the-modern-poet-in-being-modern. But within the posture's complex aggregation of attitudes there *is* a stiff one of sustained concern with *effects.* This attitude, which is not necessarily imperceptible amidst all the fine critical argument and fine adjustments of the poetic writing to this and that personally professional consideration, is, perceived, perceptibly one of sharp crassness—as compared, for instance, with Wordsworth's blunt, business-like vulgarity in his analysis of the poet's task.

(Poor Coleridge devotes many, many pages of the latter part of *Biographia Literaria* to his agonizing perplexity over Wordsworth's critical pronouncements on the practicalities of poems-making. How does the realistic, professionally common-sense view of poetry voiced in them accord with the lofty elegance—in Coleridge's loyal-hearted and wistful estimation—of some of Wordsworth's poetic writing? Coleridge pondered this wonderingly. He would have liked to be able to sustain a line-to-line course of poeticized philosophic elevation such as Wordsworth could. But he was not merely philosophically but religiously a more serious man than Wordsworth. And he was serious in his conception of the nature of poetry with an angelic philosophic seriousness. His poetic ideal was itself so elevated that he had not an ounce of professional poetic elevation in him. Wordsworth had a weighty talent in this. It was his intensely professionalistic view of poetry and of himself as a poet that allowed of his making the matter-of-fact prescriptions for good poetic practice, in connection with the *Lyrical Ballads,* that later haunted Coleridge, distressingly, when he looked back on this—and on his past association with Wordsworth generally.)

## 11.

Let those who are puzzled by the proposition that the components of poems that they tend to regard as peculiarly poetic detract, in the total appraisement of a poem's achievement, from its effectuality as *what it says* consider the traditional proposition associated with poetry, even in untraditional modes of practice of it, that *felicity of word* is its domain. How much is attention divided, in the mind confronted by a poem, between the words, in their performance of the function of meaning, and sensations excited by the words that conduce to impressions pictorially and otherwise physically interpretative of *meaning not fully delivered by the words?* That is, "felicity of word" in a poem is converted (by the basically unalterable conditions of poetic expression) into something different from straight linguistic felicity of word. It is a felicity in the circumstance of an imposed (unalterable) brevity: the poem is a *confine* from which full expression is automatically excluded. The fullness permitted is a makeshift fullness: a saying all that can be said within the confine of the poetic occasion that the poem outlines, and is. Latitudes of suggestion, sensation-excitation, evocation of feeling physically rather than intellectually associable with the actual words, an extra-marginal area in which autobiographical significances of the words for the poet are mingled with autobiographical significances of them for the reader: very much of the experience presented by a poem is only hypothetically present in it, is outside the poem experience. The words are torn between reference to themselves in their linguistic duty, and to the special duty to the poem imposed on them of compensatory reference to what they do not get said.

The conditions that poetry imposes on the use of words complicate and confuse the question of the nature of linguistic excellence; and they also complicate and confuse the question of the emotional sincerity, and that of the intellectual probity also, with which the words are used. The poet of good poetic conscience must accept these conditions. As a person of good personal and linguistic conscience also, the poet must constantly endeavor to maintain a state of mobility in which all the consciences are given their right to press their values, in the harmony of mobility, none arresting movement, bringing all under its rule. Where the conditions of the poetic profession and the conditions of personal validity and the intellectual conditions of language are all honored in an exercise of the poetic profession, the poet is headed for an ultimate extreme test by an undivided meaning of "honor."

## 12.

### On The Latter-Day Mood of Concern With Poetry

Latter-day poets have discarded the standing subjects of poetry, and much of their poet-energy is expended in subject-fabrication—from which they go to poetry-procedure fabrication. One can look back to the early phases of poetic modernism and see this happening; first, the deconventionalizing of subject, then the deconventionalizing of poetry itself.

There is that outrageous pronouncement of Eliot's of many decades ago, which continues to be quoted as respectable literary, critical, and human doctrine: "Poetry is not the expression of personality, but an escape from personality" ["Tradition and the Individual Talent," 1919]. Nothing has any independent dignity of identity from a main or stable decency of function that is an escape from something else. Personality is not a vice or an affliction if it is not perversely made so: and, if it is made so, the use of a human practice in the category of letters, traditionally honored, as an emergency-door of exit from entrappedness in it is nothing to brag about. However, the rhetorical deviousness of the dictum is the real indecency here.

Eliot was attacking the ferment of expression of personal feeling that transformed the writing of poems, in the early twentieth-century new poetic liveliness, into an almost popular activity. Poetry began, then, to seem a wide open field of literary endeavor. It was expanded in content by the injection into the categories of poetic subject-matter of multifarious individual changes-ringing on the traditional emotional stances of poets, the forms of emotional temper in which poets traditionally cast their personal identity, as it figured in their poems.

If Eliot had been a better poet, and a better person, and a better critic, he would not have committed himself, in his consciousness of the flooding of the field of poetic activity with indiscriminate experimentation in the possibilities of free-ranging individuality of emotional temper, to an assault of snob-disdain upon this as literary vulgarity. The historical inspection of poetry—of the stylistic behavior of poets—that he undertook was motivated by a desire to establish a firm distinction—applicable to past and modern poetic work—between the literarily vulgar in poetry and the literarily dignified. The disastrously potent effect of Eliot's general preachment as poet and critic sprang from the easy intellectual solution he offered, to a period of new restlessness in literary activity, for the confusion of moral purpose in which the general thinking of human beings was then enveloped, as in a climate of final enlightenment.

The grand moral definitions of religion and philosophy and political idealism had fallen into intellectual disrepute, to be replaced by a general scepticism different, in the use to which it was put, from the character scepticism has ever had in the past as a refuge in times of intellectual crisis, a temporary suspension of commitment to definitive positions. It had been itself a position of religious or philosophical or ethical bearing, a position of concern with questions of intellectual commitment. Now it became a position of final dissociation from commitments of the traditional sort.

The pivot of intellectual relationship of the new scepticism was a primary orientation to science as the definer of reality. The sceptic position became that of absolute abstinence from the engagements of the old schools of thought in the definition of the subjects of thought that have been the perpetual intellectual preoccupations of human beings. The new scepticism accepted the tenets of science as to the proper subjects of intellectual preoccupation: they were subjects that generalized themselves for definition in the experiences, first of all, of the physical actualities, not in the experiences of thought. Scientific intellectuality reduced thought to a secondary status in the functioning of human intelligence, and, with this, it made the traditional subjects of intellectual preoccupation intellectual fictions. The effect, in the special world of literary intellectuality, of the ascendancy of scepticism as an absolute intellectual position, was to narrow greatly the scope of literary *meaning*, and especially that of poetic meaning—for, that is, the intellectually self-conscious habitués of the literary world.

Eliot took upon himself the combining of the rôle of believer in the new absolute scepticism with the rôle of defender and preserver of the traditional literary-ness of poetic meaning—pinning the poetic position down to its minimum as a professional literary minimum. The gospel of poetic literary-ness that Eliot preached is still reverberating in the literary world, of which poetry has ever been an experimental element—as it has been, indeed, in the world-in-general. Poetry has become a region of continuous literary competition governed by self-constitutedly representative boards that issue the graded awards of honor with as much fluidity of standards as they can without submerging the literary dignity of the competition in the flood of their liberality.

Not "exactly" Eliot, but Eliot and those of that common time who with him, and with his volunteered help, took it upon themselves to give poetry the dignity of a well-managed *business,* a well-defined literary business, created a cultural commerce in which the differences between literary dignity and literary vulgarity of Eliot's labors of critical discrimination have been subsumed in an all-dignifying comprehensive merchandising systematicness, and advertising and distribution efficiency. The business is sham culture. The dignity of the enormous enterprise is sham dignity. The products are sham everything, as what they are offered as being, under the grand old name of poetry. But where scepticism has become the absolute human position, the sham version of anything is the real, the only, form of it. Eliot provided a legalistic definition of authentic sham, for poetry (as he did of authentic sham, for religious attachment).

Can one man have such widespread, and enduring, effect? *One man* can be more than an illustration of something existent in or implicitly possible in human behavior. When the illustration that one man, one woman, one person, makes of the existent or implicitly possible in human behavior is adopted in broad extension by other human beings as confirming actualities or potentialities of their behavior-dispositions, the circumstance is that of the illustration turning a particular fact or condition of human behavior disposition inside out. The balance between the happy and unhappy significance of what undergoes turning inside out, in such circumstances of one man's proclivities proving to have a broad correspondence incidence, is not clearly readable. I think it likely that this is because it is not on the favorable side as to the state of human dispositions—that what becomes distinctly and provocatively illustrative of the existent or potential in human dispositions has been for the most part what, of themselves, the most would not be proud to profess. Trends in ideas, in many areas of human judgement, pick up their force in a gradual growth of courage, in people, to disregard what, in the ideas, some instinctive element of their thought shies from as wrong.

# Poetry Has Ever Overtaken Itself

In poetry, truth has been both sought and hidden away in the seeking: poetry has ever overtaken itself in its resolve to surpass itself.

Is poetry, by a secret agreement among human beings, a substitute for what they secretly long to hear from one another but temper to a common reluctance to do that which might startle common desire, as if in the event of its fulfilment it might prove too much for itself?

If it be that poetry is the "other" way, to how we speak, the way of care for our words that they be our sense transmuted into knowability to the other—the sense *and* the very delivery of it *at the same time*? The way of speaking in which the engagement between oneself, speaking, and the other, hearing, succeeds—oneself, saying, and the other, attending? The way of entire sincerity and seriousness—the one in expressive purpose, the other in purpose of comprehending the expressed?—But who have cared about that "other" way, in caring about poetry? Who have not yielded to the attraction of a poetic *alternative* to that other way?

How much bartering between effort for a perfect meeting, by another's wish and one's own, in the unity of sense in which a word can lock one and another, and a busy ease of letting minds brush against each other with some rustle of word-sound, promising a next-time of perfect possibility, makes up the occasions of poetic encounter? Who have sworn themselves to try their all to help their minds make the care for what is said the leading care—*since words are being uttered?*

Did not the impossibility at last show, of poetry's proving itself that which human beings hoped of it, in sleeping expectancy? There is no relief, in poetry, no waking, after a word-fond dream of hope, to a new day of spoken sense, nothing left behind in the darkness of the unsaid.

Is it not clear that poetry is now a ground of old hope covered over with a growth of desire for yield of words that has nothing to do with what that old hope proposed of the happily imaginable, in word-yield? It used to be a wishing-ground, a place of wishing with words for better than wishing—for a full revealing of what words are empowered by the human desire for truth to reveal. The imagination of the possibility was allowed to play the part of the actuality. The results could be no more than pleasurable faith in a destined rescue of the human soul from the demon of silence-of-mind by the angel of language.

Poetry has had the realness of a place where tribute is paid to the redeeming powers of words. The anxious soul could take comfort there in the virtue words possessed because of what they *might* bring to pass, if they were summoned lovingly enough to make their peace of truth between minds—and first of all between minds and their universal nature, and between minds and themselves. But poetry has lost its franchise as a place of word-reverence. Words themselves have lost their meanings, in minds. They have been converted into the coin of an exchange of understandings in which the significance of being human is broken up into myriad minor importances—a busy commerce, everyone well-educated in the opportunities and invigorations of buying and selling, and no major sense knitting the whole into a common *point.*

Poets, operating now *anywhere,* not on the reserved special ground of poetry, set up their claims, their titles of place, as all-privileged squatters. Their operations are not, actually, upon the historic ground of poetry. They call every individual spot they seize upon poetic ground, and call what they produce, there, poetry. The operations are, actually, on a personally pre-empted piece of public ground declared private property, in poetry's name; and the verbal activity performed for public witness on each such personal preserve is, in each case, a peculiar individual issue of talk, disquisition, recitation, harangue, outburst, meditative pronouncement, in a loosely conventionalized new version of poetry, not more specifically describable than as verbal performance *in the poetic manner.*

I have written here in a spirit partly sorrowful (with respect to what has been) and partly condemnatory (with respect to what is). Altogether, I regard these things as inevitabilities (what has been, as to poetry, and what now is). But inevitabilities are lessons that spell themselves out very, very late; and, even when they deliver their messages in the form of actuality become patent fact, it can be very long before eyes are immediate to the fact, intelligences active to the lesson. "How long?" is the underlying spirit of what I have written here.

# Reading for the Library of Congress

Quite long ago I was invited by Robert Penn Warren in the name of the Library of Congress to come to Washington to read from my poems, for a recording of the reading.[1] A rather long time before then I had renounced poetry, after two decades of loving concentration on the practice of it. I declined the invitation, wanting any public presenting of my poems after my renouncing of poetry to be accompanied by a reference to that fact, suitable in its substance to the occasion. I had not yet succeeded in formulating to my sense of the fully adequate the view of poetry I had come to have that led to my renouncing of it. Not until early in the 'sixties did I feel able to provide the definitive account of my decision that I judged its seriousness to require of me.

The seriousness of my decision was not of a funerary order. It derived from my seriousness about poetry, and being a poet, which was related for me to the solution I understood poetry to offer to the problem of our using words in a way that effected distinct presentation of experiences of consciousness felt by us to exemplify essential qualities of the life-experiences of human beings as minds. I took and take this understanding of poetry— poetry seen as a long-sustained activity endowed with this function and conceived of as capable of fulfilling it—to correspond with the traditional place that poetry has had among the historically certified human importances.

By the time I entered into the continuity-course of poetry, its historic impressiveness, emblematic of the urgency felt by human beings to give eloquent report of all that is humanly experienceable, had begun to weaken. It wore the old cloak of

1. [See Friedmann, *A Mannered Grace*, 426.]

acknowledgement of human identity as an intimately active involvement of the human state in an embracing universal reality; but in the new century concern with poetry was shifting further and further towards a different conception of its function and importance. It was gradually acquiring the character of a place for free presentation of experiences of self-preoccupied consciousness felt to exemplify the life-nature of the individual life-experience of human beings as uniquely particular personal entities. The world or universe of traditional poetic thought gradually receded into a background of literarily metaphoric myth. The property of distinctness as the natural objective of fully expressive report of human experience as having a natural universal scope disappeared from the prescriptive expectation of what poetry might provide. The verbal character of poetry—poetic diction—changed, in intent, from that of precision of phrasing and linguistic excellence in the entire substance of poetic argument to effort for the mark of individuality of poetic style: eccentricity of expression became the substitute for originality in poetic diction, and instability in standards of the linguistically fitting, the way of life in the twentieth-century world of poetic activity.

The pattern of human experience as one of uniquely universal scope—not personally or biologically or otherwise an idiosyncratic, particularized experience—disappeared from the historically verified equipment of sensibility that had, until our times, marked the poet, and the poetic function. But its disappearance was for quite long invisible, lost to view in the sweeping disappearance of the property of distinctness in poetic word-use that converted twentieth-century poetry into a field of personalistic bravado, the words serving private functions assigned to poetry, not the general human ideals that had been embodied in the linguistic and moral constitution of poetry. It was just that property of distinctness in word-use, and just that pattern of human experience as the universal accessible to human sensibility, that I made the basis of my commitment to poetry as a form of realization, in human beings, of speaking presence of mind to the whole existence-compass of being.

The mood of twentieth-century engagement in poetry became a mood of daring—daring to use the occasions of poetic utterance, which had been understood in sustained commitment to a fixed conception of poetry as a kind of speaking reserved to urgencies of thought and feeling, utterance-needs above the level of private triviality, petty commonplaceness, for verbal improvisation for the sake of the satisfaction it might afford as intellectual adventure, emotional pastime. This daring became so elaborate and diverse, the private trivialities and petty commonplaces so weightily sustained, that the scales of measurement of the poetically urgent lost applicability: anything and everything was legitimate poetic subject-matter, and *nothing* was necessarily an essential or fundamental element or principle of engagement in poetic composition or comprehensive concern with poetry. The field of poetic writing expanded into one of democratic release to liberties of enlargement of the importance of private sensation, personally individualized problems of experience. It also contracted, concurrently, as a field of elevation of the concerns of human thought and feeling. That is, it became a variable of private spirituality; the poetic realm of the ideal was pluralized into whatever mirrored the individual poet's sense of individual higher need, the factor of spiritual elevatedness in the poetic temper no longer a common human mark of aspiration. Inwardly and outwardly, poetry became, in the twentieth century, a changeling—a new literary form that continued to be given the name "poetry" but that grew emptier and emptier, in the century's course, of the animating impulses of human aspiration of which poetry had been the lifted-up voice intended to redeem human utterance from its surrenders to the demands of the impatient, greedy minutes of practical time, practical speaking— "ordinary speech." The special voice of poetry was flattened into extinction by the construing of poets of themselves as, each, an autonomous poetic voice. In the critical language, the lexicon of critical terms, of the century, the criterion of authenticity applied to the work of a particular poet has come to be a poise of self-confidence in his individual conception of what poetry is, ought to be, or can be made to be—the attributability to him of a "voice," a poetic voice all his own.

I have used the masculine gender in referring to the poet of characteristically twentieth-century temperament—one who conforms to the new dogma of poetry, poetry as a speech-realm of personal demarcation where the poet makes bold to be the presiding "voice," inventor-in-charge of the particular kind of poetic objective matching the spiritual appetite of the particular poet-self—because I have found that the century change nullified the traditional, humanly universalized figure of the poet, of masculine identity by historic presumption. There ceased to be the ideal type of human sensibility that poetry stipulated as the ideal level of human experience. The figure of poet that issued on the stage of twentieth-century literary—and human—change was the individual male human being liberated from the moral and spiritual compunctions typifying the traditional poetic ideal of transcended sexually specialized identity. The model of twentieth-century poet-personality early stabilized itself as the male spokesman of the human state daring to probe the content of human individuality as the reality displacing the mystery of the human state itself, and that of the mystery of a universal reality presumed to envelop it.

The literary clamor of the new poetry of human individuality, represented in speaking-postures of new, self-emphasising, male-natured human identity, caught numbers of the contingent of women drawn to venture in the chances of success in the new poetry in a net of self-emphasizing female-natured human identity. This semblance of new opportunity provided them with no more than imprisonment in a delusion of literary, psychological, and social liberation from the cultural bounds of the old poetry. As poets, the women writers of the new poetry have achieved no more than imitations of the male-voiced exemplifiers of it in female-voiced exemplifications of the purportedly all-human realism of the new poetry. The male-female liberalistic ideology of the new poetry is a conspiracy of wilful confusion imposed on the production-site of twentieth-century poetry by all who place their poet-identity under the protection of this ideology. The male conspirator affects an all-human allegiance that is but boast of male-naturedness as identical with honesty. The female conspirator canvasses femaleness as a new, humanistically realistic ground in the new poetry—committing the absurdity of killing off the transcendence of female naturedness to a unitary all-human naturedness that has an instinctive, ever-potential immediacy in the personal constitution of women.

Present-day understanding of the idea of poetry—its history

and relation to the idea of the human being as fulfilling an ideal lovingly evoked in the human form of being—is heavily encumbered and obstructed by the ideological confusion of new sexualistic influences that have infiltrated themselves into the century's laboratories of literary theory and critical dogma. But the systems themselves of new prescriptions of what poetry "is," which severed its connections with historic human identity and connected it with a philosophy of self-created individuality, vaguely scientific, vaguely political, definitively nothing other than spiritually nihilistic (rising from Nietzschean death-of-poetry pyres to phoenix-new forms of poetic vitality), are the crux of the disaster of acquisition of manifold spurious identities that befell the ghostly remains of poetry. I feel a need of touching on the theses of critical argument that were widely circulated in the first half of the century to scare off assaults upon the poetic "new" by proving it the only possible living successor to an unresurrectible "old."

A ferment of preoccupation with a need felt to replace old forms and uses of human powers of mind and sensibility with new ones marked the consolidation of the new-numbered century-date into a time-structure rearing itself up as a world of change. The change manifested itself in a widespread sense of human ineffectuality, that was not allowed, however, to plumb itself with the depth-rods of despair, but was doctored with nostrums based on new, complexity-abbreviating conceptions of what constituted the human effectual. The old regimen of intellectually intricate philosophic speculation, and the old morally intricate religious regimen of emotional discipline, were supplanted by new philosophies of science, new sciences of philosophy: the pace of intellectual activity was quickened to curtail the dilatory extravagances with which the old rationality was now charged. Problems of the life of personal identity (of character) and the life of human identity (of association) were relieved of subjection to old patterns of distinction between good and evil, truth and falseness, and transferred to the care of new simplified rationalities of distinction, based on psycho-biological interpretations of human nature and human behavior. Previously important principles of thought were stripped from the processes of thought. Meaning-values previously of organic presence in the word-conscious elements of these processes were reduced to the fictional conveniences of a new kind of human mind, keyed to change, uncertainty, a universal environment no more than a coherence of incoherencies. Thus came it about that, everywhere in the thought-centers of human life where the air of the twentieth-century "new" touched down, old familiars of human consciousness either underwent redefinition or expulsion into the void that had been thought of as a universe—an all-containing vessel of meaning. Locales of the "new" in literature and art the world over became compulsively busy with the devising of theories that made the nothingness of the *table-rase* of the "new" the rationale, or magical irrationality, of effectual methods of literary or artistic functioning under twentieth-century conditions of change.

In twentieth-century poetic radicalism, Gallic and American theory was preoccupied with identifying the new in poetry as time-compelled change in its linguistic constitution. Gallic poetic radicalism tended to treat the words of poetry as entities different, by the nature of their use, from the words of general linguistic use. While the emphasis here was on the physical attributes of word-make-up, the theoretical concern was with a sensuous artistry of utterance. Germanic philosophic scientism and general European psychoanalytical moral scientism contributed to the breakdown, in all twentieth-century quarters, of the old conception of poetry as integrating language, the speaking human being, the all-attendant universe of being, in a coherence of healing non-partiteness. But the Gallic version of the poetic "new" was a unique theatricality. The American version of the poetic "new" was also marked by emphasis on the physicalities of utterance—and by random influence-intrusions into poetic theory from both European and American versions of the twentieth-century scientistic intellectual "new." Indeed, the American redefinition of poetry and the Gallic, in the importance they gave to the physical effects and potencies injectable into it, had a bridge of critical sympathy between them in the theatricality that Edgar Allen Poe popularized as indispensable rhetorical strategy in poetic composition.

But what emerged as the dominant tendency in the "new," in American twentieth-century poetic theory and practice, was neither to outright revolutionary overthrow of traditional principles of poetic intellectuality nor to resort to devices of theatric novelty as escape-route from the underlying promptings to revolutionary stands. The American poetic "new" early resolved itself into dedication to a politics of personalism: literarily, linguistically, intellectually, psychologically, poetry emerged as the scene of exploration of the possibilities of success of the individual human being with himself, himself in an absolute (indistinguishably physical and spiritual) detachment from the public worlds of nature and human sociality. That is, American rescue-work was performed upon the remains of poetry in twentieth-century literary life. That gave it a semblance of vigorous survival in exercises in privacies of verbally daring self-experiment. The poet of the American new way of poet-being did not wage war against old ways of conceiving of the privileges and limits of the personality of the poet in his fulfilling of the poet-rôle; he acted under the authority of a declaration of new poet-independence, and of the constitution of a new united state of poetic freedom: poetry was now the realm of the illimitable open spaces of the universes of private personality. The gender-reference I use here is apposite. Poet self-identification became, automatically, personally individualized, in the new customs of poetic behavior and, automatically, also, concretely male for general practical inference. The female counterpart to this development, though comprising novelties of experiment in poetic behavior, was a shadowy image of it, of no substance itself as something new in poetic theory and practice. The force of new programmatic purposefulness was confined to, concentrated in, the male-gendered focal points of poetry-propaganda.

The names of Pound, Eliot, and Williams resound in the corridors of twentieth-century poetry-centered literary criticism as hauntingly echoic of a profoundly influential view of past poetic theory, principle, practice. Other poet-names of American national identity are associatively intoned in this music of attribution to the new century as an instant-antiquity-ground that brought forth a new poetry, in full bloom at birth with the maturities of a tradition all its infant own. Poet-names of French national identity figure with solemn ring in the myth of poetry's having been redeemed from an extinct history by the acquisition of a new twentieth-century historicity; and honors of hymnal mention are visited upon poets of other identity-location as pioneers in the rewriting of the history of poetry, the fashioning of a new *Genesis* for poetry to rid minds of the new times of superstitious notions about poetry inflicted on them by the *Genesis* of the old literary regime.

Understanding of the relation of my poetic work, and of myself as poet and mind actively concerned with the historic fact of poetry, to the peculiarities of twentieth-century literary experimental play with the fact—reflecting and reflected in the experimental play with the fact of the human state of being that became the century's obsessive, general, all-round interest—requires some specific evocation of the century scene that was its temporal, but not its historical, background. The fact of my being a poet and the spirit of my devotion to the fact of poetry did not have their generation in the spirit of revolutionary experimentalism that pledged itself to the re-invention of poetry and of the human being himself (herself, according as the new prognosis of the individual as universe might prove or not prove adaptable to the still old, old differences between *him* and *her*). I did not choose the work of poet to change the nature of poetry or the nature of myself as a being possessed of that distributive intelligence that calls itself "human." Misascriptions peculiar to critical and personal commentary on my poetic work and my character as a poet derive, all, from a reading of twentieth-century literary history in which the identity of poetry and that of the poet have been altered beyond any containment within the norms of aspiration, the bricks of human and linguistic potentiality with which the edifice, poetry, was built. There is no edifice, now; the poet is no longer, by a ritualistic commitment mixedly literary and spiritual, member of a special community of the faithful ministering to the promise sheltered by the edifice for the sustenance of human hope through the weather-changes of time on time.

I have singled out three American poets as main proponents and example-setters of what should be done to and with poetry to accommodate it to new twentieth-century ideas about poetry, human life, *everything*. One of these, Eliot, found a need of bracing his self-confidence as a poet of the new order of culturally political intellectual daring with credentials of climatically British literary professionalism. Pound, whose revolutionary daring had nothing in it of an inner melancholy diffidence towards the dignities and glories of the superseded poetic old, tore into the resources of the general history of poetry as into a museum of artistries become the property of poets of the new order—trophies of their victory over the old order, freely theirs for the uses of their originality. Williams, as a theoretician of twentieth-century revolutionary doctrine and practice, clung to home ground. He defined his principles of stylistic, linguistic, thematic innovation in terms of "structure." But this is not a principle of radical architectonic scrupulosity in poetic composition: Williams's "structure" is a counter-discipline to the proprieties of diction and of content that were implicit in the critically literate traditional conception of what was *good* poetry, poetry written in the English language. Williams meant a poetry of plain speech and subject-matter, a defiantly American poetry. The identification of the plain and the American as to what was to be rated as *good* poetry in the new twentieth-century literary and worldly times was no more intended to be a prescriptive narrowing of the range of interests and breadth of cultural potency of the poet of the new order than was the fancy literary cosmopolitanism of the Pound-Eliot programmes of poetic change intended to convert the poet-status into merely that of membership in a new exclusive intellectual aristocracy.

The change in the driving reasons of poets for concern with poetry, in the twentieth century, had its start in the general trend in modern ideas towards substitution of individuality of being as the unit of human identity for the universal measure of the human presence in existence that has served as a truth-mark on all the idea-systems presented for human acceptance. The American contribution to the accommodation of poetry to the system of ideas that made the particular personal "I"—being seen as an isolatedly existent power of self—the central reality in the problems of consciousness and knowledge was in all its numerous component poet, poet-critic, parts unreservedly on the side of an all-round success for poetry, for *poets*, in the intellectually and philosophically revolutionized politics of human thought, purposes, affairs, with which the twentieth-century human world busied itself. There was less of the specialistic—culturally, literarily, critically—in American experimentation in a new identity for poetry than in any other quarter of twentieth-century poetic change-making. The Americans dared to experiment where others have experimented in daring, with the result that, in other quarters of twentieth-century rewriting of the story of poetry, the emotional basis of courage for the risks of poet-being under the new conditions of evaluation was much more compromised by self-protective native mannerisms advertising the element of daring in the new poet-behavior to be autochthonously spontaneous.

Thus, vanity of national, linguistically, historically, and culturally distinct, identity has come to mark the literary posture and personal tone of English poets of twentieth-century change in ideas about poetry and poet-being. The moral support of self-assurance that is an important element of English strength of character—admixed, along the British literary course-of-things, with twentieth-century bravadoes of male-tongued and male-brained liberties-taking with the solemnities of human fact—has become the literarily officialized virtue of British-bred poetic innovation. The vanity-element in other national poetries of the twentieth century is more quixotic. These are not so tightly consolidated into monuments to themselves as is the case with British poetry of the era of experiment. The vanity-element in the American poetry of this era is more fragmentary, lightweight. The initial spirit of daring, here, was free of fear. No shadow of risk of loss hung over the vision of possible success. There seemed to be nothing to lose: the only possible *something* was the chance of gain. At the least, the American version of twentieth-century consciousness of a crisis in the historic human sense of an imperishable value of truth, affecting the importance-status of poetry, and of human existence itself, was a consciousness of an emergency calling for some immediate practical action.

A busyness of individualistic diversity of experimentation in how to be a poet under the new order of ideas about poetry kept the American poetry scene lively-looking, loose-strung— vaguely a scene of hope. My own behavior as a poet in the environment of early twentieth-century questioning of the importances had no element in it of forced response to sudden apprehension of a state of human circumstances of unignorable seriousness. I came to have the kind of behavior as a poet that my poems from early to late in my life as a poet manifest from an internal sense of my relation to the fact of human existence and the fact of the existence of language and poetry within an all-encompassing existence-fact. My initial acquaintance with these facts was not filtered through impressions imposed on my mind's young knowledge-appetencies by the new experimental thinking and writing of early twentieth-century times. That my encounter with these facts was personally direct, not generated by special emotional or mental influences, was owed in part to my being by nature stimulated in thought more by inwardly arising impulses than forces of external suggestion. My ways of mind and feeling were also affected by the limits of intellectual concern in a household in which socialistic ideas were the exemplary stuff, the moral standards of the serious. As they were rather old-fashioned ideas idealistically associated with "good" literature and philosophic thought of respected scholarly status, they tended to be, on the whole, in my young life, patrons of freedom of values-determination and protectors from erratic revolutionary intellectualist propaganda, literary, philosophical, or other, [rather] than the reverse. And so my commitment to poetry was open-mindedly general, free from any bias of sectarian revolutionary poetry-politics. It had no iron pinnings in the English poetic traditions; and no flair of journalistic or sentimental new-world or new-era Americanism distinguished it, or literary-period fashionableness. It did have—had for the entire length of my poet-being—a sustained ring of practical intent: but of concern with poetry and engagement in it as an activity of purposeful language-employment, aimed at successes of new broad human significance, not of new verbal dramatizing of human nature as a phenomenon of self-possessed, self-determining, self-referent, individual being.

The spirit of my commitment to poetry, as the energies of purposefulness developed in it, was revivalist, not revolutionary. The growing intensity of my devotion to it as a sphere of activity was related to my sense of a deficiency, in the human beings of the world of immediate life of consciousness, of primary elements of the experience of being humanly alive. It was not related to a literary-critical sense of a deficiency in the utility of poetry, question of its pertinence to the problem of self-respect, self-valuing, seen as faced by the individual human being after an ultimate dissolution of various unities devised by rational ingenuity in past time as antidote to confusion and uncertainty in human self-understanding. I was innocent of special purposes in choosing poetry as a work-path, and I never lost that innocence. But I never, so long as I labored as a poet, broke with the general purpose to which I had understood my commitment to poetry to commit me. This was, the general human purpose I saw infused in the existence of poetry with more practical earnestness and sincerity than in any of the other forms of human spiritual exertion. My purpose was to uncover more than had been revealed—crucial parts of what had not yet been revealed—by poetry of that purpose.

Poetry has carried forward earliest human consciousness of the impulsion in human consciousness towards expansion of consciousness. The elementary love of knowledge of the human mind early made a home for itself in poetry, with vision of attainment to a human wholeness of being a partnering occupant of the space of language's inner properties of truth that poetry took into proprietary charge. The taint of pride in poetry's creed of virtue was the least corruptive of virtue, among the creeds of virtue by which men published laws of life matching the versions of virtue they chose as honor-earning ones to live by. Poetry has had, in its domestic identification of itself with the truth-processes internally concentrated in words, a moral counter-poise to the pride in spiritual aspiration that kept the heights of philosophic and religious visions of success of the human lost in speculative mist or tumbling, ever, into faith's ready hands for instant re-elevation. Poetry has had the advantage, over all other forms of spiritually serious human self-commitment, of uniting the spontaneous appreciation of the human mind of the breadth of experience within reach of human consciousness of the actuality, being, with the practical capacity of the human mind, vested in the harmony of its functional processes with those of its natural instrument, language. This advantage may be termed, the appeal, the authenticity-mark, of *sensibleness*—a superiority of simplicity where other areas of virtue have armed themselves with powers of complexity of explanation and self-justification, simplicity-over-whelming rhetorics of persuasion.

So it happens that poetry has had, and has rightly had, the strength of a creed—of virtue, or honor of mind—surpassing others as coming closest to the instinctive in human purposeful-ness, and especially so as to the inner human sense of what words are "for"—their simple truth-potentiality, within the external di-versity of complex rhetorics of argument, and of the confusions of special private-purpose word-use of so-called "plain" or "ordi-nary" speech. I believe in its having had in it this strength, and the merit of a sensible spirituality. The historical record shows it to have been more actively stimulative of the instinctive human love of knowledge and truth, and the good, than other moral and spiritual influences having assigned seats in human society. It has also happened that poetry came to be assigned a literary seat in Society's academy of importances; and in consequence of this poetry has suffered of a progressive dividedness between its spiritual nature and its nature as a feature of the varying cultural dispensations that human societies have visited upon themselves on their way to seemingly endless change. I believe that by the time I chose poetry as a guiding point of spiritual orientation, its essential nature and identity as a creed of redemptive potency had become submerged in the ideas of imperative revolutionary change—of an all-new "new"—that flooded into the twentieth century in chaotic overflow from nineteenth-century repressed restiveness. Faint intuition of poetry's unique spiritual and lin-guistic credentials has survived only in rituals of critical rhetoric touched with the jargon of the philosophical, psychological, an-thropological, new. The character of my identification of my pur-pose as a devotee of poetry with a purpose inherent in poetry's nature was, from my beginnings as a poet, and remained, alto-gether disparate from the conception generally governing the sense of their relationship to poetry of the practising poets of the century.

My concern with poetry was not attended by a literarily spe-cialistic concern about poetry's course and fate in the immedi-ate world of competing cultural officialities. My concern with poetry was in terms of direct concern with the special course and fate of human life to which poetry had maintained a historied standing as its most intimate spiritual mentor. The effect of my operating as a poet with this, by literary convention, unliterary concern has been that, while I made a strong impression as a poet-figure in twentieth-century literary-world contexts of literary performance, my poetic work has been dealt with, in these contexts, both before and continually after my renunciation of poetry, as extraneous to the main interest of those concerned with poetry, whether as poets or professional students of poetry, or in private amateur intellectual attachment to it.

Robert Fitzgerald, reviewing the 1938 collection of my poems, described them as outstanding from all others, in the self-consciously modern literary period, for purity of poetic character, and as the most "advanced" and "personal"—by implication, as attaining to a new degree of humanly successful utterance in the poetic use of words.[2] Yet it is the very outstandingness of my poetic work as poetic utterance of a remarkable directness and perfectly natural distinctness that has caused it to become increasingly, in the century's advance, an outlaw from the regular ritualistic mentions, references, topics of study, indispensable choices for anthological treatment. I did not attempt to inject something poetically new into the idea and compositional procedures of poetry. I rejuvenated something poetically old: a serene offering of itself of the human consciousness as having extension of personal presence and speaking witness to the entirety of the existent, a taking of all into loving knowledge-care. No one before me, man or woman, had done what I did in my respect-paying to it as a way of utterance by which step-by-step rightness of word might open human vision to a full prospect of successful human-being—had shown how, in the scrutinies of poetic word-workmanship, the principles of fulfilment of the human destiny of truth-uncovering innocently revealed themselves (without breaking of locks, plundering of language for gems of poetic diction). What I did excited interest here and there, but it produced, always, more discomfort than comfort.

Long before I renounced poetry, poetry had been remodelled into a field of literary composition in which all sorts of fea-

---

2. [See note 1 on "Prologue: Description of Planned Work."]

tures of poetic style were employed without grounding in any general prompting of purpose identifiable as *poetic,* by the internal sense of "poetry" as concerned with the unities of human nature as a unity of truth—the virtue of speakable being. Against my poetic writing there was, from its beginnings as a twentieth-century representation of the historically verified human actuality, poetry, an ever-enlarging display of the uses to which the external mannerisms of poetic writing-style could be put for the uses of platform exhibitions of virtuosity in dignifying the incoherencies of the modern vision of human life, nature, purpose, as a self-universalising principle of individuality with formal or formally informal vestures of poetic coherence.

I have been asked by someone who, though professionally involved in the contemporary cultivation of poetry, as an authorship-activity offering unlimited opportunities of personal literary success (a poem, a test of will and the right of the individual mind to be heard, and by more than itself), feels drawn in conscience to weigh my view of what has been happening in twentieth-century concern with poetry against the evidence of her experience: Is the preoccupation of poets, now, with "performance," and the special development of what has come to be called "performance poetry," explicable in the terms of my judgement of the status of poetry in twentieth-century literary affairs? Yes!—I judge that there has passed from presence in twentieth-century concern with poetry the core of problems of central moral and spiritual concern round which the armature of protective linguistic technology was built that differentiated poetic statement as intended to hold good beyond the limits of particular speaking occasions. The sense of poetic statement was supposed to transcend its own particularity, to marry the precise and the universal. When universality disappeared as the presiding theme of human spiritual preoccupation, and, in poetry and other creeds of virtue, individuality replaced it as the general logical principle of human reference, the language cares of poetic nicety became superficial solemnities redeeming enfeebled inner human solemnity from *its* superficiality. Yes!—I judge the character of twentieth-century poetic composition to have become increasingly, and to be now hardly not other than exclusively, that of personal performance, individual self-description (or self-defining, as the procedure has been called with congratulatory implication) using the hand-me-downs of poetry's commitment to the theme of universality as its platform. Yes!—I judge poetry to have lost its identity in exercises in unidentified spiritual vulgarity.

I ought to point out that there was some riddance effected in my poetic work of a feature of poetry so deeply ingrained in it as to have gone altogether unnoted and, presumably, unnoticed. I refer to the intonations of man-pride that insistently abound in the dogged resolution with which the patterns of poetic movement are maintained from one line's end-abruptness to another as if part of the natural course of things poetic. But a general aura of masculinity has hung over poetry throughout its career as one of the major forms of spiritual testimony and practice. The ideal conception of the human being that is at the heart of poetry has pervasive reverberation in it of an association of humanness with men as emblematic representations of it. Works of poetry until very recent time were almost solidly the work of men. The reason of virtue that poetry has left as an echo-impress of its nature on the history of human achievement has, undoubtedly, an initial strong connection with the appeal to men-minds of the prompt, near-at-hand solace of relief to burdens of consciousness that poetic modes of utterance provide. The moral instincts speak themselves first in men-minds in the form of a sense of guilt. Poetry, thus, as a creed of virtue, has answered, for men, to primitive aspects of their moral and spiritual needs, as well as serving them in the maturing of their sense of themselves as human beings. Women's nature as moral beings is not in laddered pieces. Women are more immediately timed than men, in their nature as women, to their human nature: there is more immediacy of the human in the responses of women to the calls of life in the life of human beings than in those of men. I touch here on such matters of broad human pertinence only to bring into view the necessary manifestations of them in the course of poetry's taking form and maintaining continuity of identity as an institution dear to the most urgent human affections. Features marking the persistence in poetic customs of composition of procedures following dictates of a male version of human sensitivity have had long presence in poetry with acceptance as the poetically natural; for the aura of masculinity that enwrapped the age-on-age offerings of poets won by its own treating of itself as an atmosphere of virtue the name and credit for them of the humanly natural.

My comments on the history, in the history of poetry, of a dominance of the problem to men that their humanity peculiarly makes for them belong to no venture in men's-studies activity to fill out blanks in women's-studies maps of special fields of human history. I have never been troubled by the fact that poetry owed its coming into historical existence and perpetuation to the assiduous development of it by men, largely and especially as a plane of practical spirituality—a plane on which to elevate the language-functions to powers of human expressiveness above the level of the physically convenient or temporally expedient of what is called "ordinary" speech. The pull of the externals of aliveness on man-nature is relentlessly commanding; and the internals of human nature, in men, can take on a force of counter-pull giving the internals an odd, quasi-natural character of external potency. Every creed of virtue, institution of spiritually motivated human practice—poetry, religious or philosophical commitments, the commitments of the loose aggregate of loosely spiritual commitments that generalise themselves as literature and the arts—has had this problem of the pull of the external, to which man-nature is peculiarly subject, intertwined with the special form of spiritual concern the creed made its individual own. Or, the matter of the problem of a difficulty peculiar to the male human being of reconciling his outward-directed male-naturedness and his inward-directed human-naturedness is inevitably, inextricably, present in every form of endeavor to solve the problem of the relationship of human beings, as possessed of consciousness of universal breadth, to the fact, the reality-substance, of the universe of experiences. A self-detaching propensity has a primitive force of suppression-resistant recurrence in male-natured human beings. It has been as if every creed of virtue—of a principle of universality as the inherent nature of human nature—has had to keep reconstituting itself against an eternal primitiveness in the male nature of human beings, an instinctive clinging to the disjunctive powers of physical individuality, as against threat of annihilation in a contract of spiritual peace with human identity as putting the wars of individuality of being behind the truly lived human state.

In my contenting myself with poetry as a field and creed of work—for long making it the center of my general writer's concern with the work of ordering thought into the truth-forms into which it could be cast by humanly honest and linguistically honorable use of words—I did not evaluate poetry as any other than, more than, a field of work, and a creed, of best promise for the possibility of finding the way to true living of the human state. I read no fixed culmination of the linguistically and humanly possible in the past records of poetic achievement. There is evidence in my poems, as there is in all other writing of mine, both before and after my renouncing of poetry as "the way," of my having an open-eyed awareness of all the frailties in the attitudes to one another of human beings, and failures in their arrangements for associating with one another as such—and a wide-ranging perception of the still unresolved difficulty of comprehension that the differences between man-nature and woman-nature present to human beings in their still-confused sense of themselves as divided in identity within the fold of human identity. I have long seen the separatist identity-sense to which male human beings are instinctively inclined as the mainspring and model of preoccupation with individuality as essence of human identity—as, that is, the seat of delusion and self-delusion as to the nature of human nature (and latter-day philosophic dismissal of the idea that there is any "essence" quality in "being" human). I have long seen an intrinsic property of humanness in the way in which female human beings treat their human identity—which is as something in natural personal hold. But neither within nor outside the fold of poetry or poet-being have I diverted my concerns into channels of linguistic or literarian assault on maleness-trends in features or modes of literary composition. I have indicated here in a single reference to a settled feature in poems-composition that I believe that I introduced into it trial of a tempering of line-ending necessities to necessities of continuity-grace such as operate automatically in prose writing, without producing poetic prose effects or making musicality a solution of problems of poetic form. I believe that I effected generally in my writing of poems changes in poetic language-climate from an overhanging aura of masculinity that I have identified as pervasively attendant on it to a spacious air of the all-human issuing from the all-immediate fact of language. But I offer these suggestions as to differences from the "old" to be found in my poetic work as possibly helpful to an understanding of the very different differences existing between my poetic work as having some sort of "new" in it and the various examples and types of the poetic "new" recognized in the official critical catalogues as of pure twentieth-century pedigree.

In my poetic work, in all my writing, in my thinking, findings, definitive courses of disposition in feeling and thought within and outside of the limits and reaches of writing, there has proved to be that which prompts responses of the extremeness of love or hate. There has been little response to what I present authorially or in personal address that is not at least love-like or hate-like in its trend. In between the extremes and response-manifestations bordering on them, there has been little-to-nothing. Avoidance of commitment to response is not attributable, in the particular case of my poetic work, either to its being dismissible as of poetic old-hat character or as not meeting, in its new-hat features, the requirements of the twentieth-century poetic consciousness. What articulated dismissal of it there has been has not amounted to more than complaints of it as calling for efforts of understanding discouraged by initial suspicion that they would be unrewarded. Interest in poetry, in the twentieth-century poems-readership, became centered, increasingly, in verbal experiment conducted increasingly for the enrichment of the expressiveness of poetic diction in the possibilities of linguistic *play* (this according with a taste for linguistic play stimulated in the general literary readership of the century by the verbalistic revelry of Joyce, and others). There is much in my poems to interest readers disposed to pleasure-taking in enrichment of the expressiveness of poetic diction. But what I accomplished in my poems, in the fortifying and expansion of the expressive powers of poetic diction, was feat of linguistic *work*, not linguistic *play*.

*Play* has been the twentieth-century cure-all for all the human uneasiness mounted-up within the century's fences against life as an eternity; word-play in literature, as play with the visual media in art, acquired in this century an authority replacing that of the linguistically serious, so that to be taken seriously by any literary readership, a work must reveal itself as a product of hard linguistic play-work. My poems have overtried the forbearance of a large number of those who classify themselves as lovers of poetry by the consistent dependence in them on word-work—where literary reading has become so much lighter work through the time's lifting of the curse of linguistic seriousness from serious literature.

Finally, to characterise the love-hate proclivities of response to my authorial presence in the century and to the personal reality of this presence in terms of my matured sense of their significance after long and varied experience of them—lasting, even with multiplication, into these later days of mine. From the earliest in responses to my poetic work there have been certain ones of a kind, that, though rather mutely unparticular and yet rather vaguely general, belong on the (very) favorable side of critical judgement. I find myself able, from wealth of familiarity with such responses, to reduce the element of the laudatory extreme in this to a plain essence, natural and reasonable in sound: *"There is something right about this."* Yet there is something inflammatory in effect in what strikes others as having something right about, or in, it. It excites compulsion to love, an emotion of dutiful love, but it can also excite resentment in which hate smoulders. Extremes of the condemnatory in responses to my poetic work (as to the entire authorial and personal quantity bearing my name) have a ring of outraged objection to what is suspected of possibly having something right about, or in, it, as to direct exposure to an unanticipated indignity of forced acceptance of something as having something right about, or in, it. Indeed in the love-responses to my poetic work (and the entirety bearing my name) I have found a potentiality of flare of impatience with, haste of inattention towards, the loved something right. An intellectual policy of suspicion of the human intelligence as having something generically wrong about, or in, it has prospered in our times; the more persuasive the impression made by works or acts of human intelligence of having something right about, or in, them, the more subject they are to a dictate, as of human intelligence, to look for something wrong about, or in, them. A general confusion now prevails in human minds as to comfort in the human state that makes accommodation to it as having itself something wrong about it the key to an intelligent piety, faith in a something right about, and in, this something wrong as the given of existence. The stamp of a something-right on my work has engulfed it and myself in this confusion, which has kept repeatedly obscuring—or annihilating—its and my messages of comfort in the midst of it.

There could be much said on the perverse advantage to themselves that certain poets have derived from the injection into their work of echo-effects of my something-right, and on the perverse irresponsibility of critics in their excluding me from, or sometimes, including me in, their strategy-systems for positions of influence in literary-world fields of power. But I have wanted, here, to dwell on central things. In my reading from my *Collected Poems* I shall choose from the later ones, as having more concentratedly present in them the concern central to the whole.

# [From] Twentieth-Century Change
## in the Idea of Poetry, And of the
## Poet, And of the Human Being

Poetry has explored an involuntary conviction of the human mind that there is concentratedly secreted in human beings the meaning-will of the comprehensive reality of being—that what it is "like" is individualized into revelatory expression of its identity in them, as if *it* had direct presence in the speaking presence of human beings to one another. That is, poetry aimed at improving on the religious definition of the human being by attributing to human identity a quality of personhood of universal nativity and force of presence: to exist humanly was to live in individual person the whole reality of being as one's truth—and for one's life to be its truth in interlocking corroboration. But poetry made its story of the human person an after-story to the life of human beings lived in the broken reality-pieces of historical time: the immediacy of poetic time has the evanescence of the vision of reality that completes the incompletely defined with the imaginary. Truth, in the setting of poetry's telling of the human story, is, thus, only partially a necessity. The immediacy of its narrative content falls short even of the prophetic.

After I came to that breaking-point in the poet-course of testing the possible in language, the shape of the immediately[1] full possible—of language filled out to its full capacity of truth-yield—flickered through the fading, darkening shapes of the newly numerous languages of lesser yield, in the century's swollen

---

1. [The published text has "immediacy," but "immediately" is the reading in the Berg manuscript.]

verbalescence. I offer a picture I composed of the taking-shape of the filled-out language-possibility, in contemporary crises of the sense of human identity and of poet-identity, and in the struggle of human intelligence between the calls of practicality and ideality. The scene changes, in the picture, to one of revelation: a strict eloquence of unity of the human and the universal replaces the mingled language-modes of human speaking out of human incompletion.

## The One Language. Self-Revealed

The number of tongues is as the number of the reasons of speech. The tongues of justice, truth, and love, are, have been, self-perpetuating languages. But hate, wrong witness, denial of the due, have engendered ever-dying dialects.

Then a tongue began urging itself, at last, as a new word-way. In it, the reasons of speech become one. Giving myself into its waiting simplicities with a waiting readiness, helping it to help me speak my mind in the language of its temporally undivided senses, I have learned to hear with a same recognition a rejoicing, in my being, as a private resounding, and as a ring of time overcome, in being's vast patience.

Then began, begins, the translation of all that we call ourselves into its essential grave fittingness or sad unfittingness: there is only the speakable, or the unspeakable. We cross over from the several halting reasons of speech into the realm of revelation—of the impatient necessities of the language we are. All else would be horror: is horror, by the light of the single dignity of the sweet single reason of speech—that being be well spoken.

# II
# Poetry Log

# Random Choices

## As To Certain Conditions Governing Poem-Making

There is much in the way in which people are poets that is as engaging with a mirror rather than with a someone who may read the poem. Why is this possible with poems, poetic writing, peculiarly? Because the extent to which one can engage with *the words* in a poem is limited. The poem-engagement restricts the actual *quantity* of words devoted to a *period* of thought; it restricts the *time* of the period, the timing allowances of the succession of periods. The period of thought does not set the pattern of the period of utterance: the pattern of the period of utterance, which is the quantity-timing relationship, is predetermined in a *general* rhythmic pattern that the poet must have preliminarily incorporated in the idea-of-the-poem, from which the poem is to be externalized, publicly actualized.

How the poem issues under set conditions of thought-presentation, and what is to be said, must be generally pre-adapted to them. Then, in the formation, it is continually fashioned and refashioned to fit the developing evidence of possibilities of utterance within the quantity-timing pattern-development: herein can be perceived the imposed engagement of the poet with "a mirror" rather than with the words as bringing poet and auditor into co-presence.

I shall not proceed to speak here on the development of the

poem-form of utterance, which combines freedom of utterance with limitations of a strictness, even severity, that imprison it as it were in itself, and is thus an example to people of both the good and the impossible. That would be lengthy in commentary on the influence of social delineation of the forms of good. But, perhaps I have said enough to prompt imagining of how preoccupation with the public effect of the poem, its appeal to the chosen, envisaged, literary audience, haunts the poem-making occasion, and has been and is greatly present in poetic literature as the genius in the mirror that is at once the poet's critic and admirer, in the intimacies of authorial reflection. This social motivation, to which the poet is subject by the force of many historical influences operating within the conventional literary frame of authorial responsibleness, is capable of dominating every other.

# On Thought, In A Poem

Speaking with a friend, I had said, in reply to a question put to me on my later view of poetry, that the conditions of poetry (the artistic requirements of sound-appeal, rhythmic pattern, and rhetorical imposingness) made it impossible for the thought underlying any poetic passage to be brought to fully right expression in the passage: the poetic form forced deviations from the natural thought-line. My friend asked whether it could be perceived (if my thesis was true) where, in a poetic passage, the expression began to go wrong, from the point of view of the underlying thought, the original thought-impulse. I said that I guessed this to be impossible, because the process of deviation began the moment the poem began to be written, so that the character of the original thought-impulse was no longer exactly perceptible—the poet himself might not, probably would not, be able to recall exactly what it was after its transformation, in the poem. The consciousness of deviation would be diffused, for the poet, in the pleasure of having succeeded in carrying some of his thought-impulse through the formalities of poetic presentation to distinct expression. Later, reflecting on the point my friend had raised, and looking at poems and poetic passages with this matter in mind, I formed the conception of what happens that I present here below, and I communicated it to my friend, in a letter.

"Examining closely the occasion of the poet's beginning to compose the poem, on the basis of my own experience and of what poetic texts reveal as they proceed away from their beginning, I have concluded that, in the very first of the action of beginning the composition, some of the underlying thought is put aside, to facilitate a dramatically effective beginning. Once an element of the original impulse is loosed from the rest, taking on a certain special force, it is never quite possible to put the whole together. Then, the stylistic requirements of the poem, generally, necessitate important thought-omissions, a jumping to this, a curtailing of that, and a continual adapting of thought-material to the exigencies of poetic modes of expression. The extent of the difference between the given background thought-material and the express poetic result varies from poet to poet and poem to poem, but there is always evidence of some degree of such difference, in intellectual inadequacies that do not at first sight show (the purely poetic features of the poem or passage conceal them). The presence of such inadequacies is so general in poetry that they cannot be attributed to individual failures of poets to present their thought in faithfully developed form: the evidence is that poets work, whatever their personal limitations as poets, under impediments inherent in poetry that none can overcome, whatever their personal talents as poets."

# Not Mere Vulgarity

Reading a prose paean of John Ciardi's some years ago in which "What The True Poet Offers" was enumeratively set forth, I felt in the presence of someone outlining almost all that has been wrong with poets, and, because of them, what has been wrong with poetry, apart from what may be found intrinsically wanting in poetry, by its nature.

He said: "the gift of the true poet is always the gift of life." What is the not-true poet? Is it one worth the distinction? Suppose one says, just, "The gift of the poet . . ."? The gift of the poet is the poem. The idea of a poet that he "gives" life is vanity in the sense of a superiority in the possession of access to that to which others do not have access. "He traps us in joy" through language which "haunts us from nature releasing our truest ghosts to us, because imagery opens a theatre in the mind's eye and transports us to the experience of being alive with our senses spinning. . . ." And rhythm carries us along with it in mysterious suggestions of sense "whose power is infallible upon the willing reader. . . ." This is a description of the poet who seduces his poem's hearers, readers, with the lie that he is a magician of language, and can make them, with his words, feel wonders of life they could not themselves, with *their* poor words, raise up for their imagination's delight. There is a good deal more, but I prefer to quote as little as possible, not only to avoid copyright infringement. It is the stuff of the vice of poetry that is put to the uses of self-elevation above the generality, made a means of attaining distinctions of experience to which *it* can attain only as audience at the theatre of the poet's own, enacted for its emotional witness.

"The good poet cannot fail to shame us, for he proves to us instantly that we have never learned to touch, smell, taste, hear and see." There is more. " . . . he stirs us to an energy of being that we could not have known by ourselves." "We" are helpless to "shape experiences—and therefore live them—" as he does with his superior capabilities, except as he "quickens and extends us to his higher power."

Although this might be viewed as excusable by the evident unconsciousness of the absurdity of its conception of the glorifying-shaming distance between the poet and the commoner, the principle of the boast is the foundation upon which rest many edifices of poetic construction. Elaborate, respected, literary monuments stand upon this foundation that are the work of play-actors in rôles of superiorities, powers of the beyond, which the audiences of poems can know only as a stage made real as life. That is: the hypocrite, the pretender, the expert in false art, can hide the vice-capacity in poetry. What of those who are shamed, who humbly accept "the gift of life," seeing the shape of their experiences upon the poetic stage? These are the least affected by the vice. The most are the poets, and the poetry-connoisseurs, who have forgotten the armor, once donned by custom, for resisting the temptation poetry presses upon vanity to make a vice of it.

# The Road To, In,
# And Away From, Poetry

The sense of freedom excited by poetry opened up vistas of what there is to be communicated with words that goes unsaid, uncommunicated, amongst ourselves. I poured into my poetic work a great fervor of hope, which became a faith, of the possibility of realizing in poetry that perfection in speaking which is *truth:* I believed that in poetry could be uncovered the standards of purity of meaning and fullness of communication that are inherent in language but are garbled in the ever less-than-clear and less-than-wholly-expressive words of customary usage (good and bad, alike). In my writing generally, but in my poems especially, I tried to use words as words belonging to a real language, a vital, organic unity of words—and to train my thoughts towards *them,* rather than towards the makeshift verbal entities of haphazard meaning that pass amongst us for words.

The conditions of poetry, in their difference from the conditions of ordinary word-use, seem to offer prospects of fulfilment of the triple ideal of goodness of word, goodness of speaking, goodness of being, that language nurses in us. But the artistic discipline of poetry, concerned with emotionally effective use of the physical properties of language, is in fact a grudging host to the discipline of truth, which must always take second place to it: the conditions of poetry are unalterably unfavorable to the use of words in it with *entire* truth. In ordinary word-use, meaning is the primary matter, however ill-managed it be; in poetry, the status of word-meaning is clouded over, though the illusion of perfect expression produced by sensuous effects conceals this. No poet who became clearly conscious of this could with sincerity continue to practise poetry. In my own case, the effort to make the artistic discipline of poetry and the discipline of truth coincide was so intense that it was destined to end in absolute discovery of the impossibility of its succeeding.

When I put away my implements of poetry, I felt for the first time the full difficulty of the linguistic task of truth. The difference between words as real words, words of a real language, and the imitation-words that crowd the mind I saw to be a far greater one than it had appeared to be under the auspices of my faith in poetry as capable of embodying the very spirit of language. Much of the impression of superior linguistic quality that poetically used words make comes of sheer stress on them as physical entities, that leaves their reality as distinct meaning-entities incompletely substantiated. Though the physical apprehension of words is incidental to the internal apprehension of them (in which their meanings give them their identity), it easily acquires more than due importance as seeming to compensate for weakness in the internal respect. (Thus, a special physical forcefulness of utterance often goes with illiterateness.) Where the general course of word-use is a slack effusion—as it tends everywhere to be or to become—poetic word-use, with its compelled insistence on the physical and sensuous potencies of words, allures the word-lover by a deceptive appearance of extraordinary vigor of expression. But the words of poetry are never so expressive in cool examination as they seem in the heat of poetic impact to be. There is no short-cut, poetic or otherwise (some believe that there are scientific short-cuts), to word-wisdom.

The pursuit of reality of word, which is nothing other than pursuit of the fullest possible knowledge of meanings, became a vastly more serious endeavor for me after I had abandoned poetry than it had before been. The urgency, the imagination, behind the endeavor had to be transplanted to the common speaking scene, in which there are no possibilities of partial, shadowy, merely emotional successes in capturing the meaning-essences of words: here, in the open of general linguistic experience, goodness of word and the ordinary standard are opposed extremes. Take away poetry—and the conflict between the truth-motive in the use of words and the host of others that so readily combine against it makes itself felt oppressively, nakedly. I knew that the alternative to the prevailing loose-tongued verbal habits lay in a linguistic scrupulosity more extensive and thorough than anything achievable by poetic devices; it would have to be radically different from poetry, be a radically better human linguistic best than it.

The language-problem was never for me a mere literary problem. I was neither a literary verbal rebel nor a literary stylistic purist. I had my eyes on a general human emergence into a state of complete linguistic responsibility, in which the life-quality of words and that of the use of them would be the same through adherence to meaning-values as truth-criteria. Poetry seemed to me to have secreted in it such a potential because of the freedom from certain conditions of word-use, obtaining elsewhere, it offers. But it imposes, itself, certain conditions which are obstructive of the use of words with entire truth: this I finally discovered—after long putting of extreme faith in it. Nevertheless, I kept my eyes throughout on the relationship of goodness of word, goodness of use, goodness of being; and it was while I was still active, and firm, in my faith in poetry that I conceived of a reintroduction of people to their words in more orderly and decisive definitions of them, emanating from a (new) view of them in their total integrity, and individual sanity, as language.

My faith in poetry was at heart a faith in language as the elementary wisdom, with every word charged with the principle of good-judgement animating languages—and in the English language, in particular, as a language of uniquely large reference-scope and uniquely robust verbal constitution. My loss of faith in poetry was but the shedding of the superstitions that had endowed the physical properties of words with illusory capabilities and functions of expanding their ordinary expressive power. It not being possible (as I discovered) to bring the rule of meaning-fullness and the rule of poetic physical artifice perfectly to meet, I put my whole linguistic faith in the former; and I gained by that single rule a more just notion of the part of physicality in words. The physical properties of words are related to their existence as differentiated meaning-entities; these properties inhere in their manageability as such under the physical conditions of utterance. The physicality of a word is important, but only incidentally important, procedurally important. My consciousness of words as things entire, possessing by what they mean substance and identity, character and form, meaning what they mean intrinsically rather than symbolically, led me into poetry, and led me out of it. The words of poetry are not our natural words, that the spirit of speaking in us ever nostalgically seeks, in its straying: they are perforce more potent in sensuous influence than in expression.

But where are our natural words to be found? The words of common talk are shreds, slivers, dabs, blobs, sometimes no more than shadows, or vapors; they are scarcely language, rather the refuse of repeated haphazard word-using. The words of more formal or more stylized use, of contrived address, are in the main imitations of real words—"good" imitations, in the higher literary levels; in their best use of words, people rarely do more than use plausible versions of the dimly-known originals. However, our words—the *real* things—are at hand, at mind, all the while. Though we speak things less than they, they are the language we speak. They are to be found in a knowledge of their meanings that is a knowledge of the language.

It may seem that I put a mystical stress on the character words have as language, attach a mystical importance to language. I advance nothing regarding language that does not come within the bounds of its evident nature, and of our human own. If a language is, truly, known, so that in the speaking of it the person and the words are one, and is so known by all its speakers, then there is community of being between them in the possession of the language: the language, known, yields up to them the whole of their humanity. The knowledge of a language, which braces minds with the force of the unifying spirit that generates humanity, completes the otherwise fragmentary person. The importance of the language is that this spirit moves one through it—if one knows it. All the superfluities of mysticism vanish in using words that are transparent with one's knowledge of their meanings, and, functioning thus, reveal one's human fullness of being.

# Other Selections

## Entry in *Twentieth Century Authors* (1955)

Laura Jackson (as the author asks to be styled) writes: "The previous record [1942] I wrote just after I had ceased to live as a poet, when I was just beginning to live again on the common plane, after twenty years of absence from it. I became a poet because I was filled with hope of human good, but could see no room for my hope except in the isolation of poetry. The life around me I found a disorder of personal patterns unrelieved by any common loyalty of hope. Especially was I unhappy in the language I heard spoken everywhere—sordidly chaotic to my ears; I felt my tongue tied, from a sense of the impossibility of speaking mere truth in the manner in which people habitually spoke. Poetry was for me a form of living, a state of being in which the redemption of human life from its deadly disorder by truth could be looked forward to. Although I had no company in that state, I sustained myself in it in the happy certainty that there was a destined fulfilment of common humanity in truth.

"I foretold in my poems the coming of a time of truth; the necessity and imminence of this was with increasing force their inspiration. In following that single vision, not distracted by literary or ideological preoccupations, I circumvented the inveterate unveraciousness of poetry as an art of creating simulacra of truth. My whole art was an anticipating of the intonations of truth; thus my word-style had a peculiar rectitude of accent. My words were still, however, the words of a careless tradition of speech, and their intractability as such drew me ever closer to the crux of the human problem: the question of the validity of words. The same while, I was gradually approaching the end of my ability to endure in a position of hope alone, with living truth a continuously suspended actuality. At last the time came for the proving. This was the road by which I travelled to the making of a dictionary: the meanings of words, I had come to feel, had to be known with perfect distinctness before they could be used with perfect truthfulness. My husband reached the same decision[1] by a road of his own.

"We knew that in the task we set ourselves (we are speaking of it jointly) we would have to break with lexicographical tradition—to what extent was not at first clear to us. Existing dictionaries and word-books define words by suggestive generalizations that correspond with the indefinite ideas of words' meanings entertained at large: we would have to define them with orderliness and exactness, holding them to the internal consistency of the language. For long, however, we found words resistant to such treatment. We did not fully understand the character of the mental operation required for definitions of the kind we wished to make until we perceived that we must liberate our minds entirely from the confused associations of usage in which the meanings of words are entangled—and that, for us, the act of definition must involve a total reconstituting of words' meanings. Much of our work has been done upon our own minds, rather than upon words directly: and we have proceeded very slowly, in consequence. We know now that slowness was inevitable; also inevitable, probably, was our inability to foresee this—but we regret, nevertheless, the expectations of early completion of our work we excited during its first stages. It is still far from completion, but we must leave the matter of time to nature. Perhaps, under the pressure of a sense of the public need for such an unfolding of linguistic realities as we are making, we shall be moved some time to publish a separate

---

1. [One typescript reads "destination."]

portion of the work, preliminarily. Personally, we are resigned to continuing slowness and difficulty, as our part of the mental punishment all must in one manner or another suffer from the common human sin of tolerating confusion in language.

"The previous record is out-of-date in these respects: my husband resigned from *Time* many years ago; we live in Wabasso, Florida—where we have sustained ourselves by shipping and growing citrus fruit."

# Early Note on Poetry Re-evaluated

The illusion that poetry creates—both in the reading of it and in the making of it—is that the kind of use of word peculiar to it fulfils a potential of human utterance not otherwise fulfillable. Every art is an illusion-creator. But in poetry the illusion created is taken to have the qualities of the reality; it is indeed taken to be as near the reality as one may come, and to be "for all practical purposes" (as the sceptic saying goes) identical with it. The distinction between illusion and reality gets lost in poetry, as it cannot in the other arts, which must provide a point of return for the temporary belief in the made-up reality of the work-of-art—the work-of-art must stay within its art-boundaries, *cannot escape them.* Poetry invades the ground of a general human potential for its motivation, but retreats to an art-position, imprisons the motivation within art-confines, transmogrifies it. The potential that poetry exploits is a capacity of human beings to speak *from* the vital center of being, with perfect trueness of relation therefore between speaker and the things spoken of, and, through this, between the things spoken of themselves; and in a state of perfect active unity of being with all other human beings occupying their natural human placement of vital centralness in being.

{Later note on this—This centralness of position in being is the position of the speaking function, which gives the human character, in being, its identity. The human being is "for" the speaking of the sense of being, in real concentration of presence in the total reality of being.}

# [From] A Commentary of 1967 in Introduction of *Epilogue* Volumes I, II, and III (1935, 1936, 1937)

[. . .] In my own writing in *Epilogue* and elsewhere, in my poems themselves, I conceived my activity in terms of the furtherance of an identification of general complete human self-realization with a general human responsibility of spelling-out the finalities of truth lodged unspoken in the universe[. . . .]

It may be helpful to those who wonder at my seeing a possibility of literature's domiciling functions of a primary redemptive order, exceeding the merely cultural in human importance, for me to emphasize the central importance that I attributed to poetry, among the literary activities, and to point to the intense preoccupation with words that it exacts. If one honors literature as the area of human activity where language is most honored, and accepts poetry at its traditional value of being the exemplar of linguistic perfection, then one's bearings are literary because they are, essentially, linguistic: one is preoccupied with words intensely not because of literature, not even because of poetry, but because of language's great part in the (still more foreseen that actually begun) achievement by human beings of concentrated, clear, fully determined and comprehended being. This is how it was with me.

The elucidation of the being of beings by beings is, necessarily, *linguistic* action—one cannot but know this, knowing language. Only by the government of the Word can human existence become consistent with itself, break through the barrier of inconsistency of efforts dividing it ever from itself as the Good in the form of articulate life. Where to find this government? The search for it has been philosophy's most serious object, and religions' most serious passion; and when, as now, human beings decide to attempt nothing more of *that* sort, fearing to come face to face with ultimate failure, they are all inconsistency—and use their human talent to piece themselves together from moment to moment. I thought, at the time of my laboring for, and in, *Epilogue,* that poetry could yield us the government of the Word we needed, to pass from the history of ourselves to ourselves—beings who *can* live wholly, not brokenly. Poetry seemed the least spoiled by history's touch, of all the life-saving devices of the past. Indeed, so it was! But its government modifies the Word by the little by which it is history's; and that little is too much. Eventually, we must leave behind everything that is not language's own government of the Word, which does not modify what-is-to-be-said, uniting in itself the universal and the human necessity of truth. When we go with only language and ourselves as our equipment for the way, we take with us nothing to bar the way; and the way itself has no barriers built across it.

But who wants to go all the way, really—to go immediately, to go in all the senses of "going," to reach the end of the broken forms of being, and speaking, and by a full speaking enter into full being (veritable life)? With this question of the "Who?," human beings, waiting upon one another, loving the common pace (from kindness, strengthened often by timidity), have lingered much in the way, making one another's company the leader. In *Epilogue* I tried to find a common pace that would be also a pace of movement, not merely treading in one another's standing-places. Though the "who" who are one's others are the indispensable condition of one's self-realization, since one must realize human existence as an entirety in order to realize oneself (realize the significance of human existence in oneself in order to realize oneself), one must choose one's own movement, where there proves to be no common pace but that of waiting, waiting, for the other to move. So I moved; and I think I am much closer, for having chosen my own movement, to keeping the ultimate appointment I have with others—we all have with one another[. . . .]

# Miscellaneous General Reflections

*( from a span of years—but the numberings are*
*not indicative of a time-order)*

## 1.

An assumption implicit in the utterance-opportunity offered by poetry is that of a longer allowable period for the choice of word, words. The expressive instinct is thus invited to direct itself towards the pursuit of possible finalities of expression—where the general allowances of non-poetic speaking and writing stop, variously, short of even the *aim* of full explicitness, exactly expressive utterance. However, the poetic condition of utterance is not, actually, one of absolute freedom to pursue the discovery-route of the final, or the perfect, in linguistic expression. The mere *temporal* allowance, within the necessarily limited rhythmic scope of the poem—that is, the poem is always within a physical frame of *timing* of expression-phrasing—is restrictive of word-choice in a way that substitutes, for finality of expression in relation to truth as the ultimate in explicitness, a finality of the possible within the timing-frame of expression phrasing the poem.

Whether the rhythmic condition imposed on a poem is of metrical definitiveness or the seeming non-definitiveness of "free verse," any poem, whether metrically regular or rhythmically individualistic, *is* linguistic expression within a frame of constrictions of a physical order that the poet imposes on himself-herself as *in imagination* speaking, writing, in an occasion, a temporal situation, in which he-she has (ideally or theoretically) common presence with some other, or others. This orientation to a pre-construed particular opportunity of utterance-perfection, truth-expressiveness, tends to incite a straining of the physical appurtenances of verbal utterance beyond the degree of their natural involvement in the processes of linguistic expression: physical incidentals tend to be worked to compensate with their definitiveness of temporal finality of forceful immediacy for the inevitable failure of the poem to attain to the completeness of expressive finality that is *implied* in the idea of poetry from which it derives its historical authority.

These features that I have sketched of the circumstances of poetry's presence in human life as a mode of fulfilling certain human impulsions, needs, objectives, ideals, presumed to be not otherwise fulfillable are hardly recognized and comprehended, with respect to what they signify as to the nature of poetry, and of human engagement in the practice of it. One of the consequences of the bemused attitudes to poetry that prevail among poets themselves, and the professional critics of poetry, is a linguistically, critically, and—broadly speaking—poetically irrelevant idealization of the physical appurtenances of verbal utterance as constituting the essence of the *poetic,* in language. I hope that I have provided in this little reflective exercise some useful suggestion as to what is wrong with this kind of cultural legislation of poetic law.

## 2.

Someone paid tribute to me privately as having written my poems with a "voice" identifiable as the "voice" of poetry. This conception of poetry's having a special order of "voice" has come to be one of the fixtures of critical rhetoric in sophisticated literary quarters—part-sentimental, part-ritualistic, in *its* voice-quality. I have used the word "voice" myself, in a speaking of how poets speak; and I may have some responsibility for its present currency. But my sense, in using it, has been closely related to the actual personal tonalities employed. I have, for instance, spoken of "the voice of truth," meaning, the qualities of personal intonation peculiar to speaking animated by a will to truth of expression.

I commented, to the person who paid tribute to me as to using a "voice of poetry" in my poems, that in my later view of poetry I did not identify "the voice of poetry" ("in so far as one can reasonably speak of such a thing," I said) as the voice of truth. "I think the poetic 'voice' is a hybrid, varying greatly in its composition among poets, having at least *some* truth-force intermixed with its other components. My poetic voice was high in an approach to purity (that is, for me, truth-voicedness), relatively, because the main elements were two (by my evaluation) that were congenial though not identical. I see them as the truth-element I have just mentioned, and its kindness-element {I had mentioned this in a comment not reproduced here}. This latter element I consider to be an essential woman characteristic. I use 'woman' here, in a spiritually categorical sense, including importantly in what it names as a distinct identity of nature of personal being a disposition, as intrinsic in the nature, to kindness of consciousness of those of the partner-identity named 'man,' for no other reason than that it has consciousness of itself as a partner-identity in the great comprehensive opposition in personal nature of being that attends the human state. This man-woman matter is some unfinished universal business that has attached itself to the human state despite or because of the unities of generality in character of being that in tendency predominate in the human mode of being. That is, I think that there is in the traits of nature possessed by women as personal beings a prime sensitivity to the principle of *the entire* as the principle that is the ultimate decider.["]

Where someone has spoken of "the voice of poetry," in my poems, another has characterized the "voice" of my poems as a voice of glacial abstractness. I believe that, given unprejudiced audition (unprejudiced in one and another direction, literarily and personally), it will be found to be, in and out of the poetic conditions of utterance, an "all-round" voice, one evoking, in the individual occasion of utterance, the potential context of the entire.

Aristotle distinguished three voices of poetry, the voice of the poet speaking in the lyric, and that of the poet as composer of a drama, the characters, here, being voice-instruments of the poet, and that of the poet as narrator, combining, by Aristotle's theory, the lyric and the dramatic vocal qualities. This structure of analysis collapses into itself because the distinction between the voice of the poet in the lyric and the voice of the characters in the drama dramatizes the lyric, and the distinguished narrator voice, supposedly a combination of the first two voice-manners, dramatizes the narrative. Poetry is reduced here to an art of verbal mimetic. The distinctions are characteristically Aristotelian: they simplify a broad field of things into an arbitrary unity, attributing complexities to the unity that are themselves arbitrary. The device of such distinctions becomes a convenience of rhetorical discussion; they become principles of rhetoric, keeping rhetorical discussion within the bounds of a watch kept by rhetoricians on one another in their use of them as common terms, marks of sophistication on which the dignity of the profession rests, and for pressing into the service of their individual careers of rhetorical argument.

Aristotle reduced every subject he studied to a cadaver, for the delivery of an anatomical treatise on it. His depiction of the intricacies of the art of poetic construction is a nightmare-model of learned literary criticism, "everything" covered, all the technical, aesthetic, and moral aspects of poetic production, nothing left outside the grasp of practical formulation: it is comprehensively conventionalized explanation. The great extent to which literary criticism has submitted to the influence of this model, its potency as inspiration to the ambition to subsume the actuality—reproduce it, replace it in *explanation*—has hardly been perceived. A like goading influence of the Aristotelian model of explanation has had part in the explanatory devices, elaborately anatomical, of contemporary linguistic criticism—i.e., "linguistics."

Wherever systematicness in thought is the purpose of intellectual activity, there is no real subject: there is no object of *understanding*. The mind is not being used for understanding the subject of consideration, but for reacting intellectually to it. Paul Valéry is responsible for very much of the devastation of the modern critical sense of poetry. Dismissing it as something not having a content of existence, an inner reason in human performance for its having come into existence, he pitted his mind against it as a mere phenomenon of potentiality, and fashioned an idiosyncratic mode of poetic performance that was a mere product of intellectual reaction to the performance-invitation that poetry constituted for his detached condition of mind.

"Detachment" is the refuge of modern-literary criticism from the burdens of "understanding." Those who make it a critical function, corresponding to a relation of poets themselves to poetic experience as something in itself, existing in quasi-physical detachment from all other experience, are substituting a criticism of the character of a literary business or science for the actual thing, criticism, and a poetry of the character of a literary business or science for the actual thing, poetry.

It is a far throw from Aristotle's postulations as to the matter of "voice" in poetry to reference in contemporary literary criticism to a something of individual essence conceived to inhere in what poets put forth to which the term "voice" is applied, with reverential connotations. I have found evidence, in the contemporary use of the term by literary critics of serious professional dedication, of unawareness of its harking back to Aristotelian rhetorical terminology. Eliot is thought of as the patriarchal founder of the use of the word as a key term for poetic criticism. I think Eliot himself, in his account of "the three voices of poetry" [1953], gave no indication of Aristotle's being the founder patriarch of the application of the term in criticism (i.e. in rhetoric, the ancestor-study of the processes of literary composition that modern literary criticism, practised as a system of doctrine for the analysis of the processes of literary criticism, has made its historical model).

I shall not dwell lengthily here (in this particular area of reflection) on the element of preoccupation with terminology—the use of words endowed with special professional significations—in literary criticism. I shall just record, as a closing word for this brief looking into the subject, that I regard all written use of words as having in it necessarily a continuity of utterance-force reproductive of the actuality of the person speaking in physically delivered utterance. The mind does all the work of speaking in the written utterance-performance; the voice of the person speaking, in the written presentation, cannot be other than there as the animating force in the maintaining of continuity in the delivery of the words of presentation for sense-making of their sense. An attribution of a peculiar something denominated "voice" to a poet, poets, different from the general human vocal actuality permeating any writing in which the mind is at work directing the transmission of the force of personal utterance to the page, converts the poet into *an actor*. Such an attribution corresponds to what has been extensively happening, in recent literary periods, in the pursuit of poetry: poetry has come to be used as a stage for the enactment of verbal exercises in self-consciousness as having a public interest and value to be identified with the historic dignities of poetry, and poet-identity.

The implications of the attribution to poetic performance of a peculiar poetic phenomenon of "voice" open to view the decline in appreciation of its dignities that has befallen poetry, and poetic criticism along with it. Weak innovations in the criticism of poetry and in poetic activity itself have been superimposed upon sagging traditions of poetic practice and critical practice. The habitués of both fields, the poetic and the critical, are driven by a desperation to prove that there is no contemporary want in due understanding of fundamental principle and the proprieties of temporal circumstance, and of confidence in ability to accommodate practice to these as opposing poles of literary necessity. The strain of this desperation makes such a term of critical reference as "voice," and the conceptions solidified into it, as it does in the case of others formed in a hurrying for new authority for poetry, and its critical arm, a security-refuge from assaults of self-doubt, to which poets and critics who practise a private honesty are subject: such terms *are* being used *seriously*. The most important issues for human resolution can seem already resolved, or on the way to being resolved, when the content of the seriousness with which they are viewed is left unexamined—as if seriousness were itself substance of good judgement.

### 3.

I have been aware of there being considerable awareness, in the English-speaking poets of this era, at least, of my pronouncements on the linguistic and spiritual flaws of poetry—its "failure." Reference to my later views of poetry, and of my renunciation of it, is generally avoided, and not because my views, and my act, are dismissed as, just, bizarre. Poets have made use of what I have in later time presented as to poetry for being on their guard. I have a speculative inclination to believe that many of them scrutinize themselves and their work uncomfortably, with my findings as to poetry in mind. I don't conceive of their or their poems' benefiting from such scrutiny: I think the case is one of a settled, almost involuntary irritation with me.

# Some Thoughts On Poetry, Mind,
# Body, Life, Truth—Loosely Bound

As to the management of one's utterances, of which I have spoken: this is a working direction of one's thought towards its being as fully developed to articulateness as one can make it, by one's own intellectual and linguistic faculties—which is to say, by virtue of its strength as one's own thought. This matter of strength has relation to the physicalities that manifest themselves in the use of words.

The tonal course of utterance, which is of one nature with its enunciatory course, is the course of the union effected, by the person, of the sympathetic disposition of the physical sensibilities towards concentrated functioning of the person as *mind* and the generous patience of the mind as a personal actuality with the diffuse functioning of the person as an individual body. The physical part contributes to the union a force of undefined expectancy. This force becomes distinctly individualized in its conjunction with the mind's force of concentrated aim at fullness of thought with distinction of thought: the mental force and the physical force are tempered to each other's difference in a manner to corroborate their both belonging to one all-embracing life-function.

The union of the mental and the physical part, in the utterance of words, the putting of them "out," whether into the open air or the open space of the page, bring together as a necessary one *the spirit of life,* which cannot be other than indivisible, and *the living thing* that knows itself as alive with the spirit of life, as a life unto life, not a thing unto itself. It is too much, the utterance of words in which is verily realized such a bringing together, to be contained in a *category* of utterance.

There could be no more, in the category of utterance called "poetry," than protestation of a belief that the utterance of words should be of this genius, and trial at exemplification of what it would be like if it were so.

The tonal quality of such utterance will be a mutuality formed of the generous patience of the mind towards the bodily part and the desire of [the] bodily part to prove itself the match of the mind's varied anticipating of the voice of the soul. When words are of such sort and such delivery, they will be the words of beings of whom the first description will be: "They live life with truth." And what was called poetry will be seen to have been either a labor of love of truth before the time of the ultimate living of life with truth by the users of words, or a labor in that time of brazen self-love, performed with heroic lying[,] or an evasion of the attempt of truth in fictive sagacity or show of empty nobility—cowards' rhetoric.

# Poem-Reality

One might say that in the theatre of poetry the lighting is metaphorical: that is, poets have tended to employ metaphor to give a glow of realness to their poetic scenes. Such employment of metaphor encourages the poet in assuming an "artistic" necessity, in poems, of inducing illusion of the real—stirring sense of encounter with the real by artificial means. The metaphorical lighting-up of the poetic scenes creates a dramatic effect of natural lightness, deceptive life-likeness. But, along with this kind of employment of metaphor, there is the linguistically reasonable employment of it for the assistance of expressiveness with the emergence of accuracy of suggestion, which is the ordinary, non-poetic, principle of metaphor. There is found in poetry much confusion in the ways in which it is employed. Now the employment is theatric, now it is for the service of meaning, as in standard linguistic procedure. This confusion contributes to the extensive confusion that exists as to just what constitutes *poetic* word-use.

Regular metaphor in and outside of poetry can have a certain literalness, the metaphor being meant, carrying a substitute for a meaning. Theatric poetic metaphor does not have meaning as a main motive. It is merged, in its motivation, with the other theatric equipment of poetry: the rhythmics of form, the auditory peculiarity of the verbal out-landness of poetic text, forcing the reader to be mentally a sayer-over of what he-she reads.

Poetry "is" linguistically impure! It lets its ideal purpose and its immediate intent strike a bargain of difference. There is a dramatic part, the part in which immediate intent is enacted, and a part that figures in the poem as that which is supposed to follow from it for the understanding: the climax of the experience of the poem lies outside it, beyond it, by the formal nature of the linguistic construction of the poem. The "real" experience of understanding that the poem supposedly engenders is only dramatically suggested. The poem may or may not be such as to prompt beginnings of intellectual vision of a fresh kind. But, if it does, there cannot be a following development of the beginnings: there is not, in the poem, in the *words* of the poem, enough to make the rest, the unsaid (that extraneous accompaniment of every poem) determinately speakable (in terms of sense continuing from the poem).

# [From] Statement in
## *Contemporary Poets* (1970)

[. . .] Up to 1940 I considered myself centrally a poet, with every
other writing activity coming under a government of values (a
unity of values prerequisite for truth) that I conceived of as centrally poetic. This moral and spiritual emphasis on poetry I took
to be practically justified by the linguistic urgency in poetry towards rightness of word; poetry seemed where the verbal maximum could be one with and the same as the truth-maximum.
When, after long-sustained faith in this seeming poetic potential,
and pressing of the linguistic possibilities of poetic utterance towards further and further limits, I comprehended that poetry
had no provision in it for ultimate practical attainment of that
rightness of word that *is* truth, but led on ever only to a tempo-
rizing less-than-truth (the lack eked out with illusions of truth
produced by physical word-effects), *I stopped.* I stopped—but I
went on to search for the way to that rightness of word that is
truth, and as the natural yield of words cultivated for truth's sake,
not as the product of an *art* of words. . . . And in so doing I did
not, renouncing poetry, transfer allegiance to some other form
of literary procedure. I intensified my application to the problem
of the knowledge of the meanings of words, and, for the rest,
dedicated myself to the saying of what I might be able to say with
a more far-reaching trueness of word than I had attained in any
special literary climate, poetic or otherwise[. . . .]

# Background Statement on a new edition of *Collected Poems*— Laura Riding (1938), planned for 1979, authorized and edited by Laura (Riding) Jackson

Not long after the publication in 1938 of her *Collected Poems,* gathered from nine previously published books of poems, Laura Riding found a necessity of renouncing poetry, which had been to her, as one committed to faith in language in its aspect of service to the human effort of truth, as the best-assured "way" of truth. In the preface to the 1938 edition of *Collected Poems* she recorded her conception of poetry as allowing of fulfilment of the ideal of truth that she took to be naturally implicit in language, and in the nature of human identity itself. There was no sign in this preface of any questioning by her of her long-sustained faith in poetry as a sure course of redemption from the loss of the spiritual potential of language in the impromptu formations of the circumstantially determined utterances of ordinary verbal intercourse. Her view of poetry comprised the view that the linguistically indecisive character of the verbal ordinary could not be overcome in even the most intellectually deliberate utterance-practice, i.e., the studied movement of prose composition.

What brought about Laura Riding's renouncing of poetry was, rather than an experience of a sudden loss of faith in the truth-potential of poetry, an experience of gradual learning of the full potential of language that culminated in a crucial comprehension of what, practically, this promised. The comprehension spelled itself out to her unignorably: the linguistic ideal of perfect expressiveness, the human potential of truth, was not, as by linguistic pre-ordainment, the special property of the linguistically segregated precinct of poetry. She graduated as it were from poetry into the discovery that this potential belonged to the open ground of human utterance constituted of the generous provisions of language itself, in its one-mindedness with the human conscience of the necessary universality of the inborn human concern with truth. She relates this discovery to the intensified attention paid by her in and out of her poetry-orientated thinking and writing, as the decade of the 'thirties mounted towards its term, to a proposition that her mind had early adopted as its principle of self-instruction: *words mean.*

The impression that the poetic work of Laura Riding made in the periods of its general availability was strongly related to her looking in the poetic area of word-use for a fuller realization of the meaning-reality implicit in words, there, than in other areas. Words were seen to retain their intrinsic properties as words, in her poems, with a distinctness of reality as meaning what they mean as linguistic entities that is hardly found even aimed at in poetic verbal practices generally or suggested as not unsuitable for out-of-the-ordinary, individually outstanding high points of expressiveness in other forms of literary verbal practice, or in occasions of rhetorical importance in ordinary literate speech. The effect of the union, in her poems, of the aims of poetic and linguistic purity, and the achievement in them of a fusion of personal fidelity to sense-expressiveness and fidelity to the standard of truth of word, was keenly felt by some. The significance of her testing, thus, poetry and language with and against each other was in large part lost, especially with those who drew upon her poems as a source of poetic devices for the enhancement of the intellectual and linguistic distinction of their own.

Against the judgements of a not small body of hostile critics (among these, poets doing a double literary duty)—(her poetic work treated as in violation of reigning conceptions of the modern poetic "best," it conforming to general poetic and linguistic standards, not to any of the particular styles that had established themselves as critically appropriate to twentieth-century poetic modernism)—are to be set such evaluations of the total force of her poetic work as the following excerpts from reviews of the 1938 *Collected Poems* convey.

*Criterion*—October 1938

. . . By her practice and influence Miss Riding has helped several poets to write simply about abstractions, to avoid trivial decoration and irrelevant music and to preserve the integrity of their words.

*Boston Transcript*—January 4, 1939
    *John Holmes*

. . . She recreates words. She refreshes one's understanding of the plainest words, so providing excitement of a rare sort in poetry. . . . It is poetry without metaphor for the most part because she seeks to see the thing itself, rather than to find out what it is like. . . . Her preface is one of the most clear-headed statements of the whole business of poetry of recent years.

*Irish Times*—February 4, 1939
    *Padraic Fallon*

. . . In her, perhaps for the first time in literature (one cannot exclude Hopkins, whose discipline was that of the Church he embraced), poetry becomes a sort of day-to-day discipline, an attempt to define conscience by living up to it, a civilization of the senses by matching to them their mental equivalents. . . . She never surprises emotions by comment; for emotion and comment, even when emotion is loud and insistent, are always one.

The tension—to use this term straight, not as the psychological cliché—she was able to maintain throughout the course of her poetic writing between the utmost in effort to meet the highest in the categorically poetic requirements and the highest in the categorically linguistic requirements continually renewed her faith in the ideal that poetry offered to the linguistic conscience of a perfect compatibility between poetry, in its difference from ordinary linguistic practice, and the potential of the perfect in word-use that language, in its abundant substance, abundantly promises. But her very success in maintaining this tension gave her, in the period immediately following the completion and publication of *Collected Poems,* a special strength of perception for distinguishing between success in poetic expression and success in word-use judged by linguistic standards of rightness of word, irrespectively of the bearing upon the word-use of poetic sensitivity to verbal proprieties.

From engagement in the latter years of the 'thirties and the first of the 'forties in new intensive study of words as distinctly knowable and definitely employable entities of meaning, Laura Riding formed an idea of the organic meaning-potency possessed by the individual word as an instrument of expression integral with the comprehensive instrumentality of language. It became possible for her to compare the linguistic quality of her poetic word-use with a quality of word-use in any circumstance of sense-expressive utterance that, inhering in the linguistic nature of words, *must* exceed the poetic as a quality of truth of word. Thus it came about that the trial she made in poetry of the possibilities of virtue in word-use assisted her, by poetry's hospitable encouragement of such trial, in the discovery of the limitations of the poetic use of words as a truthfully expressive mode of verbal utterance, in comparison with language's unqualified allowances for the truthful utmost.

Laura Riding's poems reveal of what order of verbal utterance the truthfully expressive is—to a degree beyond the accustomed in experience of poetic word-use—it being very largely a stranger to general experience in modes of word-use. They are capable of revealing, when there has been achieved some direct apprehension of the expression-potential that the individual word possesses in any use, in the simple force its meaning possesses as a linguistic concentration of sense, hopeful possibilities of truthful excellence of expression as a common rule for literate verbal practice, irrespective of poetic or generally literary standards: the outstanding peculiarity of word-use in her poems is its linguistic naturalness where it seems at its most successful poetically. (Incomprehension of the free extent to which, in her poems, the poetic and the natural in linguistic exactitudes of expression have happy meeting, as being of this character, has produced the characterization "difficult," also that of "too intellectual," of them, in critical comment that illuminates more the defects of the criticism than the qualities, adversely or otherwise properly describable, of the poems.)

The poems of Laura Riding perform the service to the historical dignity of poetry of exhibiting how the poetic use of words is a fraudulence unless its governing motive is to accomplish the utmost possible in truth of word in every feature of it. They perform the service to the living dignity of language of exhibiting how poetry at its most honorable objectifies this aim, while leaving fully realized truth of word to be its own witness to itself. They take the mind that goes all the way with them in their exploring of the possibilities of poetic-word-use to the ultimate threshold where the possibilities that language stores in it for the fulfilment of the general human necessity of truth of word lie unlimitedly accessible.

# III
# Points Made Briefly

# The Tentative Nature of the Excellent In Language as Exemplified in Poetry

The broadest generalization that can be made on the character of poetry as the mode of a tradition of speaking (whether actually oral, or written, speaking) sustained in special practice from earliest to latest human customs in the use of words is that it is a speaking in a certain way that differs from all other ways by a certain excellence in its verbal quality. But it is the curious predicament of poetry that, although it is especially committed to verbal excellence, and so to conformity with standards applicable to all linguistic practice, it conforms to these standards in a way peculiar to it, not convertible into a generally practicable excellence. The explanation of this predicament is that poetry originates in a premonition of there being a potential speaking in which human beings, *without* such departure into peculiarity as characterizes poetic speaking, may realize language's capacity for yielding utterance of complete excellence to a matching *general* human capability of achieving this effect in the use of words. Thus, the title of poetry to exceptionality of verbal quality seals it in a fate of ultimate desuetude. It has predicted the realization of an ideal implicit in language and in the human linguistic faculties. To treat the prediction as itself the ultimate is to allow poetry the hope of that ultimate to the verity of which it eloquently testified.[1]

---

1. [The last sentence read, before L(R)J's holograph correction of it: "To treat the prediction as itself the ultimate is to corrupt the virtue of poetry, and use it to belie the hope of that ultimate to the verity of which it eloquently testified."]

# [Note Concerning] *A Pamphlet Against Anthologies,* 1928 (1964)

Of course, this is a sensible book, if the point of view is taken, as it was in the writing of it, that Poetry has an intrinsic and sacred excellence. But let me here put a 1964 footnote to the book, to my collaborator-share in it.

That presumed excellence of Poetry-in-the-large is itself but a stop-gap. If we think of the anthology-area of Poetry as an anteroom and Poetry in its undesecrated entirety as the inner room, then it can be said (I would say) that those who do not content themselves, or are not made to be contented, with visits to the anteroom, but have direct inner-room acquaintance with Poetry, will find (if they are literally looking for the *perfect in saying*) that they are only in a further anteroom, larger, better furnished, an anteroom having no opening into a further room because of its attributed character of ultimate innerness.

Poetry, visited in its wholeness, will not answer to ultimate tests of wholeness: and, if the matter of Perfect Saying is left at that, at Poetry as the saving alternative to our common saying-habit, the way-of-access to truth is *destroyed.*—Thus goes my 1964 colophon for the book, my personal colophon.

# Foreword to "Further on Poetry"

Of what profit to myself, and to others, my endeavoring thus to mark out the region of poetry on the spiritual map of human life, and, because I have found it not what I at first, and for long, took it to be, to show what it is by showing what it is not? Would it be wiser to spare my strength for labors by which that might be accomplished, possibly, or made capable of accomplishment, possibly, which poetry (as I see it) closes out while promising it? Who will thank me for this? Even those inclined to sympathy will wonder why I have so much passion over the matter, and think, somewhat, "The overvaluing of poetry shakes down; the world is not continually a fool over things over which it is sometimes a fool; poets themselves have a sort of sensibleness in their foolishness over poetry." It is this very contradictoriness in the matter that keeps me from believing that it has taken, or is taking, or will take, care of itself. I do indeed have to go out of my way to make my map, tell my story, argue my experience and view; there is awkwardness in the proceedings, from my conducting them under the difficulty of having good reasons for doing something else—and in a solitary position, without benefit of company in my renouncing of poethood, and with some effect of seeming renegade in my censure of poetry. But I feel we are safer in my assuming this elusive responsibility (in its being assumed by someone).

## As To "What Next?"

Poetry had no other reason than that of allowing for the presence, in the human kind of being, of a speaking consciousness of a principle with which the whole—the self-manifesting all of being—is animated. The credit of poetry as humanly respectworthy has inhered in its nature as a continuously existent form of action by human beings in which they speak in acknowledgement of the presence in them of mind-aliveness to such a principle. But this courtesy-paying to the principle became, in poetry's ageing in human history, as the honoring of a principle of human self-regard. Poetry, by the grace of time's patiences the speaking of a language of human witness-bearing to a universal principle of being, lost presence to the attending ears of the principle itself. It has been busy equipping itself with ears of its own. When they ask of me, "What next?," I cannot say other than: "Do not call these extravagant auditory enterprises 'poetry.' Speak only for the waiting ears secreted in the grace of the universe we know as time. This will bring speaking and being together, in the unity that language and the universe have longed, speakingly, listeningly, to describe—prove livable."

# Notes for the Time
## of Ultimate Candor

How much of what human life—human ways of living, being human, thinking, behaving, acting—is becoming, is characterizable as a vulgarization of what have been its better parts, its higher levels in intelligence, purpose, imagination of the good, vision of the happy? The whole of it began in this century to be converted, with chaotic speed, into a property for human beings to rob themselves of. Nothing must be set apart for the perfect use of it. Nothing must be left to shine of itself; all must be dragged forth into the glare of a united greed. To have, to consume, be done with wanting, waiting, finding the fitting match to desire: the all of human sentience become a mob.

Apply this to any of the treasured forms of the human best. Apply it to poetry. Poetry now is, much, a foppery of new casual word-wit. Old vulgarity is made, in it, a preciosity of a new vulgarity; poet-wisdom readies itself for promenade in the mirror of a new literary worldliness; and there is a playing upon the instruments of metaphor and measure, with a resolutely careless air of modern ease in the technicalities of traditional poet elegance and eloquence. There is an everything of exhibition of capacity to string out line and line of poetic verbal agility; and a nothing of straining love of the rare truth-sound and truth-sense long dreamt of under the name of poetry, and given a tremorous reality by the unhesitant bearing of poems—as to say "We speak of the best speaking."

[Do] I think there will be an end of this nothing, this poetry of a time of human levelling of the essential grace of the human to the floor of self-ignorance upon which the human first knew life? The human has returned itself to this floor, all that it had learned collapsing, from failure of the mortar of self-knowledge. I believe there will be no end of the nothing that the human has made of itself until, above the din of the mob-music of the private patter and chatter of this poet-many, there rises as above a loud silence, heard only by itself, a smallest number of voices calling upon each other from lonely afar-s. "Speak best! Speak best!—or the human fact will die of the fast-descending estimate it is making of itself as a low-cost mass-pride."

# Introduction to a Reading of "Lucrece and Nara" for Australian Radio, as a condition of permission (the condition was not accepted)

This poem deals in the form of legend with the theme of immortality, from the point of view of a belief that, under the condition of perfect love, a mutual immortalness is possible. The underlying conception is serious, not fanciful; but the poem, because it is a poem, a thing of compulsory artifice, does not allow of a direct and natural, and fully serious, development of the conception. A climactic degree of development seems to be attained in the poem, but this is an illusion. The theme is dealt with beautifully, evasively, uselessly. It is left to be dealt with veritably at another time—and in poetry another time never comes.[2]

# Poetry As Image of Poetry

I have declared that poetry had exhausted the possibilities envisaged in the vision of the utterable that engendered it, and become a stage for postures of poetic utterance, contests of skill in exhibiting vision of oneself, and oneself, as theme of the uniquely all-utterable. And I have pronounced on the male temper of this invention, this poetry of a relativity of innumerable absolutes, varied with female reiterations of it in the proud

2. [A fuller reconsideration of this poem forms the basis of "What, If Not A Poem, Poems?," written by 1967, *Denver Quarterly* 9(2) (1974), and *Reader,* 239ff.]

rhetoric of a new petulance of the self. The literary consequences are disguised in poetic ceremonials in which the striking of notes of the music of the self is mingled in with the sounding of rhythms of meaning, as if enhancing them. But the music of the self devours the music of meaning. The product is neither something spoken nor something sung. It is a playing upon language, as an instrument borrowed from life, to make the players seem alive.

# Poetry With A Difference

The standard of poetic performance subscribed to by contemporary poets of sophisticated ambition—which includes a conception of what can be successfully offered as corresponding with contemporary sophistication in literary taste—is complexly simple. All past standards of the poetic have been atomized, continually more and more finely split, into the minute transparency of the verbally *ingenious.*

Display of verbal ingeniousness has become entitlement to the identity "poet." All ranking of poets, backward from this governing standard, is brought under its one-value value-system. The entire range of the history of poetry is absorbed in this frame of solemnified linguistic frivolity. In one form or another of the practice of poetry in the century's ageing course, poets ape the models they make of poet-wit, poet-finesse, poet-idiosyncracy of statement-style, whatever the statement-subject. All sins of poetic performance of the past are thus cancelled, and, with this, all the virtues: nothing is any longer adjudgeable as poetically right or wrong. The poetic criticism of the past is itself nullified as irrelevant to contemporary circumstance; the contemporary standard of verbal ingeniousness is held adequate to all problems of statement, judgement, sensibility, proper to poetry. Poetry is now presumed to dispense a magic of being painless. The words themselves, anaesthetized, do not feel what is done with them; and, taken into mind in the forms of ruthless bravado of poetic style, they do not hurt.

# A Dour Remarking on Poetry

We must prepare ourselves for a journey of the spirit; and, though it is a journey on which we never start, a mythical journey, the preparation has some residue of disciplinary worth, of which perhaps we can make use for a real journey. One might thus judge of religion. But in no case of poetry; the residue is all loss—the ear for truth is spoiled for its natural accent of truth, the tongue for innocent utterance of it, free of persuasion's meddling, the mind for its generous rectitude. As the best in language we hold up to ourselves high-purposed verbal models, that, intended to lift up the hearts from the down-weighting of ordinary speaking-custom, swell them up with the vanity of the word, which turns a human being into a speaking bird and the listeners into would-be changelings.

# Poetry and The Prophetic

My identification of poetry as ideally committed to the end of truth of word is borne out in my poems in the observance of a linguistic code of honor and in an ever-present and increasingly definite element of the prophetic. Commitment to such observance and to a prophetic function as inhering in poetry (its human foundations) has been lapsing so fast and so widely that, in my recognition of the commitment, and sincerity as a poet in keeping faith with it, I became an oddity as a poet in my literary time. That there has been little hospitality offered to my poetic work is largely attributable to the treatment of time in it: time is seen in very long view.

Is not "prophetic" a too popularistic—an almost political, it might be said—characterization of the long, long, time-view peculiar to poetic vision, by traditional identification of poetry's contexts of significance? This depends on how much weight of religious associations the word is made to bear. The religious associations are pragmatical—localized to event of circumscribably human experience. What poetic associations "prophetic" carries release the time-sense to conceptions of event calling for terms of experience of universal reality-force. This suggests that poetic vision is of an order of experience larger than life—of what is not livable within the dimensions of "life" according to the categorically human definition of it. Indeed, one might describe the poetic impulse as intuition of a vital discrepancy in the humanly localized definition of life anticipating the necessity of accurate definition for the full encompassing of life in life. Nothing but fulfilment fulfils: prophecy warns of this!—as if truth declared itself the not-yet-told all, the all not-yet-exactly-spoken, into life's exact all.

# The Matter of Metaphor. Addenda[3]

There is to consider how the resort to metaphorical devices of expression, in poetry, to an extent beyond the customs of the linguistic usual, seems, can seem, to effect a greater exactitude of expression than is possible within the usual linguistic modes: the poetic metaphorical can seem peculiarly fitted to effect the precision of expression that makes for *truth*. It should be considered, in evaluation of the effectiveness, the expressive utility, of metaphorical devices, that they are, fundamentally, *comparisons*. The only element of possible exactitude in a comparison is that of the comparability of two things brought into a relation. But, there being exactitude in presenting them as comparable does not establish identicality. The care exercised in the poetic use of metaphor to establish the perfect rightness of the implied or explicit comparability—to effect precision of comparison—can cast an illusion-spell over the metaphoric areas of expression, for both poet and reader: what is phrased has the verbal air of exact specification of an appearance, a quality, a feeling—whatever is the subject of the expression-effort. Much of the special impressiveness as true that poetic statement can have comes

---

3. ["The Matter of Metaphor," an extract from *Rational Meaning*, had appeared in *It Has Taken Long, Chelsea* 35 (1976).]

of the vividness of metaphorical suggestion that has so much part in the verbal style of poetry; the mind is persuaded to accept what is suggested as a complete identification.

## To A Poet, on Myth As Modern Matter

. . . For me, generally, the modern propensity towards delving into myth-matter for imaginative suggestion is part of a condition of mind of sagged imagination: all that myth-matter, resort to myth-substance, I view as artificial stimulation to the natural modern imagination (what it ought to be, in vital actuality).

. . . Myself, I have to put me on record as regarding the resort to the evocative force of relics of ancient humanity's devices of inventing *sense* where instinct, and life of understanding, kept much closed from perception, inventing it for imagination-fill for the time-being, as resting at not taking the contemporary powers of instinct, and immediate life of understanding *in* us, seriously enough to move and move to meet the possession of these in resolute responsibility.

# IV
# On Other Poets

# Kinds of Poetic Excitement,
# Kinds of Poets

## 1.

Poets excite the minds of people in different ways: some, by the manner in which they say their say, and, some, by *what* they say, and, a few, by what they are, or seem to be, *doing*, in saying a poetic say.

My opening generalization fits the case of all poets, I think— up to the contemporary era, in which there is little excitement of mind associated with poetry itself where there is interest in it, either for poets or their readers. Contemporary interest in poetry is diffuse in kind, is a varying medley of interests to which no definite character-pattern is veritably attributable. The minds of people, including those of poets and of readers of poets, are now excited, more than by anything else, by their own disorder; it would be difficult, therefore, to discern classifiable differences in the impact of poets upon people. Yet, amidst the general infatuation with disorder (treated as being perhaps the ultimate order of things), much of the established modes of reactive behavior persists, in irregular manifestations. People now are, in disorderly mixture, both what people were and what people are differently from what people were; and this obtains no less in the behavior-field of poetry than in other behavior-fields. Something of the characteristic, long-term responses of people to poetry continue into the present, though people are too distrait generally for organized responses to it (even where the interest in it is on the plane of criticism) and what is called poetry is more and more weakly possessed of the historic identity of poetry.

I linger in these thoughts, after my opening generalization, to avoid being misunderstood as to my choosing to write on the poet Rimbaud. I am not under the illusion that the fact of Rimbaud is now of fundamental concern to anyone despite his being still one of the choicer literary reference-mentions, serviceable for demonstrating sophisticated breadth of literary background. I have no conventional literary purpose in writing of him: this is not an exercise in either literary appreciation or literary derogation. I write this without thought of benefiting poets *or* poetry or the criticism of poetry, or people in relation to poetry, through it. I judge poetry to have consumed its justifications, and to offer, now, only opportunities for unvirtuous verbal display. The mission of words, I have reason to believe, has emerged unfulfilled from its traversal of poetry. But, the better the poetic course of that mission is understood, and the nature of its failure, the freer will be our truth-instinct to find out the course that will lead it into fulfilment.

Such is my spirit, in writing now newly on Rimbaud, a little. I have begun with a theory as to kinds of mental excitation produced by poets, according to their kinds—of which I distinguish three. This theorizing should be regarded as commonsense credentials presented by me to my readers. I am aware that my generalization would be extremely difficult to apply to contemporary poets, where not impossible, because, they having lost the animation of distinct poetic purpose, there is hardly any functional distinction between them—they are not going about a historic profession in the historically typical ways but merely behaving "like" poets in a confusion of personality-differences. I am also aware that there is very little "real" facing into poetry in these times, as there is very little "real" production of poetry. I am not naïvely insensitive to how the realities that were incorporated in the existence of poetry have been smashed up, battered out of shape, in the contemporary prosecution of disorder as a higher order than order. In resurrecting the shape of them, which haunts the scene of our understanding (not only of poets and poetry but of ourselves and our total experience), I am talking in general contexts of moral retrospect, not in any special contexts of the shambling literary consciousness of the "day."

# 2.

To return to my specification of three general modes of poetic functioning, in terms of kinds of excitement produced in the minds of people—the readers, the hearers: I described the poetic quality of poems as centered, varyingly, in the manner in which what is said in them by the poet is said, or in *what* is said in them by the poet, or in what the poet is *doing* or seems to be doing, in saying the say said in them. Into this divisional pattern will fit, I think, all poets whose productions are entitled to the name of poetry by being written somewhat, at least, for the sake of poetry as an activity believed to have virtues commanding its perpetuation—written, that is, with a historical sense of poet-function. Rimbaud is very easily identifiable, by the test of these general differences, as belonging to the third class. I do not think that this necessarily establishes him as a very "good" poet in this class; it only establishes that he was, in being a poet, endeavoring to live by the words he formed into poems, and endeavoring, in forming words into poems, to form them of words he might live by. This position towards poetry involves the most sincerity on the part of poets, in their dedication to poetry. There is no back-stage area in it for literary self-management; the whole operation of being a poet is out in the open, the stage has no backing, no wings, is not a real stage. The poem is a real human location, where the poet is engaged in the real action of speaking: the poetic speaking is a way of life. There have been more false aspirants to membership in this class than to any other, for it seems to require more bravado of word than work; and the false aspirant's intoxication with his sense of the "realness" of his verbal adventures and escapades can induce in the public a feeling of witnessing the poetic action in the life. Rimbaud was a true member of this class.

I wish to avoid lingering in an enumeration of others as qualifying or not for this title, and in specific assignments of poets to the other two classes, for my scheme of distinction is but a lantern-light I carry here to help readers see what I see. But I think that with some brief specification I can swing my lantern about quickly over my opinion-ground, and give them thus some initial familiarity with its contours. Therefore I shall say that I consider Dylan Thomas, whom I have seen likened to Rimbaud in his attitude to his poems, to have been a sensationalist, judged in terms of the classes I have distinguished. By this I mean not that the members of one of the three classes are thus denominatable, but that he endeavored, by whipping his words into a frothing progress, as if he held the reins of a fiery group of poetic chariot-steeds, to give them a dramatic character of action: he sought for himself, from them, sensations of action, and assumed the production, by them, of a like effect upon others. This kind of procedure generates by its intensity continual stimulus for the poet—his own writing excites him to write on; and readers find themselves drawn irresistibly into following the poetic impulsion to action. But there is no increment of satisfaction in such procedure either for reader or poet. The intensity of the drama of sensations has the quality of thirst; the excitation is of sensations of thirst for action. There is no quenching, and there is no tragic experience in the imagination, either, of the passing of thirst without a watering of it.

Both Sylvia Plath and Dylan Thomas foundered in the use of poetry as a substitute for action—foundered both in their management of themselves as poets, and as persons. In poems written in this emotional condition, the poem exhausts the emotions. With such a one as Rimbaud, the poem-experience has first of all authenticity as an experience of the imagination: the words are used to give it reality as such, to make it real *as such.* There is an ulterior objective of establishing an equivalence between the poem as an event or occasion or experience in the realm of the imagination and as a life event or occasion or experience. But the intensity of expended, and induced, excitement is of a poetic, rather than dramatic, emotionality. The action—what the poet is doing in saying his poetic say—is not an as-it-were real-life episode in the dramatic raw of representation: there is poetic refinement in the "doing" aspect of the saying.

W. C. Williams illustrates the concentration of poet-interest, and excited reader-interest, in *manner.* He tried to generalize the poetic manner of saying, in a distinction both absolute and simple from the prose manner. There is an effect of efficiency of statement, of a spontaneity uniting emotional and intellectual involvement in statement, that makes the poet ever pleased with himself: the poet's mood is uniform, it is "poetic." And other poets take excitement from the demonstration of what seems a basic *simplicity* in the nature of poetry: that there need be no technical problems, that there is but one poetic technique, and that is poetry itself. And readers can be at continual ease. The reading experience is like that of a guided tour. The poet takes them from one poetic exhibit to another, in a wonderland of surprises; but it is a comfortable wonderland, the surprises are easy to bear, short of shock-producing, just episodically stimulative, reminding of their having the identity "poetry."

# To A Friend on Edward Thomas— and Robert Frost—and Barnes—and John Clare

. . . There is in his poems as a poking into rural nature with a stick (walking-stick?) of sensitivity—and this turns up, out, little revelations, and the tongue becomes eloquent, but the eloquence is limited in its reaches (hardly transferable to nature in the large, that is, the natural Entirety that is "there" for sensitivity). . . . What have we then but a sadness noted that, though having the virtue of unpretentiousness, a personal attractiveness as such, does not have the virtue of fresh bravery of vision—of sensitivity loosed for enlargement of the perception-possibilities? Robert Frost as it were poked about with his stick with mind on eloquence first, the turnings-up with it, secondary, incidental to a pre-existing will-to-eloquence . . . bold, to begin with, rather than bravery-nursing; and, I think, bold rather than brave, to end with.

As to Barnes—who appears in modern literary poetic reference as a revolutionary, anti-traditional, position-taking mention.—Also, John Clare appears, in this "different" position-taking. What can be said of him (Barnes) in relation to the broad matter of poetic function? We have here a recluse poetry—made safe within philological borders—which exerts an attraction as "fresh." The Hardy connection, his interest in Barnes, prompts a special turn of look on Hardy, another recluse vein of poetry: he retired in the poem as to a privacy of "honesty"—thinking which, I believe that the content of the private self-examination matters much less than at first seems, when one moves to evaluate the thought-trend—the essence is the posture of mind naked to self, withdrawn from public exhibition (which of course, it is not!).

## On Burns, and Clare (from a letter)

. . . I think appreciation of Burns's (touching) directness of word-style and Clare's (disturbingly unresolved) simple elevatedness can run dangers of over-attribution of satisfactoriness. The comfort given down those lanes cannot last long. The lanes are short. . . . The maximum of satisfaction in the poems of John Clare, where the interest is better than that of competitive appetite for literary learnedness, I judge to be in a sympathetic, and humanely sad, sense of the kind of desperation of expectancy excited by the fact of poetry that Clare exemplifies, with a special quality of innocent resignedness before some innocently intelligent apprehension of disappointments implicit in the nature of poetry. For the extent to which I may be wrong, somewhere, in this picturing of the case of Clare, I have, I think it quite possible, provided terms for the findable flaws in the accuracy of my representation.

## On Coleridge (to a friend, December 1964)

He had a tragic massiveness of personal reality hardly matched in the persons of other poets of the general tradition—which I take to come of an intuition of how little poetry did about how much. The sense of how much operated for him outside of poetic limits—but haunted him there. And he left it at that.

# On Vachel Lindsay, and Robert Frost
## (from a letter, August 20, 1967)

All the buoyant variety of diversity of interest that characterized Vachel Lindsay, in thought, work, personal emotions, ran bigheartedly into one stream, that of a unifying will for the good; but such a will can make for *sameness,* where it swirls much in its own exuberance, as it did in V. L., and does not become in continual actuality the good thing done, or said. (But he was heroically loyal to it). . . . So, especially in the light of your suggestion of the Pearson-Yale placement, will my husband be likely to be thinking, Is there anything special about these letters, enough to justify my offering them in formal presentation to this great collection? (Offerings to you do not have for him, or myself, a categorically formal shape.) To repeat: large thanks from us both for what and how you have written. . . . I'll report to you some time after we have returned—and my husband has looked again at what there is, and put his feelings to work, and I mine assistingly—what we have decided.

We were both rather surprised by your report of the Frost letter's figuring prominently in the exhibition current at the time of your writing, and thank you very much for telling us about this.[1] My husband could not help feeling a little pang, in thought of the personal letter's having so much public life, but in offering the letter to you he was acting by the feeling, not unaccompanied by personal pang, that the letter belonged to the public domain. And so, pang notwithstanding, we are glad the letter is in your care, for sharing! . . . There is truth in the letter we think that does not speak itself to most eyes; and perhaps one or the other or both may, one day, comment on what we see revealed in some of the things said in it, as kindred with some not commonly perceived aspects of Frost's nature. He was to my husband a loved

---

1. [The letter in question from Frost to Schuyler B. Jackson was likely the one found among L(R)J's papers in her typed transcription, beginning "Dear Schuyler, You mustn't be so hasty with the slow . . ." (undated, probably 1939 in response to SBJ's review in *Time,* May 15, 1939).]

friend. I did not know him personally. But there was that in him that disturbed my husband, and myself separately . . . and we have done some thoughtful notes-comparing, in these later years. (The Frost letter contains a reference to an expression of this disturbedness of my husband in Frost's regard.) I am reminded of what I have just said of Lindsay. In Frost there is no such sameness found. He did not live in the solitude of a will for the good but liked to enrich his will for good with an animation of will that had no moral quality, being merely self-will not bent on, yet not committed against, mischief; the energetic thing done or said became thus equated with the good thing done or said. . . . This pragmatism excites, I think, rather than inspires. Please, let this talk of Frost I have subjected you to be as a mere postscript overflowing from our own interest in the letter, and Frost. . . .

## On Robert Frost (from a letter)

Frost had the American conscience—conscience in a state of freedom, not old-world guilt. And that went to many people's consciences, and to their hearts at the same time. There was, however, a quirk in all Frost's conscience-workings; it had a charm for people, without their seeing what it was. Frost had a mischief-streak in him. And I don't mean mere mischievousness. . . . He liked turning things from the line of truth into lines of self-will— and presenting these as lines of truth. What about conscience? He kept it beside him as a companion—was *very* friendly with it, sort of talked it into continual agreement with him. . . .

Now, Robert Frost I rate as a mischievous person, whose mischief has serious aspects because he chose mischief from a vantage that he liked to think was the vantage of spiritual conscience—identifying mischief with the necessary moral independence of the individual. He had always first to turn his back on something in order to stiffen his confidence in himself— which amounted, in the matter of truth, to the stand that the only way to speak truth was to turn your back on truth as the official guardian-spirit of everyone's virtue, and say your say: *that* was truth. Well, this indomitable will of his took him from here where he started to just there—and it wasn't very far from where he started, but he moved with the proud air of one who does what he does all on his own—and it had a certain fetchingness. For many kinds of audience it made a thrill: there goes a man who defers to no one, makes his own standards of good and evil. It didn't, when it was all said by him, amount to much, but right or wrong, it was his contribution. People had to take it. He seemed not to care whether they did or didn't. But he made it attractive with that pride of moral independence: they took it.

# To A Friend—a University Teacher of English—As To Eliot, Pound, Yeats

. . . As to Eliot, once again. I do not think anyone is going correctly to estimate Eliot within the favored enclave of literary evaluations. Such comparisons as "Cowley" could, in my judgement of Eliot (of anyone, for that matter, of literary identity), not take in the whole human performance, the whole performing being. For me they are not relevant to what's amiss. This holds with me for Yeats, very much. He was a much more elegant performer, with a spontaneously present ability to strike varying poetic poses. For me, the personal actuality breaks through the literary costumery, with—well, with them all. Pound I consider humanly more respectable than Eliot, he had a natural human energy of experimentation, proceeding from a desire to strike poses that had some practical sense in them, changing them, much, indeed, even within a single poem; he sought, in this and that, some sort of sense that would "do." I dislike it all, but he is more likable than Eliot, suffered more genuinely, about "how things were" in literature and elsewhere, though he cheapened his sensitivity, his discomforts, with privately concocted, quack, cures. . . .

# To Another University Teacher,
# On Eliot, Pound

I cannot share your wistfulness as to Eliot. I am deeply serious in a view of Eliot as an underminer of the potentiality of this time of fresh moral sensibility. I don't think him wicked, as I do Joyce, in this respect, but a moral fool who tried to borrow wisdom to make a whole of himself. Pound, healthier, but bent on mischief. The proponent of the anti-serious, as a modern solution, but with some unfoolish propensities in the direction of human self-preservation (in which figured his economics-preoccupation, and his idea of plundering the literature of the past so that certain faculties might have some "healthy" exercise in literary making play with them). That these—for instance—are *taught* (these three) in our institutions of education as helpful elements of knowledge possessing inherent human worth, I view as contributory to the condition of spiritual impotence with which the time is affected—where there should be what is educationally restorative. . . .

I can't know, or imagine, just what troubled your students about "Hugh Selwyn Mauberley," I can only estimate what the cause of its disconcertingness for me would be if I had to attend closely to it. What Pound's reading of it would do I can only guess at in terms of questions as to his powers of putting on a show. For, I think he had the sincerity of an actor, could mean a part while he played it. But in this poem there are so many parts to play—the open speaking autobiographical part, the teasing obscurantist, the "radical" critic of "civilization," passionate anti-war cynic, elegant literary wit—but I am tiresome. . . . I think it would be found that his poems were so made that wilful carelessnesses, occurring amidst the elegancies, were the protection from the vulgar crime (he would feel the potentiality of it himself) of insincerity: how can you accuse him of slumping from sincerity when he fails to sustain a vein of "good," when he, plainly, slumps deliberately? But, I think the habit took its toll. You can find him trapped in insincerity.

See the poem about Whitman.[2] Examine the tree-figure carefully—the *carving*, together with the root-sap aspects. It's a *mess*—and an unintended one.

# Robert Lowell
## (Written Before He Died)

The question, what, if anything, is there to say about the poems-production of Robert Lowell, has insinuated itself at times into my field of consciousness of poetry as, in the contemporary production of it, yielding a large portion of the literary news of the day. There is conspicuously much of Robert Lowell in this news. His poetic turn-out is a flow of formalized loquacity. Each example suggests that no one doubt that there will be more, and more, and that in the immediate instance the reader settle comfortably into enjoyment of the privilege of the experience of being the confidant of a mind that has disciplined itself to think with public poetic effect on all sorts of subjects, general and personal.

Having habitually brushed aside the question, what if anything is there to say about the poems-production of Robert Lowell, I find myself now, the question once again pressing its way to the attention of my conscience by the irregular routine of chance, at a point of consummate weariness with it: I shall either, now, say something, deciding that there is something to say, or, deciding that there is nothing to say, say that. The issue of my final facing of the question seems likely to be, a something amounting to nothing. For the sense of it is that the poems-production of Robert Lowell amounts, in the scales of word-value, to nothing.

Robert Lowell's use of words for poems-production requires to be judged as disquisition for which a poetical posture of delivery is assumed. The results are not poems except by imitative adoption of the poetic convention of profuse allowance for

---

2. ["A Pact."]

delivery-pauses, so that the results be rhetorically identifiable as poems. The particular production-result does not follow from concentration on an internal experience of consciousness as something worthy of an effort to put it, precisely it, in its interior realness, into words—words that are faithful to its interior quality. The Lowell model for the poem is an adaptation of the traditional model: the person inwardly moved, in the experience of consciousness, to spell out the mind's very movement in honest effort to give to self-revelation a value of actual, general, revelation—to make self-revelation *true*. Other poets of the inward course of poetry in the twentieth century have increasingly *used* poetry as a form of autobiographical pronouncement, in which, supposedly, more of the intimate life of the autobiographer is containable than in the conventional frame of autobiographical self-disclosure. Lowell stands out among them all as possessed of a delivery-poise, a self-assurance, over and above anything provided in the traditional poetic paraphernalia of precedents in positions-from-which-to-speak-as-a-poet. They have all been engaged in this new personal-platform modern poetic post-modernism, but *he* engages in it as to the public-speaker's manner born: unembarrassed, however personal the mood of confidentiality, the content of intimate thought and feeling attending the experiences selected as autobiographically poetry-worthy, he brazens critical challenge of every sort. Nothing disturbs his aplomb: he *starts* with this. He has made himself be there, above criticism, as country-music has made itself be there, by sheer force of performer self-confidence.

He has "got by" with this spacious personalism as "poetry" because everyone else taking the name of poet has been doing exactly the same thing—but without striking the notes of absolute imperturbability in the rôle of poet-autobiographer that carry his performances through to their finales of candor, their impressiveness as such drowning the actuality of the worthlessness of the material of candor.

> . . . Now, heart's ease and wormwood,
> We rest from all discussion, drinking, smoking,
> pills for high blood, three pairs of glasses—soaking
> in the sweat of our hard-earned supremacy,

offering a child our leathery love. We're fifty,
and free! . . .
. . . once, we wanted nothing, but to be old, do nothing,
type and think.[3]

In a concentration of human, literary and personal effrontery
he likened John Berryman—who boasted desperation rather
than imperturbability in his use of poetry as *the* autobiographical medium—to himself: "We both used the language as if we
made it." I leave Berryman out of this question. No one can use
the language as if he made it: what he does in treating it as his
creation is to make what is a common possession an instrument
of *vanity*. He gives not a damn about *the* language: himself is his
literary cause. In all public performance, the element of vanity
is purged by the generosity of the performing impulse, or it is
the heart, secret or open, of the performance, holding an appeal of flattery for the audience, the performer's vanity teasing
the audience's proclivities to self-kindness, self-congratulation.

Everybody "in" poetry, in the twentieth-century progression,
is doing it: the business of vanity, treated as poetry's new base of
operations. Critics are found, of course, comparing this poet
with that poet, favoring the one over the other as exhibiting a
"unity of vision" not forcefully present in the other. But emptiness of faith in poetry as having embodied something of the
faith of humanity in itself is in thin-disguise everywhere in the
continuing solemnities of literary criticism, formal and informal
(the reviewing area of literary criticism). The prevalence of vanity as the poet-posture developed in the twentieth century into a
norm for poetic literary performance needs to be seen in its
connection with the development in the general human environment of all literary performance of the individual self as the
universal cause—the focal point of professedly collective human
concern. In the total context of contemporary human existence
and activity, such a work of poetic performance as Robert Lowell's is a phenomenon of the dissipation of moral sensibility—
in its making, and in its standing as something intellectually,
literarily, and, even, spiritually, notable. There exists within the

---

3. ["A Lowell Sonnet" was published in *Time*, June 6, 1969.]

borders of the literary world no aggregation of forces of judgement in which critical and moral sensibility unite for the reminding of the populations of that world—and, by extension to the human world-at-large of sincerities excited there, for the reminding of humanity-at-large in its unlimited aliveness—that human beings are not creatures unto themselves except by self-depravement . . . : but can a major moral responsibility be placed on literary-world procedures, productions, operations?

Where is responsibility? Is any human being excusable or self-excusable from it? Is Robert Lowell, or any other literary notable, relieved of guilt by the intensity of his preoccupation with himself as a literary subject? To what is this devotion? Not to poetry, not to literature, not to all the others *en masse* or any particular ones individually, and not to any conceived-of spirit of reality found difficult to define in human terms—not to anything in the specifiable or in the abstract. It is—how else is it describable?—devotion to non-devotion. It is a putting of emptiness where the complex courses of being have put something nameable human. In my book of responsibility, language is both the essence and instrument for the articulation of being's truth, given into human charge, and the worst defections and defectors are, necessarily, of literary-world location. That world accepted, assumed, the mission, on the general behalf, of nurturing the *generous,* in human endowedness with language.

# V
# From Letters of Mine
# on Poetry

## To An Anthology Editor, to a previous anthology of whose I had contributed: explaining my special reluctance of the time to contribute to anthologies, May 1948

. . . believing then [1938] that in poems one could speak with more truth than in one's ordinary speech. I now regard the poem as a relic of past ages, with functions congruous with the social organization of their times, but now socially {and otherwise} incongruous. Each poet adapts the antique device to his personal end of lending importance to his personal say-so. {And facility in the use of the device is one criterion of importance— one's say-so is, in the first place, subject to constrictions implicit in the use of the device.} This is how the activity of writing poems now looks to me, after nine years of my not writing poems. I still believe that there is a deficiency of truth in all our ordinary speech. How that deficiency can be removed in it is now my concern. It is not to perform a personal miracle {by poetic means} of true statement, as it once was.

## To The British National Book League's Poetry Circle, 1954

{*To be noted: I speak in my statement only of the non-rational element in poetry, not of the craft-impositions it involves.*}
{I speak of having come to perceive that} the poetic use of

words attains some of its effects of expressiveness by an intensive play with irrationalities . . . that it involves exploitation of the possibilities of irrational uses of language to an extent larger than is allowable in ordinary use. Irrationality is more difficult to detect in poetry than in ordinary speech because poets tend to make free with the laws of word-meaning and so present what can seem to be a sense of the status of a "higher sense" governed by laws of their own. In this rupture with ordinary sense, the common laws of meaning, a spurious semblance of verbal success can be achieved—damaging to all who succumb to it, since it obscures the fact that there can be no true verbal success except that of perfect rationality, arrived at through observance of the standards of truth implicit in language. The theory of special standards of expression peculiar to poetry as the loftiest region of language on which poets so much lean is itself a rupture with the principle of common faith in a common language, by which alone a language can be made to work successfully.

# To A Literary Agent,
## also a friend, 1962

For I think we human beings are, all, imprisoned in a way of speaking to one another that is only part-truthful; and that poetry actually obstructs comprehension of this by seeming to free the spirit for a time from the prison-walls of the ordinary way of speaking, of using words. Even those who have little or nothing to do with poetry are affected by its presence in their environment, as I see these things; poetry either makes the ideal of an all-truthful, perfect way of speaking—of using words—seem to them something attainable only by a few, and through a peculiar talent, or it makes them disbelieve in the good sense of such an ideal. Seeing these things, I feel it my human duty to communicate my view as I fittingly can.

# To A Poet, writing to me on poetry,
## May 9, 1962

You ask, "*In what form shall we write in the style of truth?*"[1] First, I'd like to say: do not stress the word "write"—though, because of the studied effort that will be required to learn how to use words by a style of truth, the way will have to be felt out initially in written address. The form? Whatever form the words cast themselves into as you proceed in using them with perfect, or as near to perfect as you can make it, devotion to them as your guardians, your teachers, even, in how to speak true (devotion to the words in their capacity as language, as having in them the spirit that urges speech of eternal virtue). But trust in the counsels of your language. . . . There is little if anything towards which humility is a fitting human posture in a spiritual sense, a final sense—an old feeling of mine!; but I can by a tight stretch view it as a fitting one towards words (language)—these spiritual elders to our speaking life. So much for the attitude. The technique lies in using all one knows of (the) language for truth of speech, and in keeping one's knowledge of it in ever-fresh, ever-active state. (Not just assuming you know the meanings of words: *know* them. . . .) But when you say "In what form shall we write in the style of truth?" you have largely if not entirely in mind categories of literary prose—which, with poetry ruled out, seem then to constitute the total field for writing. If you go on thinking like that (you or anyone) you'll remain perpetually gripped with nostalgia for poetry. What I was talking about was not a literary style categorically, just a *constant* of human manner of utterance everything other than which is unworthy of us as human. . . . Now it is impossible to reject for the attempt at purely true speaking something in the form of a novel or play in the way in which I reject poetry—not just bad poetry, but the best. . . . With poetry, I am rejecting the poetic style of word use. A thing is not a novel or a play, as against being a piece of poetry. It is a novel or a play as against being an

---

1. [A reference to "Introduction for a Broadcast," as is "whorl of artifice" in the next extract. See also "Poetry and the Good," *Reader,* 211.]

actual record of live communication between people involved in a certain suite of actual circumstances and events. You or anyone else would just have to get the prime matter right, attain to grasp of what the use of words with perfect truth involved, before judgement could be formed as to what effect this achievement—as one generally achievable—had on the validity of the novel or play.

## Further to the Same, July 18, 1962, and February 28, 1963

Your comments . . . seem to me to presume that poetry has claims on us that bind us to try to reconstitute it, however seriously wanting in the capability of truth we may eventually see it to be. I myself recognize no such claims, no self-evident reason why poetry ought to be perpetuated, no justification for its existence in its mere being poetry . . . my position is that it is time that we all moved out of the poetic linguistic limbo. . . . There is so much prestige of spiritual and linguistic distinction attached to it {poetry} and so little habitude of vesting natural (as distinguished from artistic) grace of word with the highest importance, that to liquidate poetry must seem to take away a spiritual birthright. This I hold to be an illusion.

The distortion, the whorl of artifice, I judge to be fundamental to poetry. Remove it, and you do not have poetry. Speak true: then there is no need of poetry in which enchanting physical effects have first importance.

I will repeat here that I believe I went to the extreme possibility in poetry—one always of a vanishing verge of truth: that no further degree of advance is possible in it. . . . What do I owe to poetry that, if I should succeed in using words with truth consistently, I ought to tag the achievement with the name of poetry? What do we all owe poetry that, if we should succeed in speaking consistently with one another in the style of truth, we must drag the name of poetry into this vindication of our tongues' and souls' honor? What is there left to call poetry, if we seek only to speak true? What is it that is sacrificed if we do only that?

. . . in making a poem a person is obliged by the nature of poetry to concentrate on ensuring that it shall "hold" its audience (on trying so to ensure)—hold it not as with an ordinary piece of composition, by means of exciting and keeping *interest,* merely, but in the sense of fascination, of binding it with words, of fixing it with a certain *power* exerted through physicalities of utterance and impression even as people may be fixed with power excited through glances of eye and accompanying of face and body directed at them. . . . {There is} *another* {power}, the power of letting and making one's words take (with no forcing them into customary deviations and with entire direction of them away from those) the course of truth. . . . The two powers come into conjunction in poetry, the first seeming to hold out compensation for the failure to exercise the second substantially: (. . . in some cases, of poets, the first is the main reason for the assumption of the poetic rôle—sometimes, even, the only.)

# To A Friend (poet, writer),
# September 15, 1962

When I was still hopeful of poetry's yielding us our truth as had *nothing else,* I saw well, I think, too, what this and that poet did and misdid. Wherever I saw virtue of utterance (I did not see it in many places—but, even so, in too many!) but not enough (enough, I never saw), I wished, fretting, hoping, for more, a something poetry might yet yield us. Now, in poetic writing, I see such virtue—be it to some degree there—as wasted, self-frustrated, only, expended to no good: there is no question for me of genuine success of human utterance in poetry. And the waste, in failure, makes no literary story for me, but is directly a story of human loss, loss to us directly. Thus, I am struck by the absence of poets from the scene of encounter with ourselves at our humanest: they are the most absent, because they are using their (perhaps naturally very good) utterance-powers in dramas of self-communication, self-enactment, self-celebration, proffered as instances of essential human expressiveness. But *that* (that expressiveness) is only in the direction of one another, not in the poetic direction, which can only be the direction of a single person taking the stage from one-another.

# To A Friend, 1962

. . . I ceased to write poems, but that cessation had living point, and I went on, devoting myself to the problem of truth of utterance, for the poetic *solution* of which I had intently sought, in the poetic solvability of which I came to disbelieve.

# To A Friend, November 8, 1962

My attitude to poetry, and my poems, is not anti-poetry fanaticism. It is incidental to views as to language generally, and human self-expression generally and to work and purposes of mine in this respect.

# From Letters to Robert Nye, 1962

. . . the poetic fraction, an immensity divided by partiality.

. . . an impulsion to speak with truth and a compulsion to write poetry.

I do not ask you to reject my poems. I regard them as anticipating truth within the pleasance of poetry. They stop where they are stopped—at the walls of the pleasance. If you have indeed followed them, they will help you find a way out of the pleasance, and themselves. They have a stronger loyalty to truth within them than either to poetry or to themselves.

I am in no competition with my self of the poems. I am concerned with all our life, not the "life" of my poems, or of my subsequent utterances—not with such mortal immortality.

I am no despiser of poems-writing, am in no posture of regret towards the chances of my poems' being kept in the museum of time; I am not sobered into awe of my poems by the consideration that they might join those of the lusty blabberer {Shakespeare} in the literary *Remains*.

I am, above everything else, as I always was, interested in that first page which is not the page before the first page.[2] Everything written on that page is going to seem very dull, for quite a while: it will be quite a while before we turn *that* page.

As poetry kept falling short, and more and more I sought in it more of the means of saying-True, I drew from me a greater and greater kindness for it, which could not but be a kindness to much of human defect in it.

# From A Letter to Robert Nye, October 31, 1962 or 63

Poetry belongs to literature only because it fails to be anything else. Its erraticness to literature does not take it any further than off-centeredness to it. I touched on this category-matter in the *Chelsea* 12 writings. . . . Instead of thinking of what you do in writing poems, endeavor to see what it is that poets are doing. For one is bound to overcredit to the process the element of one's own poet-functioning that is active before there is a poem—before the manipulations of format are undertaken, before the persuasion techniques, and those of creating

---

2. [A reference to "Poet: A Lying Word"; see *The Poems of Laura Riding*, (2001), 238; (1980), 218.]

an occasion in which to bind others physically into the desire-to-speak possessing one, go to work. See them, the poets, and yourself, as one of them, together, as doing something the same; and you may come to identify in yourself where you are pure in word-motive and not yet officially poet-pure (actually, of qualified purity in motive, and result). I recommend to you again and again my notion of the hybridness of the poetic process. Mixed with the good *why* are, corrupting it with the very first words of the actual poem, a number of other *why's* not of the order of the good one. (The combination of why's varies considerably—and, of course, in many cases of poetry there is no initial good *why*.) {Then I speak of "the danger to a poet of self-idolatry—of poets' viewing themselves as achieving something miraculous in the writing of the poem . . . how this is induced by a self-hypnotic rapture with the hypnotic (for others) physicalities of the poem. . . ."}

# From A Letter to A Poet, December 27, 1962

. . . My concern is not at all with the poet as distinct from others. . . . I have no special tears for them {poets}, rather a feeling that they have built up a debt. . . .

My concern is with all, and how we all speak; that a true way be found, and held to, so that we may deliver to one another the full reality of being that is encompassed in our humanity.

. . . The renouncing I mean (by poets of poetry) is something done in the service of truth as an envisaged universal practice. I see poets who have become aware of the impossibility of going beyond the short-of-truth limit in poetry, and through poetry, as peculiarly fit to become, by self-training, good examples to others in the use of words. They are people, such renouncers, with a capability of exercising linguistic sensibilities of truth with patience in the intricacies of utterance—if, that is, they had, to begin with, the intuition of the taste, the smell, the clean-sharp edge, of truth.

. . . Myself, I aimed early at a point at which poetry should pass into sheer truth-speaking. And when I reached that point, that "should"-point, having been conscious all the way, I found the envisaged miracle to be but the old poetic miracle that consumed itself, had no aftermath. And so I had to look for a point of departure for truth-speaking on natural speaking-ground.

{I then touch on} ideals of life-redeeming utterance (my governing ideals in my poems, and what I have after them done) in dedication to which there can be no partnership except with perfectness.

# From A Letter [to a librarian], July 4, 1965

My pursuit of poetry, to which all my thinking became centered, was a very serious one. In my fortieth year, after the publication of my *Collected Poems*, that seriousness itself began making a new light in my thinking, and showing me poetry in that light; and for many years thereafter, and especially in relation to the problem of unifying the practical and the spiritual functions of language, which I believe I discovered to be an impossibility in poetry while coming very close there to the feel of a solution, I wished to steady the new light, and extend the field of its shining. My older and my newer thinking are not at basic odds, but the difference is—I consider—of crucial importance, and this not for the understanding of the two parts of my working and spiritual course but for the general capability of human beings of understanding some further things about themselves. Part of this contribution is necessarily in the form of new writing, some of which is being done in collaboration with my husband, that I am doing my utmost, under certain strains of circumstances, to accomplish. Part of it must consist of commentary of now that points up differences between my stand of then and my stand of now. I feel solemnly about this responsibility; my desire is to have everything of my former writing furnished, eventually, with some commentary that may be of use in this sense.

# To An American Publisher who wanted to republish my *Collected Poems*, on what I should want to say in my preface, 1965

*(When my preface was written, his poet-critic adviser recommended rejection of it and engaging someone else to write the preface. After I had rejected this proposal, a University Press asked to republish the book; here, my preface was rejected on the recommendation of a group of poet-advisers, and that closed the matter.)[3]*

. . . I shall write as one who attempted to make devotion to poetry and devotion to truth a linguistically successful unity, and one who regards the discovery of the impossibility of that as a disproof of the serious validity of *all* poetry.

I suppressed my poems as I could, so important to me was the question of the nature of poetry, on which I meant to have new things to say. I did not want my poems to circulate against the background of the going view of poetry, without my revised view of it in the picture.

---

3. [The prospective publishers were Holt, Rinehart, and Winston; and Wesleyan University Press.]

# Poets are ineffectual people. . . ,
## August 20, 1965 [? or 1969]

Poets are ineffectual people . . . they are, as it were, symbols only of effectual (fully so) human utterance. Morally committed, they are morally inert because they are not committed to a real, only to a symbolic objective. What happens if they become aware of this? What can happen? This depends on how ingenuous they were initially. The more ingenuous may be presumed to be there (in poetry) for a good reason; and the first people who directly, unsymbolically, unreservedly, attempt true speaking in the whole (speaking in which the Good is made live!), may well be poets rededicated, become something more "real" as believers in words.—I mean effectual word-use, use of words that will work at every point, in all its parts, and in the sum, as truth.

# To A Friend, December 14, 1971

. . . What I did, rather than "fall silent," was to withdraw into private labors of study involving basic problems of language as involving the all-basic matter of truth.

# To A Poet, Friend, 1974

{In reply to comment on my renouncing poetry}. . . I did not renounce it as inadequate to my purpose. In being a poet I had not a special personal purpose that poetry failed to satisfy. I believe I was a poet to the full. Having succeeded in being that, I learned the inadequacy of poetry to the need and hope of fullness of words from which the human speaking genius rises, and to which human lenity recommended the linguistic lenities, the kindness of utterance to which words could be bent, that were compounded into poetry to give the feel of truth. And you think *that* is the end of it all? Of course you do—with many others.

And, of course, I don't—and without many others by (indeed, I can say quite without others by, except one). I do not think you set *your* sights too low—I think you set the general human sights at a lenity-level that for long, long, human capability (of knowing and saying) has been, in somewhat stupefied state, transcending. There is a point of actual attainment of recognition of the human expressive capability that has been progressively put out of reach, from dogged loyalty to the lenities, as perennial means of kindness to ourselves in this endless piecemeal achievement, the whole dismissed unattempted as too hard for the likes of these mere ourselves. That "too hard" is the fiction that makes the lenities our reality-experience limit. What is all this "mere ourselves," this "mere insights," this "mere language"? (You say "any linguistic vehicle"—why "vehicle," why besides language do we have to have "linguistic vehicles"?) Poetry is only a prepared, given, atmosphere for utterances under a certain commitment of dedication, in which there are certain contradictions. How much is this position one of disbelief in better, wholler, less mereish, and how much fear of it? This is not aimed for response. You have set your boots into the soil of my thinking and finding on poetry, and some dust is kicked up! I mean no unhospitality to you, treading there, I have made the ground open.—And it is dust of acknowledging the visits—not quarrel-stir.

# (Further)

. . . Perhaps I ought to remind you that for me, for quite long now, there is no pure character, for a poem, of ultimate value, intrinsic totality of virtue. The value, the virtue, is in a hope-vision, as to what may be done with words, that had a sort of foster-home in poetry. I am concerned in this later time, by my experience of identification of poetry as something other than the natural scene of the vision, with trying to be and show where the vision *takes* (not where one "puts up" in having it), and the home of the ultimate in word-virtue is.

# To A Programme Associate, 1975

I thank you for your letter to me of October 1st, and the copies of *Coda* sent, and the green form accompanying your letter, and the little booklets tucked in with all this.

It is indeed a fact that I have made a very serious, besides considerable, contribution to the store of American poetry. But while I was working as a poet—which I ceased doing at the beginning of the 'forties—I was, with some exceptions, rather meanly received as a poet; and for various reasons resembling and somewhat differing from the earlier trend, the mainly mean disposition to my poetic work has continued constant. My other work, however, has not been differently received, to any marked extent, in earlier or later time. For any who are moved to do my poetic work some honor, a difficulty has to be faced. As I have noted on the green sheet, I renounced poetry, very seriously— feeling I had done the utmost within what I found, as a devotee of language, and a devotee of poetry, esteeming it as the mode by which the full of language's boon could be realized, to be limitations to that full imposed by some of the features of poetry's nature. I have since preoccupied myself with studying the potentialities of that full provided directly by language itself. The little *Selected Poems* that I name on the green sheet has a Preface in which I rather briefly set forth this principle. I have written on this matter for magazines; I have long been at work on a book about poetry. . . .

My general contemporary status is that of writer who has a substantial record as a poet, but who *is* not in any practising sense a poet: I have not—and this from choice—composed a poem since the close of the 'thirties, and published none of any later date of composition than 1938.[4] All my poetic work is in the name of Laura Riding. I do not use that name in these later years except in connection with work that was published under

---

4. [L(R)J did in fact subsequently go on to compose six post-renunciation poems, two of which are included in this book in the form of an appendix.]

that name. My later authorial name is "Laura (Riding) Jackson."
The 1970 *Selected Poems* (London: Faber, 1970; New York: Norton, 1973 [reissued, New York: Persea, 1993]) has the authorial
name "Laura Riding." My book *The Telling* (London: Athlone
Press, 1972; New York: Harper & Row, 1973 [Manchester: Carcanet Press, 2005]) has the name "Laura (Riding) Jackson."
(The latter, of course, is not poetic work.)

I am, thus, a rather moot item of writership for your listing.
I am not an "enemy" of poets, or poetry. I believe very solidly,
however, that the human way to go of truth gets stalled in
poetry; and that capability of successful exercise of it is in
discovery of what language allows of within its implicit and explicit provisions.

# [From] Comments on a study
# of my work, [1975]

. . . I did not renounce it [poetry] as the "best method of truth-telling," but as failing to yield what it implied as to itself, that it
was a way of using words having a larger potential of truth than
the prevailing ordinary modes of word-use, including other literary modes. . . .

. . . The poet-performance has got to be a non-incidental
quite big linguistic performance. But the conditions of categorically poetic utterance, the peculiar conditions, reduce the
large-spirited address (what should be large-spirited address)
painfully. Don't go rubbing poetry's nose so much in the dirt. *I*
never have done that. I never thought of poetry as an "art" in
any but accidental use of the term art in some special kind of
reference. . . . What I found was not a discorrespondence between truth and art, but that the art element of poetry (which
for any serious poet is not "art" of concept-resemblance to the
material arts, but certain kinds of instrumentalities for delivery-effectiveness) defeated over and over the full truth-potential of
poetry. . . .

# To Someone who has written to me on the difficulty of getting into the mood to "create" a poem, but rejecting this as, properly, no obstacle: there should be no waiting for "moods," 1976

. . . As to "creating" poems: what are they, at the *best,* but an effort to give express reality, in full degree of expressness, to what is felt to be a true experience of consciousness? The effort commits itself to forms of expression of very much qualified truth-potency: the forms of poetry itself are conditioned by commitment to the use of mannerisms of utterance limited to poetic utterance not by reason of their possessing a peculiar truth-potency, but by reason of an actual limitation in poetic utterance of degree of truth-potency. One accepts, in the effort of composing a poem, a struggle between the necessity of commitment to the mannerisms and a desire to succeed in expression beyond the imposed poetic limit in expressiveness. I think the hankering for a "mood" is related to a wish for a persuasion of capability of success in expression beyond the strictures of poetic technique.

The idea that there should be no waiting for moods has, I think, some relation to a reservation, quite common among poets, as I judge, by which the poet allows himself, herself, an informal, common-sense, view of the work of composing a poem as in the actual process no elegant affair, as rather, an operation a good deal mechanical. Even, I consider it presumable that there is an element of contempt of the operation in the attitude of many a poet to it, and an accompanying self-contempt in the poet as the conductor of the operation. I think this analysis is supported by the very large factor of career-realisticness that so many poets evince, in incongruous collaboration with the idealistic dedicatedness to the course of poetry and the solemn office of being a poet, requisite for a poet's being taken seriously, professionally, as such.

{I closed my response with a summary of the "point" of my writing in this way on poetry.}

. . . It is to rear up the actuality of an unconquerable in the task that a person sets himself, herself, in undertaking to compose a poem. An impossibility is undertaken *if* one is a seriously responsible user of words. And therefore, every resultant poem, in substituting a possible in the chosen mode of expression for what proves impossible in that mode, negates the poetry-animating poetic ideal.

{I append to this generally expanded reply-comment a comment I shall be making in a reply to a newly received word from a poet on the effect on her of the reading of my preface to my *Selected Poems: In Five Sets.* She described herself as so thoroughly affected by what I said there on the peculiarities and limitations of poetry that for a period (not *very* long) she halted in her poems-writing. It is part of the emotional, intellectual, spiritual and linguistic, accommodation to it that poetry enforces that there will seem to be *nothing to do,* of the rank of highest word-virtue that poetry has by uninterrupted traditional ascription, except what can be done under its seal of ideal authority. That poetry's ideal virtuous something-to-do in words obstructs vision of language's real all-to-do, of the virtuous in words, no one practised in the poetic word-mode will allow himself, herself, to believe for more than a brief period (if at all) except as the taste of truth has become a hauntingly irresistible longing on a tongue long minded to know the taste of it in poetic utterance.}

# To A Poet who has thought I might cooperate in a project devoted to poetry, October 1976

. . . I am unqualifiedly dedicated to illuminating the immediate necessity of new knowing of language, for such use of words by human beings as will release them from their present declining hold on the principles of their being. This including for me their graduating from the devices of poetry which I consider to have reached its limit as an area in which a certain kind of effort kept itself alive. I regard, I see, the continuing poetic writing-activity that is all round, in gross multiplication of past quantities in it, as exhibiting the deterioration in sense of the responsibilities of being, and speaking, to which I have here alluded. I have not written differently in my preface to *Selected Poems: In Five Sets,* or in *The Telling,* a book of which you have read. My response is no refusal, no rejection, of your proffering. What you envisaged, in the proffering, is at odds with the actualities of my present purposes, my firmly developed convictions, my belief in what must and must not be, the human point of being not losing itself.

# To A Poet, March 1977

As to the matter of "self-interestedness," the case is, to me, the difference between an objective of expression according to what words, at fullest use for their expressive capacity, allow, and endless variations in purpose to do "something" with words. This doing something with words makes the performance, in word-use, the center of the operation.

In the past, the "doing-something-with-words" condition of mind of the poem-composer could escape the worst of the semblance of self-centered performance by the choice of subject: the choice of certain subjects conferred on the poet the character of one interested in themes of a recognized common interest—a certain conventionalized intensity of general subject-appeal reduced the danger of personalistic vulgarity that has more and more haunted modern poetic production.

And I would not make self-interested a standard summarizing identification of what I found wrong in contemporary poems-production. It's a useful *clue.* The right is not "disinterested." It is interested in the what-the-words-do, by their expressive potency. The "master" character of it, if it is anywhere, is in *this.*

# To Someone, on my inappropriateness as a contributor to a magazine devoted to poetry, 1977

I thank you for the kind answering. I mean no tit for tat in pointing to a misunderstanding of yours, in what you have written of descriptions of my feelings about poetry as correspondent with feelings of yours that poetry had got too mixed up with "fashion." I have not written anything of that sort, nor do I hold any view as to a right kind of poetry not markedly mixed up with fashion, and a wrong kind as thus mixed up with it. My view of poetry has been, from very early in the 'forties, when I renounced poetry, the writing of poetry, that it, when taken to its limits of the linguistic possibilities allowed of within them, fails to meet the premise of principle on which it rests of potentialities of fulfilment in it of perfect truth of utterance. It can satisfy the hope-instinct of this that language itself excites, in its occasions, but the reality of fulfilment lies in straight full address to language's facilities of provision responsive to the purpose of truth as the human natural, the proper general expressive norm.—So, I can't see how I would fit in as a contributor. If you can't lay hands on something comprehensive of statement of mine on poetry (there is one in the preface to my *Selected Poems* published by Faber & Faber), Mr. Alan Clark could I think point you to something. He is working on a bibliography of my work, and knows it in detail very well. The difference between our views is of an order, understood, that would make you feel, I believe, very differently about my desirability as a contributor. As to subscribing: I don't seek out what is produced of poems in these times. I do see some. It is part of my view, and everything I see sustains this, that the poetic possibilities have been spent, and what has for a long time, now, been put forth, in the forms of poetry, is experimentation in the use of words for self-satisfaction as the linguistic ideal. That by which poetry endured for so long spiritually subscribed to a different satisfaction ideal.

I am sorry about the aspect of this encounter as missing the mark of personal agreement in feeling.

# On A Review in "Poetry Project Newsletter," May 21, 1983

Thank you, Theodore, for the copy of the St. Mark's *Poems* review. I may indeed have seen this (and by your kindness of sending me a copy—or, if not, the publisher's act). It has interested me to read it (again?). And I am setting down some notes on it—which you may care to see.

Nothing in my thinking gives "the word" identity as "power object." My conception of the ideal function of poetry was not to change the world but to fulfil the human function of speaking the universal sense of "things" or "existence."—I do not view my poems as having failed: they achieved, in my judgement, an utmost of the possible in poetry. I believe the failure is the failure of poetry.—My "language" is falsely understood if it is thought akin to that of Gertrude Stein, or that of Emily Dickinson. Emily Dickinson was an "ecstatic" user of words—using them for speaking from an uplifted position—the context always at some special remove. I do not monkey with the language as being of different levels of use. (Stein levelled the language to make all words nonentities—*she* the giant presiding Entity, in her use of them).— Sonia Raiziss, my good friend, was mistaken in her suggesting that my perception of truth lurks in paradoxes; that my poetry is mathematics-like.[5] Everywhere in them there is a putting finger, word, on the actuality of *much* almost meeting in all-clarifying union: this, not as caused by "the slippery nature of words," but by the problem of the resolution of the fact of materialities, and the disparity of materiality and materiality, into necessary evidence of an all-pervading general coherence, or "logic." The tension of perception of such inhering logic is not mathematical but spiritual: i.e., verbal.—The idea that in the work on language she "has found a better outlet" than in the work in the poetic field is a going-nowhere speculation. . . . The work on language began with her as a limited dictionary project, and developed into a busy—a broad and detailed—exploration of the nature of

---

5. ["An Appreciation," *Chelsea* 12 (September 1962).]

language and word-meaning. It is, simply, the mind's elementary need—where the mind is centered to the in-lodged human responsibility.—The description of my poetry as "brain poetry" is a reckless facileness.

# A Reply to Some Basic Questions Posed in Private Correspondence, December 24, 1984

I regard the contemporary human state, the state of human intelligence, as verging on total dissipation. Twentieth-century forms of identification—of the human intelligence itself, of the nature of life and of the universe—have run close to emptiness. Poetry, along with religion, used to have inhering in it a sense of fundamental connections, and of a human responsibility of eliciting them through the special capacities of human experience—the powers peculiar to the human life-constitution called "mind." Responsibility has been in these long twentieth-century times fractured into myriad self-created human identities, self-preening replacing the functions of mind, destroying mind (each one his or her own). I have not found, since I myself renounced the writing of poems, anything in the teeming production-field of modern, "post-modern," poetry that bears the mark of the sense of duty to the human factor in the universal constitution, and to that constitution, that was for long at least a *token* service of human beings to their extraordinary fortune of share in it.—The self-preening of which I speak reeks of the male fighting self-experimentalism. But women are induced to read "freedom" charters in this despoiling of the rarity of human nature in nature for the satisfactions of vanities of self-persuasive performances. "Great living poets"? The term is *robbed* from a tradition, a history, of solemnity of tribute-paying, a past sense of *possibility* of honest human generosity towards the generous human share in the universal constitution.—If I were able to, and were called on, to teach, in the field of literature and poetry, I would introduce my students to the work of

Charles M. Doughty, his poetic work, but also his *Arabia Deserta*, for learning how words might be known for their meanings, and used by what they mean by the rational honesty of the language to which they belong.—He renounced the Victorian English of his time, turned to what he believed would be a righter English. This would not be my recommendation. But one could learn from him to strip off the hideous garb of imitation-meaning that contemporary speaking, and writing, draws from its vocabularistic wardrobe-room.

# "My View Is Not Anti-Poetic"
# (From a letter to a friend who wrote to me in irritation—with some interpolated comment)

. . . My view is not anti-poetic but pro-linguistic, that is, concerned with the universal human expressive potential, not just with the expressive potential of a category of utterance (the poetic) conditioned by its professionalism, by being a pattern of the universal human expressive potential restricted to an area of verbal performance reserved from the general field of this potential. I have thought that those who, in being poets, became practised in the formal linguistic transcendence of the verbal ordinary that is poetry's gift to human life—as human speaking is a mixture of levels between the careless or hasty or the ineloquent, to the rare perfect rightness of word—might perceive a happy part to be played by them[selves], in the elevation of the general speaking level.

That there could be and should be a natural linguistic transcendence of poetry as a formal breaking away from the uneven, unsteady, ordinary speaking, ever-varying in degree of effectiveness of expression, poets ought to comprehend better than others—and sooner. That is, once question was raised, distinctly raised, of the incongruity of humankind's natural possession of language as a common facility of the mind and its failure to employ it sustainedly, uniformly, to the full of the powers, advantages, benefits, joys, its possession made accessible, how could poets, experienced in excitement with the anticipations of personal fulfilment that straining for right-wordedness in poetic performance yielded, not respond heartily to the conceived prospect of a general enlivenment of human beings with an aim of right-wordedness in all their performances of human address?

Against the possibility of a special enthusiasm for a cause of universal happy word-practice, in persons who have known the special straining for right-wordedness of poetic practice, is the failing in poets, in this century's course, of the energies of linguistic sensibility (there's little energetic concern with right-wordedness *within* the frame of poetic word-use itself). Also on the other side of possibility is the weight of jealousy of the professional rôle. The universalizing of the aim of right-wordedness, the proposing of a general effort for human word on word success in the "ordinary" human occasions of expressive performance, would nullify the honorific status poets enjoyed as specialists in the linguistic extraordinary. How much purity of motive is presumable in the attachment of poets to poetry? Is there justification for crediting poets, because they are poets, with a ready welcome for a general human achievement of speech, speech right in its choices of words, its tones of feeling and address, and in the shaping of what rises in the mind for formation into structures of utterance to the particular conditions of the occasions of utterance? Would not claims of superiority in comprehending the possibilities of combining care for the harmony with itself of what is uttered *and* in the quality of *spontaneity* of utterance hurry into battle-rank, in the consciousness of poets of their traditionally assured professional position as experts in graces of word-management in utterance-structures prepared for delivery with spontaneity-like intensity of utterance-force—utterance-structures that contain in themselves the occasion of their delivery?

How strong a sense of the linguistic natural as potentially, implicitly, identical with the linguistic right—a principle of right-wordedness of an authority of personal force uniting linguistic and human principle as being of one nature, not in truth distinguishable—could collect in minds habituated to poet-attitudes to language? Could the persuasion of the authority of the poetic natural be overcome by the appeal of a conception yielding to all uses of words, all occasions of their use, without categorical distinction between a poetic literary style of utterance and ordinary literary and non-literary utterance practices, the honors of a complete capability of linguistic rightness, linguistically right human expressiveness? The case hovers between almost total unawareness of its having been broached, or lack of a sense of responsibility for considering it where there is some awareness of a broaching of it, and a tending of the entire state of concern with poetry towards an abandonment of concern with it as a pursuit of the possibilities of right utterance outside the common range of utterance, presumed fated to fall short of an ideal fullness, for concern with it as an instrument for the development and exhibition of individual powers of expressive utterance at variance in form from the ordinary forms of linguistic activity. Concern with poetry has become diffused in the general relaxation that concern with language has undergone in the human mental constitution. Can poets be expected to be different from others, in personal mood, in this time—not to think first of themselves? To be more preoccupied with the problem of human success in rightness of word than with their own success within the confines of their special standards of special poetic rightness of word?

. . . To chide me for my thinking on poetry by bringing Homer into argument as one done an injury by my thinking is unjust to my view of Homer—which ought not to be unknown to you. . . . Homer made a beautiful mixture of story-telling and poetic wording invigorated with the energies and graces of chant. I have indicated to you that I regarded him as one who determined for the future of poetry its essence as a strictly literary order of performance—literary in the sense of being dissociated from all interests of emotion and idea other than what pertained to the enjoyability of its performances as serving the mind's love of *beauty* in the features of verbal utterance.

# Appendix

*Two Post-renunciation Poems*

## [From] As To A Certain Poem & Poetry

[. . .] After the publication in 1938 of my *Collected Poems,* I found myself halted in my commitment to poetry as the path of resolution of the truth-problem that language opened to the powers of human experience and understanding. Poetry, I saw, ritualized the possibility of the resolution of the problem. The actuality of resolution of it was distanced in poetry in immediacies of ceremonial anticipation of the ultimate perfection in words. That perfect, as the destined immediacy of constant human enactment of the laws of language, became my entire and single literary concern. I would write no more poems.— But in my recent times I have written a few poems, or statements of a poetic ceremoniality, occasions of licence-giving to myself for a rare pausing to speak (or write) in incidents of departure from my later-life commitment to the resolution of the truth-problem in ever-immediate concern with it as the literary obligatory.

A friend of devotedly serious attachment to my work and myself expressed appreciative wonder, on learning of there being these poem-rarities, at my disregarding my vulnerability—be it but in restricted measure—in resorting to the renounced potencies of poetry where some benefit seemed to outweigh the flaw of an infraction. My feeling, whether the indulgence is of private effect only or has some public extension, rests on a question of utility. Although the poetic form of language-employment, used with full literary seriousness, implicitly professes an objective of truth as its animating intent, it stops short of literal truth-achievement in a rhetoric of truth-love: its history is more a record of propaganda for the effort of "truth," in loving word-detail, than a testament of accumulative human realization of the truth-objective. I acknowledge a propagandist element in my committing these latter-day exceptions to my not writing poems "any more"[. . . .]

### In Gratuitous Witness

After I had long nursed a faith
In the promise on which poetry has thrived—
The recalled promise of language
At its careful rising in minds
To teach all, little by little,
Until life and speech are one,
Union of being with itself,
Of knowledge with the known,
Instantaneity consuming
The separating silence heard as "time,"
The beat, beat, of not-yet, not-yet—
Suddenly I saw, startling at each other,
In me, without interchange,
The plight of life and the plight of poetry,
That I had lovingly judged near-same.

Words had flocked around the plight of poetry,
Flutters of promise populating the air.
But suddenly I saw how they vanished
Between plight and plight—nothing sealed,
As nothing said, only plight and plight left.
I saw the nature of the promise:
Poetry could only echo it
From the forefelt unspoken all-speakable.

Suddenly my will changed. In me formed
A new sense of the necessary.
Poetry itself could not fulfil
The promise of language, only reveal—
Failing ever to be full wording
Of the speech of lives—promptings of desire,
The wish for utterance's utmost
Given intonations of achievement.

I have waited for the breath of life
And the breath of speech to mingle.
This must come about first in the mind.
We must think our way into our station
Of watchkeeper on the universe,
Upon the life-whole of it.
It is the station of speech.
Here the promise of language will be proved.

But poetic images of word-success
Abound in our Day, and speech-failure seems
The literarily impossible.
And the universal possible
Of life-true speech and speech-true life
Singled out in the human summation
Is being broken down into
Infinitesimal human perversions
Of the human truth-possible.

If this is what is happening,
How can the promise of language
Prosper in us and we in it,
The universe rejoicing in the event?
And when? The event broods over us
As we over the when it is,
Not knowing what when to say it is.
The answer waits upon the asking.

## A Poem: "How A Poem Comes To Be"

Within a very few years of the publication of my *Collected Poems*
(1938), I found that I had reached the limit, in what the poetic
way of using words could provide for the saying of what needed
saying with truthfulness. I renounced further trying the way of
poetry for the attaining to whole saying: I would write no more
poems—and I wrote no more poems. But in the early 'seventies
I came to have a friend whose interest in the difference between a poem and possible ways, generally, of using words was
free of categorically literary conceptions; and this enabled me
to explain my conception of the difference, which was related

to general linguistic principles, not literary preconceptions of the nature of poetry, with expectation of trustful attention. My friend's mind would be open to my fundamentally plain account of my experience of poetry, the story of finding poetry's great literary facilities failing the simple great human potentialities of language. *I wrote for him, in the 1978 Christmastime, a poem, marked as a poem for him only, giving it the title "How A Poem Comes To Be."* I kept no copy of this privately written and given poem, and forgot the writing, and the giving, of it.

I chanced, recently, to tell my friend of receiving a request for a poem to publish in broadside form for the Lord John Press, indicating my feeling some surprise that the Press's director should not have been aware that for forty years there had been no new poems of mine. But my friend reminded me that about a year ago there *had* been a new poem—the one I wrote for him; and he urged me to let him release it to me from its private status of being a poem for him only, for my responding to the request from the Press[. . . .] I give here the poem, given him, to be out in the world—give his giving out of it.

Foreword to the Poem

The Poem-experience (the reading, the hearing) is customarily apparelled in Garments of Quasi-Divinity. But I make this poem as one who as a Poet put my words under no Protection of Auspices other than that of their being, without Guile of Deferential Pride in a presumption of Inspiration by Poetry as a Divinity, Mine.

*How A Poem Comes To Be*

Necessity haunts us as an accusation of impotence:
Can you or can you not speak up,
Prove yourself present?
What you have to find to say,
To deliver the knowledge that you are
To the mercies of the believing and the not-believing
Of our kind in one another,
You may gather as you approach them,

And leave the issue of acceptance
Suspended between your offering
And its fate with them in time.
(This is named "prose"!)
Or you may call for listeners,
And not wait upon them—
Making what you find to say
Self-witnessing, be listeners absent.
(Thus does the poem construct itself:
As for delivery within narrow throw.
If there is no attendance, it yet speaks.)

Reality in a poem is inextensible.
It embraces the will to speak up,
But, if it presumes to include
Visiting will to hear the said,
It feigns Presence to it besides its own.

What else can be done?
Do we not speak to one another?
Put words into the air and on paper
That travel between us as *real*,
Under the protection of time,
Not all lost between one and another,
These, those, and their others,
Or lost all at once?

Were this not a poem
I would speak on speaking,
Write on speaking (and writing),
That saved itself for the other, others,
Constructed itself for one and all,
Or none, contained its travel-force within it,
Needed no grace of time to rescue it
From total loss.

Or I would so speak, so write,
Endeavor to construct, I mean,
Something binding our understandings
In a reality of words, selves, others,
More utterable, enterable, occupiable, open.

# Note on the Text

The author's working title for the book was *The Failure of Poetry*. She did once contemplate altering it,[1] and in the event it has been decided to add to the original title the complement-phrase *The Promise of Language*. The part titles for section headings are ones that the author either intended to use in the book—"Points Made Briefly"—or did use elsewhere.

Square brackets in the text are the editor's; the author's own square brackets have been altered to {curly brackets}. Corrections have been made silently where possible. Use of initial capitals for words in titles has been guided by the author's view, concerning the convention that lower case should be used for "minor" words within titles, that "there is no proper ruling as to what is 'major' and what is not. 'Upon,' in 'Faith Upon the Waters,' is not a minor word in meaning value, and force" (letter to Alan Clark, June 18, 1978). Her practice of giving each word in a title the emphasis she thought it should have has been respected in this book.

A number of important pieces have had to be omitted for reasons of space, but are available elsewhere. These include the 1970 preface to *Selected Poems: In Five Sets* (London: Faber) and the 1980 introduction to *The Poems of Laura Riding*, also "Poetry and the Good" and "What, If Not A Poem, Poems?" They are available in *The Laura (Riding) Jackson Reader*, ed. Elizabeth Friedmann (New York: Persea Books, 2005) or *The Poems of Laura Riding* (New York: Persea Books, 2001), or both. Some other pieces that address the theme of the failure of poetry, but which it has not been possible to include, are listed at the end of this note on the text.

In the following notes on the provenances of the pieces, *Berg* refers to The Berg Collection of English and American Literature, The New York Public Library, Astor, Lenox, and Tilden Foundations; *Cornell*

---

1. She considered the title *Poetry, Literature, and Beyond,* at a time when she was considering including in the book some of the material in her file marked "Post-*Telling*." Letter to Fran McCullough, March 1, 1976 (Collection of Elizabeth Friedmann).

refs to the Division of Rare and Manuscript Collections, Cornell University Library.

*Prologue: Description of Planned Work* (page 17): The typescript of "Description of Planned Work" is at Cornell; there is a manuscript at the Berg, bearing the title "Draft of Commentary on my 'position' on poetry presented with application for a grant for a book—which application was denied!" To this has been added her brief "Foreword" (Berg), and a related passage from a grant application of 1973 (collection of Elizabeth Friedmann); see Elizabeth Friedmann, *A Mannered Grace: The Life of Laura (Riding) Jackson* (New York: Persea Books, 2005), 431.

*Truth Begins Where Poetry Ends* (page 21): This section title is a quotation from "For Later Readers" (viii), and from the 1970 preface to *Selected Poems: In Five Sets* (15); it was one of the possible titles envisaged by L(R)J for a new *Collected Poems* planned in the mid-1960s (see note on "Then, And Now," below).

*Introduction for a Broadcast; Continued for* Chelsea (page 23): *Chelsea* 12 (September 1962). Broadcast on BBC Third Programme, early April 1962.

*The Failure of Poetry* (page 29): There are three extant typescripts, two belonging to Elizabeth Friedmann and one to Cornell, where it is part of the typescript of *Under The Mind's Watch* (Oxford: Peter Lang, 2004), to which the essay had been assigned by L(R)J in the late seventies (though not in the event published in that book). About half of the essay comprised the centerpiece of her recorded reading for the University of Notre Dame in February 1977 (see Friedmann, *A Mannered Grace*, 426–27). The original eighteen-page essay written in 1965 (with seven pages added in 1973) was L(R)J's third statement on the subject, following "Introduction for a Broadcast; Continued for *Chelsea*" (1962) and "Further on Poetry" (1964)—or her fourth, if the 1955 entry in *Twentieth Century Authors* is counted.

*Then, And Now* (page 49): In 1964–65 L(R)J was preparing material for a new selection of her poems proposed by Holt, Rinehart, Winston, the working title for which was *Poems by Laura Riding, With An Introduction, and Presenting Some New Thoughts On Poetry and an Autobiographical Epilogue*. The introduction was to consist of three parts: Part I, "Then, And Now"; Part II, "Autobiographical Summary"; Part III, "Principles of Choice, Arrangement." In the event, the arrangement with the publisher was cancelled. In 1966 she was invited by Wesleyan University Press to prepare a similar book (see Elizabeth Friedmann's note in *P. N.*

*Review* 97 (1994): 27; also letter to Charles Monteith, March 14, 1969, Cornell), the working title for which was *Truth Begins Where Poetry Ends / New Thoughts, Old Poems;* this arrangement too was cancelled. These were the "suggested larger reproductions of my poetic work" to which she refers in the Preface to *Selected Poems: In Five Sets* (London: Faber, 1970; New York: Norton, 1973; New York: Persea, 1993), 17. The manuscript, which is in the collection of Elizabeth Friedmann, is in places exceptionally difficult to decipher.

*The Otherwise of Words* (page 100): This comprised Part III of the "Harvard Recording" made on Tuesday, January 18, 1972. Part IV appears in *The Poems of Laura Riding* as "Excerpts From A Recording (1972), Explaining The Poems" (2001: 495); but this untitled "little essay" is previously unpublished. The present title has been provided by the Laura (Riding) Jackson Board of Literary Management. The typescript belongs to Elizabeth Friedmann.

*[From] Story, and Story-Style* (page 103): *Chelsea* 35 (1976).

*[From] Some Notes on Poetry and Poets in This Century, and My Influence* (page 104): *P. N. Review* 9 (1979).

*From a Notebook of Essays-In-Little* (page 106): Unpublished, except for sections 7–10, which appeared in the *London Review of Books,* September 7, 1995, under the title "The Promise of Words" (cover title "Twilight of the Poem"). Section 12 was in the late seventies assigned by the author to *Under The Mind's Watch* under the present title, "On The Latter-Day Mood of Concern With Poetry," though it was decided not to include the piece in that book, but instead to reincorporate it back into the "Notebook." Collection of Elizabeth Friedmann.

*Poetry Has Ever Overtaken Itself* (page 122): Collection of Elizabeth Friedmann; also Berg.

*Reading for the Library of Congress* (page 125): The piece was read by Sonia Raiziss in August 1985 for recording on audiotape. Collection of Elizabeth Friedmann.

*[From] Twentieth-Century Change in the Idea of Poetry, And of the Poet, And of the Human Being* (page 146): *P. N. Review* 84 (March–April 1992).

*Poetry Log* (page 149): "Random Choices" was published in *Chelsea* 35 (1976). "Other Selections" consists of selections made by the editor from the author's shorter pieces on the subject of the failure of poetry; all are previously unpublished, except for the statements in *Twentieth Century Authors* (her first public statement on the subject) and *Contemporary Poets*.

*Entry in* Twentieth Century Authors *(1955)* (page 161): *Twentieth Century Authors 1942. (Supplement 1955),* ed. Stanley J. Kunitz and Howard Haycraft (New York: Wilson, 1955), 482–83. By the volume's heading-conventions, the entry begins JACKSON, LAURA (RIDING), thus accidentally anticipating the name form not actually adopted until a decade later; see *Chelsea* 69 (2000): 178–79.

*Early Note on Poetry Re-evaluated* (page 164): Cornell. L(R)J has written on the manuscript "50s or 60s."

*[From] A Commentary of 1967 in Introduction of* Epilogue (page 165): Cornell.

*Miscellaneous General Reflections* (page 167): Collection of Elizabeth Friedmann.

*Some Thoughts On Poetry, Mind, Body, Life, Truth—Loosely Bound* (page 174): Collection of Elizabeth Friedmann.

*Poem-Reality* (page 176): Collection of Elizabeth Friedmann.

*[From] Statement in* Contemporary Poets *(1970)* (page 178): From *Contemporary Poets,* ed. James Vinson (London: St. James Press; New York: St. Martin's Press, 1970).

*Background Statement on a new edition of* Collected Poems (page 179): Berg.

*Points Made Briefly* (page 185): This section heading was of the author's own devising.

*The Tentative Nature of the Excellent In Language as Exemplified in Poetry* (page 187): Collection of Elizabeth Friedmann.

*[Note Concerning] A* Pamphlet Against Anthologies, *1928 (1964)* (page 188): Cornell.

*Foreword to "Further on Poetry"* (page 188): Berg. A previously unpublished Foreword to "Further on Poetry" (*Chelsea* 14 [January 1964]), which itself comprises, with slight rewriting, sections 1–4 of "Poetry and the Good," *Reader,* 208ff.

*As To "What Next?"* (page 189): Cornell; Berg.

*Notes for the Time of Ultimate Candor* (page 190): Cornell.

*Introduction to a Reading of "Lucrece and Nara" for Australian Radio* (page 191): Berg.

*Poetry As Image of Poetry* (page 191): Cornell; Berg.

*Poetry With A Difference* (page 192): Berg.

*A Dour Remarking on Poetry* (page 193): Collection of Elizabeth Friedmann; also Berg.

*Poetry and The Prophetic* (page 193): Collection of Elizabeth Friedmann; also Berg.

*The Matter of Metaphor. Addenda* (page 194): Berg.

*To A Poet, on Myth As Modern Matter* (page 195): Collection of Elizabeth Friedmann. The typescript is dated December 1975.

*Kinds of Poetic Excitement, Kinds of Poets* (page 199): Collection of Elizabeth Friedmann.

*To A Friend on Edward Thomas—and Robert Frost—and Barnes—and John Clare* (page 203): Collection of Elizabeth Friedmann; also Berg.

*On Burns, and Clare* (page 204): Collection of Elizabeth Friedmann.

*On Coleridge* (page 204): Berg.

*On Vachel Lindsay, and Robert Frost* (page 205): Berg.

*On Robert Frost* (page 206): Berg.

*To a Friend—a University Teacher of English—As To Eliot, Pound, Yeats* (page 207): Collection of Elizabeth Friedmann.

*To Another University Teacher, On Eliot, Pound* (page 208): Collection of Elizabeth Friedmann.

*Robert Lowell (Written Before He Died)* (page 209): Collection of Elizabeth Friedmann.

*From Letters of Mine on Poetry* (page 213): This section title was written by the author at the head of her handwritten transcription of one of the letters, "To A Poet, writing to me on poetry." The extracts in this section were selected by the author from her personal correspondence, and identified by her for possible inclusion in her "poetry book."

*To An Anthology Editor, May 1948* (page 215): Berg and Cornell. In making this extract, L(R)J made some alterations to the wording of the original letter cited in Friedmann, *A Mannered Grace*, 392. The same applies to the next extract.

*To The British National Book League's Poetry Circle, 1954* (page 215): Berg. Slightly rewritten by L(R)J from her own transcription (Cornell) of a paragraph from her original letter.

*"My View Is Not Anti-Poetic" (From a letter to a friend who wrote to me in irritation—with some interpolated comment)* (page 235): Collection of Elizabeth Friedmann; also Berg.

*Appendix: Two Post-renunciation Poems* (page 239): Of her six post-renunciation poems (all published), these two bear explicitly on the theme of the failure of poetry.

*[From] As To A Certain Poem & Poetry* (page 239): *Chelsea* 47 (1988), commenting on another of her late poems.

*In Gratuitous Witness* (page 240): *London Review of Books* 17 (17), September 1995.

*A Poem: "How A Poem Comes To Be"* (page 241): Northridge, CA: Lord John Press, 1980.

**Some of L(R)J's principal writings on the failure of poetry, in chronological sequence:**

1948   "To An Anthology Editor"

1950   "To Kimon Friar" (part-quoted in Friedmann, *A Mannered Grace,* 392)

1953   "To The British National Book League's Poetry Circle"

1954   "To A Magazine Editor, In reply to his request to reprint a short story" (part-quoted in Friedmann, *A Mannered Grace,* 393)

1955   "Entry in *Twentieth Century Authors* (1955)"

50s or 60s   "Early Note on Poetry Re-evaluated"

1962   "Introduction for a Broadcast; Continued for *Chelsea*"

1964   "Further on Poetry" (full essay published 1992 as "Poetry and the Good")

1965   "The Failure of Poetry"

1965   "Then, And Now"

1966   "An Autobiographical Summary" (published 1994)

1967   "What, If Not A Poem, Poems?" (published 1974)

1968   *The Telling,* "Preface for a Second Reading" (published 1972)

1970   Preface to *Selected Poems: In Five Sets*

1970s   "From a Notebook of Essays-In-Little"

1975   "A Reading . . . for . . . the University of Florida" (published 2000)

1976   "Poetry Log: Random Choices"

1979   "Some Notes on Poetry and Poets in This Century, and My Influence"

Ca. 1980   "Righteousness: The All-Pervading Theme" (§§5 and 8)

1980   Introduction to *The Poems of Laura Riding*

1983   "Engaging in the Impossible" (§§2–4)

1985   "Reading for the Library of Congress"

1986   "Body & Mind and the Linguistic Ultimate" (published 2005)

1987   "Twentieth-Century Change in the Idea of Poetry, And of the Poet, And of the Human Being"

(Date unknown)   "On the Continuing of the Continuing" (§10)

# Index

165, 233; as spelling out truth, 165; truth-function of, 43
human identity: attitudes to, 2; crises of, 147; and language, 27–28; man- and woman-components of, 10, 142; truth implicit in, 179; and universal reality, 126
humanity, 7; and language, 160; and truth, 161; unifying spirit of, 160
human nature, 104, 139; contrasted with man-nature, 141; rarity of, 234
human personality, 28, 35; universal essence of, 88. *See also* person

ideal, the: human and linguistic, 63, 91; in language, 110
immortality, 191, 221
individual, the, 132; spiritual versus psychological, 94
individuality: contrasted with soul, 28; contrasted with universality, 139; modern overemphasis on, 119, 126–28, 133, 135, 139, 211, 237; physical, 141
instantaneity, 32, 240
*Irish Times*, 181

Jackson, Laura (Riding): abstractness, alleged, of her poems, 75–77, 169; "difficulty" of her work, 111–12, 182; family background, 135; her poems described, 180–83, 220–21, 233, 234; her poems judged, 233; idealism of, 88; "influence" on others, 18, 73–84, 112; as "Kurt Gödel of poetry," 4; as "modernist" poet, 17–18, 112; names of, 29, 227–28; not experimentalist, 132; not "philosophical," 76–77; as person and poet, 84–85; poetic religiosity of, 71; responses to, 62, 143, 173, 180, 227; as revivalist, not revolutionary, 135; rightness in her poems, 144–45; traditional spirit of her work, 18; visionary content of her poetry, 74; what her poems are "about," 84–87
Jackson, Laura (Riding), writings of: *Anarchism Is Not Enough*, 12n2; "An Autobiographical Summary," 62n6; "Backgrounds," 12n4; "Body & Mind and the Linguistic Ultimate," 15n51; *Collected Poems*, 2, 17, 23, 40, 42, 49, 87, 145, 179–81, 223, 224, 239, 241; *Contemporaries and Snobs*, 12n2; "A Covenant," 14n35; "Engaging in the Impossible," 12n4, 15n41; *Epilogue*, 41, 73, 165–66; *Everybody's Letters*, 16n54; *First Awakenings*, 13n19; "For Later Readers," 13n24; "Interest," 10; *Later-Life Commentaries*, 13n23; *The Laura (Riding) Jackson Reader*, 12n3; *The Left Heresy*, 42; "Lucrece and Nara," 4; "The Missing Story," 10, 14n36; "A Modern Legend," 14n29; "The One Language. Self-Revealed," 10; "The Only Possible Ending," 10; "On the Continuing of the Continuing," 10; "Open Confidences," 10; *A Pamphlet Against Anthologies*, 188; "The Person I Am: The Subject in Extended Perspective," 13n23; "Poet: A

187; speaking-capability, 66; speaking-needs, 24, 51; speaking-potential, 42; speaking-urgencies, 66; spirit of, 160; as voiced, written, thought, 59. *See also* saying

Spender, Stephen, 79–80

spirit, 69, 217; of being, 71; energy of, *11;* generosities of, 67–68; and humanity, 160; of life, 174; and reality, 59; of reality, 212; of speaking, 160

spiritual, 55, 59, 233; articulateness, 89

Stein, Gertrude, 233

story: contrasted with poetry, 103; Homer's, 237; the one, *8,* 87

Tennyson, Alfred, Lord, 79

Thomas, Dylan, 202

Thomas, Edward, 79, 203

Thompson, Francis, 80

thought: fullness and distinction of, 174; and language, 104–5; in a poem, 153–54; and science, 119

time, 189, 240, 243; historical, 146; in L(R)J's poems, 193; overcome, 147; poetic, 109, 146

*Time,* 163, 205n, 211n

*transition, 13n13*

Trotman, Michael, *15n45*

truth, *11,* 19, 50, 56, 96, 146–47, 161, 194; activity distinguished from product, 110; actual contrasted with abstract, 57; and beauty, 56, 58; being's, 146, 212; clarities of, 67–68; concern with, 180; ear for, 193; as explicitness, 167; as full of utterance, 96; as the human natural, 232; and human nature, 139; illusions of, 178; and language, 17,

24, 136, 179, 225, 232; "in the large," *8;* love of, 175; love of contrasted with achievement of, 240; motive of, 69–70; natural, 160; natural clarities of, 67–68; necessity of, 166, 183; as perfect expressiveness, 179; as perfection in speaking, 56, 64, 157; as perfect utterance, 29; and poetry, 56–57, 64, 97, 215, 224, 228; potential of in words, 98; principle of, 72; problem of, 220, 239; as quality, 17, 66; quality contrasted with thing, *7–8;* as rightness of word, *8,* 61, 178; as speaking true, 110; speech of, 24, 54; spoken, not found, *8,* 98; standards of in language, 216; style of, 24, 28, 217–18; tests of, 56–58; time of, 161; truth-instinct, 26, 200; truth-maximum, 178; truth-objective, 64; truth-speaking, *2–5, 7–11,* 223; uncovering of, 138; and values, 178

truthfulness, *8,* 18–19, 241

unity: of being, 164; of minds, *7*

universality, contrasted with individuality, 139

universe, the, 85, 88, 241; of being, 130; and language, 189; reintegration of, 85; Self of, 89. *See also* World

utterance: crises of, 93–95; life-redeeming, 223; perfection of, 67–68; potentialities of, 65; problems of, 99

Valéry, Paul, 170–71

vanity, 86, 105, 134, 155, 211, 234; of the word, 193. *See also* pride

Villa, Jose Garcia, *15n49*
vision, 146, 177, 203, 226; of being, 74; historical, 97; poetic, 193–94
voice: in poetry, 23, 127, 168–69, 171–72; of the soul, 175; trueness of, 24
vulgarity, 155, 190, 231

Warren, Robert Penn, 125
Whitman, Walt, 209
Whole/whole, the, 87, 88, 189. *See also* entire/entirety
wholeness, 136
Williams, William Carlos, 131, 133, 202–3
Winters, Yvor, 30
wisdom, 42, 108
Wittgenstein, Ludwig, *13n20*
women: contrasted morally with men, 140; and human identity, *10*, 140, 169; kindness of, 169; as unitary, 128
Word, the, 165–66
Words/words, *7*, 71–72, 182, 233; attitudes to, 109; as crux of human problem, 162; expression-potential of, 182; freedom of, 98; goodness of, 62, 65, 93, 158–59; grace of, 218; as guardians, teachers, spiritual elders, 217; as harmony of words, 59; human disposition to, 62; humility towards, 217;

infallible and dependable, *4;* as instruments of truth, 59; intrinsic authenticity of, 60; irreverence towards, 109; literal spirit of, 72; mission of, 200; physicality of contrasted with intellectuality of, 106, 158–59, 168, 174; of poems, 87; potential of truth in, 98, 137; promise of, 113; real distinguished from imitation, 157–58, 160; reality dependent on, 67; redeeming powers of, 123; relearning, 70; respect for, *6;* rightness, goodness, and quickness of, 68, 70; stress by L(R)J on, 59; task of, *11;* truth-function of, 63; utmost in, 66; validity of, 162; word-meanings (*see* meaning); word-play, 143–44; word-practice, 236; word-virtue, 226, 230; word-wisdom, 109, 158; and World, 72
Wordsworth, William, *2;* contrasted with Coleridge, 38–39, 114–16; contrasted with Eliot, 115–16
World, 86, 89. *See also* universe, the

Yale University Library. *See* Pearson, Norman Holmes
Yeats, W. B., 25n, 76, 207